MUSIC and POETRY

California Studies in
19ᵀᴴ CENTURY MUSIC

Joseph Kerman, General Editor

1. Between Romanticism and Modernism: Four Studies in the Music of the Later Nineteenth Century, by Carl Dahlhaus. Translated by Mary Whittall.

2. Brahms and the Principle of Developing Variation, by Walter Frisch.

3. Music and Poetry: The Nineteenth Century and After, by Lawrence Kramer.

4. The Beethoven Sketchbooks: History, Reconstruction, Inventory, by Douglas Johnson, Alan Tyson, and Robert Winter.

The publication of this book was made possible in part by a generous gift from Gordon Getty of San Francisco.

MUSIC AND POETRY:
The Nineteenth Century and After

Lawrence Kramer

University of California Press

BERKELEY • LOS ANGELES • LONDON

University of California Press
Berkeley and Los Angeles, California
University of California Press, Ltd.
London, England
© 1984 by
The Regents of the University of California

Library of Congress Cataloging in Publication Data
Kramer, Lawrence, 1946–
Music and poetry, the nineteenth century and after.
(California studies in 19th century music ; 3)
Includes index.
1. Music and literature. 2. Music—19th century—
Philosophy and aesthetics. 3. Music—20th century—
Philosophy and aesthetics. I. Title
ML3849.K7   1983   780'.08   83-1173
ISBN 0-520-04873-3

Printed in the United States of America

1 2 3 4 5 6 7 8 9

Contents

Preface

Though the great song return no more
There's keen delight in what we have:
The rattle of pebbles on the shore
Under the receding wave.
(YEATS, "The Nineteenth Century and After")

I have stolen the title of Yeats's self-affirming little lyric not for its vision of art in decline—something I do not share—but for its singling out of the era since 1800 as a time when something that was hidden came to the surface. The nineteenth century developed a view of music and poetry as arts that are deeply interrelated, endowed with common sources and common ends. Figures as diverse as Arnold and Nietzsche treated the work of artists like Beethoven, Wordsworth, Byron, and Wagner as elements in a large cultural act of human self-definition, and they did not share our modern scholarly reluctance to interpret poetry, music, philosophy, and politics in the same breath.

My purpose in this book is to reaffirm what is viable in this attitude, though with an exploratory rather than a prophetic or polemical emphasis. The book grew out of my conviction, slow to become articulate but of long standing, that the way I read certain poems was intimately bound up with the way I heard certain pieces of music. Eventually, this intuition led me to ask about the conditions in which such convergences appeared, about why I felt they were important and what they could suggest about the two arts involved. Music and poetry had often been linked, sometimes with speculative keenness, more often in vague, unsatisfying ways. Was something better possible—a discipline that could situate the two arts in a coherent and significant context? Could such a discipline be used to provoke new ways of reading and hearing? If so, it would have to be a discipline that could embrace both arts without merely assimilating one to the other, without scanting the idiosyncrasy of either, without losing sight of particulars. The eight chapters that follow constitute a first attempt to show that these demands can be met, and met in areas of concern that are vital, not arcane.

With a few exceptions, the music I deal with here is non-dramatic, and most of my generalizations—especially those about word-music relationships—are meant to apply to non-dramatic music only. The presence of a dramatic action both alters and clarifies the bond between text and music; the relationship between music and drama is a separate subject, and it has been studied both often and well. Similarly, the poetry in question here is primarily lyric or reflective rather than narrative in form, though this generic distinction is not absolute.

For both theory and interpretation, I have drawn freely on various disciplines: phenomenology, psychoanalysis, semiology, and the indispensable "ordinary" forms of critical reading and musical analysis. But my approach is not meant to be limited to or by these resources. Its responsibilities are to the demands of its subject matter, and its aim is to speak of music and poetry in the same language, wherever such a language may be possible.

Finally, it would be useful to have a name for this kind of study, so I will speak of it as "gestural" in its concerns. The term reflects the idea that music and poetry, more than any of the other arts, define their formal shape as a function of rhythmically integrated time. A physical gesture—beckoning, waving good-by, embracing—is a complex action so integrated that it is perceived as simple; its duration can define the virtual present; and in the right context it can assume an enormous weight of implication and emotion. Music and poetry seem to share these qualities, doing over a span of time what a gesture does in a moment. Perhaps, through performance, there is even a direct (but now largely submerged) link between the expressive gestures of music and poetry and physical gestures. Some poems, some compositions, resist and fragment gestural continuity, but it is always there to be resisted or fragmented. To disturb it—to break off a poem in mid-cadence, or a tonal composition on a dominant chord—is to open a palpable gap in perception.

The concept of music and poetry as distinctively gestural challenges the conventional division of the arts into "temporal" and "spatial" forms. All of the arts organize and characterize time; what counts is the way they do it. The shapes of time evolved by the various arts may finally be more representational, more mimetic, than any pictorial, narrative, or programmatic content. Such shapes model and interpret the current of lived experience, as, perhaps, do the shapes of work, play, and seduction. My effort in this book is to bring those esthetic shapes—or one of them—into the productive activity of critical understanding.

Acknowledgments

A book like this one necessarily owes more debts than can be recognized, let alone acknowledged. Special thanks go first to Joseph Kerman, who read the entire manuscript with great care and generosity, and responded with suggestions that have a great deal to do with the final shape of the book. His continuing support and encouragement have been invaluable. I am also grateful to Marjorie Perloff and Thomas McFarland for commenting on various portions of the manuscript, but my debts to them go deeper as well, to years of encouragement and conversation. Emily Wallace's judgment and support have also had special value. Stuart Curran, Frederick Grab, Morse Peckham, and Charles Rosen all read portions of the manuscript in earlier versions and made valuable comments. Frederick Harris, Lia Lerner, and Eva Maria Stadler, my colleagues at Fordham University, Lincoln Center, have provided both encouragement and assistance. Finally, there is the unique contribution of my wife, Nancy Leonard—no Preface Spouse but a colleague whose critical acumen and personal presence combined invaluably during a long and often frustrating project. Thanks also go to my editors at the University of California Press, Mary Lamprech and Doris Kretschmer, and to Danielle Gastall and De Anna Tidmore, who worked with me on the index.

I would also like to thank the staffs of three libraries: those of the library of Fordham at Lincoln Center, The New York Public Library of the Performing Arts at Lincoln Center, and the Van Pelt Library of the University of Pennsylvania.

Earlier versions of several chapters were presented as papers at Modern Language Association meetings and at Bard College, and provoked helpful comments from many who were present. A portion of chapter 6, in an earlier version, appeared in the fall 1978 issue of the *Wallace Stevens Journal*; an earlier version of chapter 7 appeared in *Beyond Amazement: New Essays on John Ashbery*, (Cornell University Press, 1980). My thanks go to the publishers for the right to reprint this material.

Wallace Stevens's poems "The River of Rivers in Connecticut" and "A Completely New Set of Objects" are reprinted in America by kind permission of Alfred A. Knopf, Inc., from *The Collected Poems of Wallace Stevens*, copyright 1954 by Wallace Stevens. In Britain, the poems are reprinted by permission of Faber and Faber Ltd., from *The Collected Poems of Wallace Stevens*. Yeats's "The Nineteenth Century and After" is reprinted in America with the kind permission of the Macmillan Publishing Company from *Collected Poems of William Butler Yeats*, copyright 1933 by Macmillan Publishing Co., Inc., renewed 1961 by Bertha Georgie Yeats. In Britain, the poem is reprinted by permission of Michael B. Yeats, Anne Yeats, and Macmillan, London, Ltd.

A Note on Sources and Musical Symbols

Primary poetic texts are quoted or translated from the following sources throughout. All translations are my own:

Charles Baudelaire. *Flowers of Evil*, bilingual edition, edited by Jackson and Marthiel Matthews. New York: New Directions, 1955.

William Blake. *Poetry and Prose*, edited by David V. Erdman with commentary by Harold Bloom. Garden City, New York: Anchor Books, 1965.

Hart Crane. *Complete Poems and Selected Letters*, edited by Brom Weber. Garden City, New York: Anchor Books, 1966.

T. S. Eliot. *Collected Poems 1909–62*. New York: Harcourt, Brace, and World: 1963.

Johann Wolfgang Goethe. *Gedichte. Versepen*. Frankfurt am Main: Insel Verlag, 1970.

Johann Wolfgang Goethe. *Faust: Der Tragödie erster und zweiter Teil*, Gedankensausgabe, edited by Peter Boerner et al. Nördlingen: Deutscher Taschenbuch Verlag, 1962.

Heinrich Heine. *Das Buch der Lieder*, first edition. Hamburg: Hoffmann und Campe, 1827. (The edition used by Schumann in composing his Heine songs.)

Friedrich Hölderlin. *Poems and Fragments*, bilingual edition, translated by Michael Hamburger. Ann Arbor: University of Michigan Press, 1966.

John Milton. *Paradise Lost*, edited by Merritt Y. Hughes. New York: Odyssey Press, 1935.

John Milton. *Paradise Regained, The Minor Poems, and Samson Agonistes*, edited by Merritt Y. Hughes. New York: Odyssey Press, 1937.

Rainer Maria Rilke. *Werke in drei Bänden*. Frankfurt am Main: Insel Verlag, 1966.

Arthur Rimbaud. *Oeuvres Complètes*, edited by J. Mouquet and Rolland de Renéville. Paris: Bibliothèque de la Pléiade, 1954.

Theodore Roethke. *Collected Poems*. Garden City, New York: Doubleday, 1965.

Percy Bysshe Shelley. *Poetry and Prose*, edited by Donald H. Reiman and Sharon B. Powers. New York: Norton, 1977.

Wallace Stevens. *Collected Poems*. New York: Alfred A. Knopf, 1954.

Wallace Stevens. *Opus Posthumous*. New York: Alfred A. Knopf, 1957.

Walt Whitman. *Leaves of Grass*, Comprehensive Reader's Edition, edited by Sculley Bradley and Harold W. Blodgett. New York: Norton, 1973.

William Carlos Williams. *Selected Poems*, expanded edition. New York: New Directions, 1969.

William Carlos Williams. *Paterson*. New York: New Directions, 1963.

William Wordsworth. *Poetical Works*, edited by Thomas Hutchinson, revised by Ernest de Selincourt. London: Oxford University Press, 1969.

William Wordsworth. *The Prelude, Text of 1805*, edited by Ernest de Selincourt, revised by Helen Darbishire. London: Oxford University Press, 1960.

William Wordsworth. *Home at Grasmere*, edited by Beth Darlington. Ithaca: Cornell University Press, 1977.

William Butler Yeats. *Collected Poems*, second edition. London: Macmillan, 1950.

Music in copyright is quoted from the following editions:

Elliott Carter. *Syringa*. New York: Associated Music Publishers, 1981.

Charles Ives. *Second Pianoforte Sonata—"Concord, Mass., 1840–1860,"* second edition. New York: Associated Music Publishers, 1947.

Arnold Schoenberg. *Das Buch der hängenden Gärten*. Vienna: Universal Edition, 1941.

Beethoven's letters are quoted from the following edition:

Ludwig van Beethoven. *Letters* in three volumes, collected, translated, and edited by Emily Anderson. New York: St. Martins Press, 1961.

The following system of musical symbols is used throughout:

Chords and keys are labeled with upper-case Roman numerals if major, lower-case Roman numerals if minor. Augmented triads are marked with a plus sign, diminished triads and seventh-chords with a degree sign. Augmented-sixth chords are indicated by the abbreviation A⁶; Neapolitan sixths by N⁶. To simplify presentation, chord inversions are not indicated except in the case of six-four chords with their special properties; thus, for example, the notation V⁷ may stand for any inversion of the dominant-seventh chord, not just the first.

When register must be specified, notes in the octave below middle C are represented by lower-case letters. Higher octaves are indicated by superscripts, lower ones by capitalization. Hence the note C as it appears at different octaves on the piano keyboard is: $\bar{\text{C}}$ C c c^1 c^2 c^3 c^4.

Definitions of musical and literary terms appear in a glossary at the back of the book.

1

Introduction

In the beginning was the song. Poets, at least, have always been content to say so, and the association of song with primal creativity has persisted in poetry since the days when

> World-famous golden-thighed Pythagoras
> Fingered upon a fiddle-stick or strings
> What a star sang and careless Muses heard.
>
> (YEATS, "Among School Children")

It is easy to concoct a miscellany. Dryden represents the divine Word as a "tuneful voice . . . heard from high" on the first day ("A Song for St. Cecilia's Day"); Hölderlin writes that to "ripen song" for only a single autumn is to live, for that time, like the gods ("An die Parzen"). Milton describes a "divinely-warbled voice" heard at the nativity as both a recollection of the creation and an anticipation of apocalypse:

> Such Music (as 'tis said)
> Before was never made,
> But when of old the sons of morning sung,
> While the Creator Great
> His constellations set,
> And the well-balanc't world on hinges hung.
> . . . .
> Nature that heard such sound
> Beneath the hollow round
> Of *Cynthia*'s seat, the Airy region thrilling,
> Now was almost won

> To think her part was done,
> And that her reign had here its last fulfilling.
> ("On the Morning of Christ's Nativity," st. 12, 10)

Shelley, evoking an apocalypse that *is* a creation, makes the same links between first and last, singing and being, and adds to them the figure of Orpheus—Milton's Orpheus, Rilke's Orpheus—that archetypal singer who is also the archetypal poet:

> Language is a perpetual Orphic song,
> Which rules with Daedal harmony a throng
> Of thoughts and forms, which else shapeless and senseless were.
> (*Prometheus Unbound*, IV, 415-18)

The basis of these images, and of the many others I could have chosen in their place, is the mythical union of a lower reality embodied in language and a higher one embodied in music. Through song, usually the song of a disincarnate voice or of a figure touched by divinity, language is represented as broaching the ineffable. Carried by the singing voice, poetry approaches the source of creation by uniting with the "harmony" that its words cannot express. (That is why poets habitually call poetry song when they want to represent it as vision, epiphany, or prophecy.) For an ancient writer like Cicero or a Renaissance writer like Milton, the ineffable element in music is its analogy to the unity of the cosmos, "the most delectable music of the revolving stars."[1] For a Romantic writer like E. T. A. Hoffmann, music transforms language like a "wondrous elixir" by steeping it in "inexpressible longing" and a sense of the infinite.[2] Either way, music has the privilege of transcendental immediacy; poetry is transfigured by it.

Composers might plausibly be expected to revel in this traditional supremacy of music over words, and of course they do. As Schoenberg put it, complaining over a publisher's request for titles to his Five Pieces for Orchestra, "Whatever was to be said has been said by the music. Why, then, words as well? If words were necessary they would be there in the first place."[3] Yet at least since the Renaissance, music has been recurrently anxious to be less than—or is it more than?—ineffable. Often enough, to alter

---

[1] John Milton, *Prolusion* "On the Music of the Spheres," quoted and translated in *Paradise Regained, The Minor Poems, and Samson Agonistes*, edited by Merrit Y. Hughes (New York: Odyssey Press, 1937), p. 208.

[2] E. T. A. Hoffmann, "The Poet and the Composer," from his *Die Serapions-Brüder*, translated in *Source Readings in Music History: The Romantic Era*, edited by Oliver Strunk (New York: Norton, 1965), p. 36.

[3] From an entry in Arnold Schoenberg's diary, January 1, 1912; quoted in the booklet accompanying *The Music of Arnold Schoenberg* (Columbia M2S 709), v. 3, p. 5.

Pater's dictum, music has seemed to aspire to the condition of poetry. In Monteverdi's *Vespers* of 1610, the trinity is praised by the movement of three voices from a triad to a unison; in Elliott Carter's 1976 Symphony of Three Orchestras, the opening trumpet solo is supposed to evoke the soaring gull that Hart Crane describes in the first lines of *The Bridge*. In the centuries between, both vocal and instrumental music have repeatedly engaged themselves, often in dialectic, with the possibilities of poetic expressiveness.

In the nineteenth century that engagement is particularly intense, heightened by the development of program music and by the enormous prestige of Beethoven's Ninth Symphony. Not that composers were willing to surrender their claims on a tangible transcendence; even Liszt, writing in defense of programs, exclaims "Heaven forbid!" No one, he goes on, should "assert that the heavenly art does not exist for its own sake, is not self-sufficient, does not kindle of itself the divine spark, and has value only as the representative of an *idea* or as an exaltation of language."[4] Yet many nineteenth-century instrumental works are written, in effect, as expressive glosses on valued poetic texts, including Liszt's own renditions of Dante, Goethe, Lamartine, Lenau, and so on. Debussy's *Prelude to the Afternoon of a Faun* virtually has the function of elucidating the opaque Mallarmé poem that it evokes, as the poet acknowledged in a little inscription to the composer, who is represented as blowing light through the faun's flute. And the idea that the tensions built up in a large-scale orchestral work can be resolved by the climactic arrival of a poem—the pattern of Beethoven's Ninth—is followed by Liszt in his *Faust Symphony* and by Mahler in a pair of symphonies, the Second and Fourth. Mahler, unlike Liszt, is genuinely ambivalent about the word, but he is even more compelled by it.

In the beginning was the song. Is it fair to add that, once separated, music and poetry tend to become nostalgic for each other? Both Beethoven and Wallace Stevens seem to have thought so:

> If you go to the old ruins, remember that Beethoven has often lingered there. If you wander through the secluded fir-woods, remember that Beethoven has often poetized or, as the saying is, composed there.
>
> (BEETHOVEN to Nanette Streicher, July 20, 1817)

> A music more than a breath, but less
> Than the wind, sub-music like sub-speech,
> A repetition of unconscious things,

---

[4] Franz Liszt, "Berlioz and his 'Harold' Symphony" (1855); translated in Strunk, *Source Readings*, p. 108.

Letters of rock and water, words
Of the visible elements and of ours.

(STEVENS, "Variations on a Summer Day")

On the evidence of habitual metaphor alone, the two arts demand to be understood together as well as separately. After all, we praise music for its poetry and poetry for its music; composers write tone poems and poets write preludes and nocturnes. More importantly, music and poetry are arts uniquely dependent on the immediate, tangible organization of the flow of time. Their structural foundation is in that sense the same. Yet though a literary critic might try to unpack the analogy that Whitman drew between Italian opera and "Out of the Cradle Endlessly Rocking," though a music theorist might point to effects of irony or imitation in *Die Winterreise*, music and poetry are most often left to their separate provinces. Surprisingly enough, twentieth-century advances in literary interpretation and musical analysis have done little to foster an interdisciplinary method. To put it bluntly, none exists. In fact, the gradual formalization of technique in each discipline, with its concomitant specialization, has drawn attention away from issues surrounding words and music that the nineteenth century found compelling.[5]

This situation, of course, is neither inevitable nor irreversible, as the well-developed study of poetry and painting, the traditional sister arts, ought to suggest. And contemporary techniques of analysis and interpretation can just as well help as hinder an interdisciplinary approach. In this book, I would like to ask when and how a poem and a composition can be rewardingly discussed in tandem. Can we identify a level of analysis, a plane of interpretation, on which, say, a Beethoven sonata and a Wordsworth poem are commensurate—and this not just in a general way, but in enough detail to support an extended consideration of both? If so, would the same be true of a Handel concerto grosso and a poem by Pope? And where would vocal music fit in? What follows is an attempt to open—in some cases re-open—questions like these.

II

To begin with, how do music and poetry compare as forms of expression? It is important to emphasize that this question is aimed at the *arts*, not at their media—sound and words; the arts themselves must be understood as "speech media" which, according to Nietzsche, serve "the desire to speak

---

[5] For a discussion, see Joseph Kerman, "The State of Academic Music Criticism," in *On Criticizing Music*, edited by Kingsley Price (Baltimore: Johns Hopkins University Press, 1981), pp. 38–54. Also published as "How We Got Into Analysis, and How to Get Out," *Critical Inquiry* 7 (1980): 311–32.

on the part of everything that knows how to make signs."[6] How, then, do these arts make signs?

Both music and poetry juxtapose elements that are referential, mimetic, or conceptual with purely formal patterns that are largely independent of external meanings. The degree of emphasis on either aspect varies from style to style, but even at the esthetic extremes of aleatory music and automatic writing both are present, even if only as raw material. This duality corresponds loosely to the linguistic distinction between semantics and syntax. The mimetic—call it the connotative—dimension seems to look outward toward the world or inward toward the self; it invests significance in realities or fictions outside the work of art. The formal—call it the combinatory—dimension relates the parts of the work to each other alone, for instance by uniting a word to its rhyme or a dissonance to its resolution. The exact status of these processes is a matter of considerable debate, but purely as phenomena they seem to establish the inescapable basis of our musical and poetic experience.

In both arts, the alliance of connotative and combinatory features becomes significant in two ways: intertextually, through allusion, generic affiliation, and the play of stylistic codes; and intratextually, through rhythmic design and the play of likeness and difference among particulars. Even by omission, these elements are always interlaced with each other, and what I call their "play"—their suppleness, inventiveness, balletic energy—joins the sensuous and emotional satisfactions of music and poetry to the play of critical intelligence. To say this is to reject the formalist equation of pure music with pure form, if only because any listener who responds emotionally to a composition is implicitly investing it with connotative content. Likewise, the extreme poststructuralist view that poetic language (indeed all language) is non-referential, a prison-house that endlessly reflects back upon itself, may be a valuable way of "opening" texts to speculation. But no such view can overrule the rooted feeling that poetry addresses reality, even if that feeling rests on an illusion. The pattern of mediation and *différance* may, if we like, overwhelm the imaginary experience alluded to by a poem, but the "free play" of formal terms is always anchored by a referential fiction. The fictive experience, the sense of presence or world or being, underlies the shifting instability of meaning, like the weight in one of those toy clowns that cannot be knocked down.

The central difference between music and poetry, contrary to the usual assumptions, is not a lack of referential concreteness on the part of music. Some poems are considerably less mimetic than some compositions; Liszt's "Les Jeux d'eaux à la Villa d'Este," for instance, arguably creates a referen-

---

[6] Friedrich Nietzsche, *The Will to Power*. Translated by Walter Kaufmann and R. J. Hollingdale; edited by Walter Kaufman (New York: Vintage Books, 1968), p. 428.

tially richer fountain image than the refrain of Baudelaire's "Le Jet d'eau," which is mainly intertextual and self reflexive:

> La gerbe épanouie
>   En mille fleurs
> Où Phoebé réjouie
>   Met ses couleurs,
> Tombe comme une pluie
>   De larges pleurs.

> The sheaf (spout, shower) in full blossom
>   With a thousand flowers
> Where jocund Phoebe
>   Lays her colors
> Falls like a shower
>   Of large tears.

What really separates music from poetry is a complementarity in the roles that the two arts assign to their connotative and combinatory aspects: each art makes explicit the dimension that the other leaves tacit.[7]

Musical meaning, even when focused by a text or program, is always non-predicative and inexact. Its connotations are peripheral, always somewhat displaced—not so much vague as unlocalized, at a third remove, like a name on the tip of the tongue. Music achieves its unique suggestiveness, the power (first identified by Hegel) to embody complex states of mind as they might arise pre-verbally in consciousness, by resting its tacit connotations on an explicit combinatory structure that is highly charged with complexity, expectancy, and tension. In poetry, this expressive balance is reversed: poetic meaning, as it unfolds to an interpreter, is a virtually limitless play of explicit connotative relationships—predications, tropes, displacements, allusions, associations, ironies. Supporting this is a combinatory structure that varies in the degree of its formality with different styles, but that manifests itself in the rhythm and sonority of the verse. It is experienced tacitly, peripherally, by most readers, for whom it represents a tangible continuity that cannot

---

[7] I take the terms "tacit" and "explicit" from Michael Polanyi. An object is known tacitly when we attend *from* it *to* something else. Polanyi calls the mediating object "subsidiary" and the object attended-to the "focus." These concepts help to resolve the old question of whether music expresses feelings and states of mind or elicits them—the answer being: neither. When we listen, what we attend to is the music itself as it unfolds its combinatory sequence; this is the focus. The connotative element—which as Polanyi would predict seems to be internal to us—continuously involves us in (and guides and shapes) the activity of listening. In a complementary way, the combinatory play of rhythm and sonority in poetry involves us in a reading of—a reading of ourselves into—the connotative play of the text.

See Michael Polanyi, *The Tacit Dimension* (Garden City, N.Y.: Doubleday, 1966) and "Sense-Giving and Sense-Reading," from *Intellect and Hope*, edited by W. H. Poteat and T. A. Langford (Durham: University of North Carolina Press, 1968).

be reductively equated to an explicit description of metrical, phonetic, or syntactical properties. As Milton suggested when he described the movement of poetry as "the sense variously drawn out from one verse into another," poetic form is realized as a kinetic aspect of meaning.

Direct attempts to put poetry and music together are obviously doomed to founder on this asymmetry in semiotic structure. Analogies between the tacit and the explicit can hardly help being loose to the point of limpness. Aside from identifying similar stylistic resources, like the folk elements in Yeats and Bartók, it is hard to say anything with much point. Elgar's *Enigma Variations* may encipher portraits of the composer's friends, but no amount of interpretation can enable them to X-ray an ego with the merciless complexity of a Browning monologue. And a critic who tries to find genuine elements of sonata form in the repetitions of Eliot's *Four Quartets* might as well be on a snipe hunt.

Impasses of this order have undoubtedly helped to discourage an interdisciplinary approach to music and poetry, but they also indicate very clearly what is required for one. Any discourse that hopes to embrace both arts must, so to speak, be mobile. Its mobility would consist in the power to treat both connotative and combinatory structures with equal exactness, agility, and sophistication. An interpretive language with this property would have access to both the tacit and the explicit dimensions of music and poetry alike; its structural argument could incorporate materials as diverse as parallel chords and parallel metaphors. One possible resource for mobility on this scale is psychoanalysis, which has a distinctive, even a preeminent, claim to it. As we will see shortly, gestural and psychoanalytic methods of interpretation tend to maintain a constant dialogue.

Meanwhile, we can set it down as a first principle that any language mobile enough to take in both music and poetry must always be focused on process. As I have already emphasized, music and poetry are the two arts most saturated by time, the arts most dependent on giving a tangible contour and a distinctive texture to the lived present. In contrast to the teasing, disjunctive movement of narrative fiction, the movement of music and poetry becomes compelling not by fastening value on the outcome of imaginary events but by enveloping the reader or listener in a kind of polyphony of periodic forms. And it is just this hyperbolical "timeliness," this insistent transformation of time into form, that can make music and poetry mutually intelligible. In principle, a composition and a poem may shape the flow of time in commensurate ways. If that should happen, any interested party could proceed to demonstrate a proposition of Geoffrey Hartman's: "Interpretation is like a football game. You spot a hole and you go through."[8]

---

[8] Geoffrey Hartman, "The Voice of the Shuttle: Language from the Point of View of Literature," in his *Beyond Formalism: Literary Essays, 1958–1970* (New Haven: Yale University Press, 1970), p. 351.

III

Music and poetry share a kind of temporality in which the experience of passing time is concretized and perceptually enriched between a definite beginning and a definite ending.[9] These characteristics represent an antithesis to the free-floating, perceptually tenuous, vaguely bounded time-sense that informs many of our routine (and some of our urgent) activities. Our experience of these extremes, together with our protean passages between them, involves our shifting relationship with what the phenomenologists call the life-world (*Lebenswelt*)—the plane of "our common, immediate, lived experience."[10] The temporality of music and poetry resists the immediacy of a work just enough to intensify it, to invest it with certain forms of expectancy and desire. The process is very accessible to phenomenological clarification, and it is by that means that we will begin the effort to bring music and poetry into a single discourse.

When I read a poem or listen to a composition, I am aware of a heightened and strongly directed continuity among its various segments—lines, phrase-groups, stanzas, motivic statements, harmonic progressions, sectional divisions, and so on. Heterogeneity in the material is more likely to enhance this impression than to diminish it. The segments are subject to an interweaving and overlapping of their *presences* which does not at all depend on a blurring or running-together of their immediate shape or meaning. The result is a coalescence of distinctness and at-oneness which is comparable at any moment to the effect of the juncture between two words uttered in a single breath. Each segment is braided together with its counterparts in the sustained process of unfolding that realizes itself in the activity of reading or listening.[11] Taken as a whole, this richly shaped unfolding is like a reified or slightly distanced form of the consciousness of internal time by which, according to Husserl, we become aware of our own egos. Its feeling as a process is succinctly described by Rilke as "lasting squeezed out of elapsing" ("Dauer, aus Ablauf gepresst").[12]

---

[9] On this "framing" effect, see Edward T. Cone, *Musical Form and Musical Performance* (New York: Norton, 1968), pp. 11–31; and Elliott Carter, "Music and the Time Screen," in *The Writings of Elliott Carter*, compiled, edited, and annotated by Else Stone and Kurt Stone (Bloomington: Indiana University Press, 1977), pp. 343–65.

[10] Joseph H. Kockelmans, "Life-World and World-Experiencing Life," in *Phenomenology*, edited by Joseph J. Kockelmans (Garden City, N.Y.: Doubleday, 1967), p. 195.

[11] I am assuming that reading and listening are active, not passive, occurrences that proceed with minimal lapses of attention—reading as a silent recitation, listening as inner performance. Obviously, these are ideal conditions, fully achieved (even fully desirable) only part of the time, and sometimes subverted by the works that they address.

[12] Rainer Maria Rilke, "Gong." Robert P. Morgan (in "Musical Time/Musical Space," *Critical Inquiry* 6 (1980): 527–38) has pointed out how musical progression migrates to

To organize time in this way, several forms of periodicity have to exist at once, from the immediate levels of pulse or phrase-structure—which realize the shaped flow sensuously—to the consummatory level of a whole musical movement or poetic unit. At any such level, the periodicity depends on, and is perceived as, the accumulation and release of tension. This "layering" of the work need not be wholly systematic, and it may leave gaps, but there must be enough of it to engage several different time-senses simultaneously. As the levels of periodicity expand in scope from immediacy, they come to articulate the expressive meaning that we find in the work. Except in very brief works, our concrete experience of reading or listening generally attaches to a variety of intermediate-range levels of action. These, in turn, find their context, their horizon of significance, in the highest level—the pattern of tension and resolution which spans the whole. It is the highest level through which we constitute the expressive process that our concrete reading or listening experience acts out. And it is this level, too, with its large-scale temporal shapes, that under certain conditions can form the basis for the tandem interpretation of a poem and a composition.

In *Musical Form and Musical Performance*, Edward T. Cone argues that musical form is basically rhythmic. "Just as, in a normal musical period," he writes, "the antecedent phrase stands in some sense as an upbeat to its consequent, so in the large forms one entire section can stand as an upbeat to the next. And if, as I believe, there is a sense in which a phrase can be heard as an upbeat to its own cadence, larger and larger sections can be so apprehended. A completely unified composition would then constitute a single huge rhythmic impulse, completed at the final cadence."[13] Cone goes on to make the important point that these larger units are not defined metrically, as the smallest ones are; they are unfolded on the basis of a more flexible "rhythmic principle that supports the melodic and harmonic shape of the phrase" at every rhythmic level.

Poetry, no less than music, embodies a multi-layered structural rhythm as it unfolds, though at the large levels the constituents of that rhythm cannot be determined in advance; they may be images, tropes, levels of style—any rhetorical construct whatever. In *Poetic Closure*, Barbara Herrnstein Smith defines poetic structure (what I call structural rhythm) "as consisting of the

---

the rhythmic/melodic surface against a harmonically "frozen" background in much twentieth-century music. Similar effects abound in modernist poetry with the abandonment of conventional forms of narrative, descriptive, or argumentative coherence. The frequent result in both cases is to heighten the continuity within blocs of material by stressing "lasting" more than "elapsing," and to weaken the continuity between blocs. In this tradition, the dynamic relationship between "lasting" and "elapsing" becomes dialectical.

[13] Cone, *Musical Form*, pp. 25–26. "The single phrase," Cone adds, " . . . is a microcosm of the composition."

principles by which [a poem] is generated or according to which one element follows another." She goes on: "The description of a poem's structure, then, becomes the answer to the question, 'What keeps it going?' To think of poetic structure in this way, rather than as an organization of, or relationship among, elements, is to emphasize the temporal and dynamic qualities that poetry shares with music."[14] Smith denies the prospect of more concrete structural links between music and poetry; but if I am right, large temporal structures like those that she and Cone identify form the basis of the links that must exist, unless the intuitive gestures of a good many composers and poets are insubstantial.

My argument is that a poem and a composition may converge on a structural rhythm: that a shared pattern of unfolding can act as an interpretive framework for the explicit dimension of both works. Alternatively, especially in vocal music, the structural rhythm of one work may provide an interpretive framework for the structural rhythm of the other. Either way, the poem and the composition involved would form an intelligible pair—not in a vague or trivial way, but concretely and significantly. The overdetermined play of poetic connotation and musical combination would cohere through the mediation of the rhythm by which both turn time into form. And with that mediation as a context, even the less discussable, more sheerly qualitative tacit dimensions might take on new associations.

Just when and why the structural rhythms of certain works engage each other in these ways remains to be examined. Initially, a sense of the basis of convergence can rest on a second phenomenological look at structural rhythm itself. Earlier I drew a contrast between the temporal movement characteristic of music and poetry on the one hand and the movement of narrative on the other. The contrast can be usefully continued, though in terms that are somewhat idealized and are not meant to rule out mixed forms. On the whole, narrative form is opposed to the heightened rhythm of connection and association that is typical of music and poetry. The arts of narration—enigma-making, deferred disclosure, the use of unreliable and multiple narrators, manipulation of time-frames and point of view, multiple plotting, and so on—all tend to disrupt the continuity of a work. The sense of continuity must be realized by the reader's resistance to narrative mystifications. Music and poetry thus stand apart from narrative—even when they incorporate narrative elements—by embodying the other major way to organize time. Their structural rhythms embody a surplus of connective processes that in some cases—certain poems by Whitman, Apollinaire, Ashbery; certain compositions of Ives, Schoenberg, Carter—produces a vibrant fluidity that baffles the will to distinguish and interpret. This is the kind of

[14] Barbara Herrnstein Smith, *Poetic Closure: A Study of How Poems End* (Chicago: University of Chicago Press, 1968), p. 4.

temporal movement that I call gestural, and its existence both authorizes and focuses the study of convergence.

The contrast between gestural and narrative organization can be further sharpened by reference to what Wolfgang Iser calls consistency-building.[15] This is a preconscious process by which, according to Iser, the textual segments of a literary work are linked together to ensure the feeling of "good continuation." When applied to narrative, consistency-building produces a subliminal, background feeling of coherence which allows the reading process to proceed. Applied to a gestural text, and by analogy to a composition, consistency-building begins to affect the foreground of awareness. Instead of integrating actions into meaningful sequences, gestural consistency-building evokes the quality that is sometimes called "voice": the feeling of a continuous plane—or several interwoven planes—of intentionality.[16] (It does not matter whether we accept voice as somehow real or regard it as a logocentric illusion; it is the material at hand in either case.) The sense of good continuation that belongs to voice is not left half-conscious but is projected into the work, where it participates in the rise and fall of tension and manifests itself as a rhythmic/sensuous quality rather than as a conceptual one. The overdetermined, multi-layered rhythmic movement of the poem or composition supplies voice with its temporal shape, subordinates narrative elements to it, and sustains its physical, prereflective appeal. Baudelaire, who could heighten the sensuous aspect of voice to the point of hypnosis in poems like "Le Balcon" and "Harmonie du Soir," wrote suggestively about it when "dream[ing] of the miracle of a poetic prose, musical, without rhythm and without rhyme, supple enough and rugged enough to adapt itself to the lyrical impulses of the soul, the undulations of reverie, the jibes of conscience."[17]

IV

At this point an example of convergence seems to be called for. Example 1 is the entire score of Beethoven's Bagatelle in C major, Op. 119, no. 8, an easy piece to sight-read if anyone is inclined to it. I want to connect the bagatelle

[15] Wolfgang Iser, *The Act of Reading: A Theory of Aesthetic Response* (Baltimore: Johns Hopkins University Press, 1978). See especially parts III and IV.

[16] Intentionality: the directedness or orientation of consciousness toward its objects, real or imagined. In Husserl's phenomenology, intentionality is defined by the principle that consciousness is always consciousness *of* something. Musical intentionality is customarily referred to emotional states; Peter Kivy's *The Corded Shell: Reflections on Musical Expression* (Princeton: Princeton University Press, 1980) discusses the history of this practice and offers a philosophical justification of it.

[17] Charles Baudelaire, *Paris Spleen*, translated by Louise Varèse (New York: New Directions, 1970), pp. ix–x.

to Hölderlin's little poem, "Der Winkel von Hardt" ("The Nook at Hardt"), which I also give complete, together with a very literal translation:

> Hinunter sinket der Wald,
> Und Knospen ähnlich, hängen
> Einwärts die Blätter, denen
> Blüht unten auf ein Grund,
> Nicht gar unmündig.
> Da nämlich ist Ulrich
> Gegangen; oft sinnt, über den Fusstritt,
> Ein gross Schicksal
> Bereit, an übrigem Orte.

> Down sinks the forest,
> And like buds inward
> Hang the leaves, to which
> From under blooms a valley,
> Not quite inarticulate.
> For there had Ulrich
> Come; often there broods, over his footprint,
> A great destiny,
> Ready, in the left-over place.

EXAMPLE 1.   Beethoven, Bagatelle in C Major, Op. 119, No. 8.

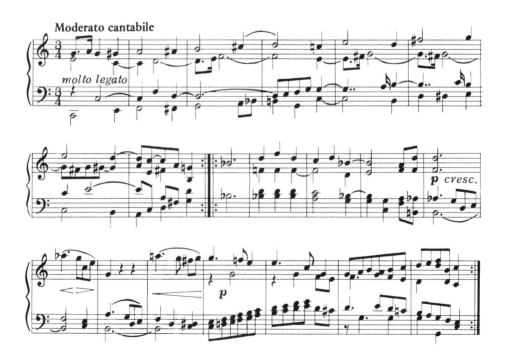

Beethoven's bagatelle, a tiny interlude of utterly relaxed lyricism, falls into two unequal parts (mm. 1–16, 17–20) that do not coincide with the more balanced division of its binary form (mm. 1–8, 9–20, both sections repeated). The piece is initially concerned with the unhurried resolution of several chromatically altered chords—augmented triads—that represent the surface intricacies of a simple underlying tonic-dominant pattern (mm. 1–8). There is also some prominent chromatic ornamentation, which eventually extends to chromatic harmony (mm. 9–12) before the music turns back toward a somewhat wobbly dominant (mm. 13–16). Measures 17–20 abandon all of these features for a bright, severe, almost modalized tonic-dominant surface. The structural rhythm suggested by these shifts in texture is a gradual movement from a nuanced, gently mystified version of C major to a blunt, clarified one, with the dominant progressions of mm. 13–16 forming a transitional area. This shift can be taken as a large-scale projection of the expressive voice-leading in mm. 1–4, where augmented triads resolve in turn to the subdominant, dominant, and (with some mediation) tonic triads of C major.

But Beethoven's design has a curious catch to it. For all its enhanced dissonance, the first part of the piece remains firmly centered on the tonic; its harmonic obscurities are local, not structural, and there is no genuine modulation. In fact, the tonic orientation tends to grow richer and stronger as the harmonic details grow more involuted; every mystification yields a greater transparency. This process begins in mm. 1–4 and reaches its height in mm. 9–14. The augmented triads of mm. 1–2 affect only the harmonies adjacent to them; they alter the preceding chord and resolve to the following one. The augmented triad in m. 3 is more expansive; it begins a broad cadential progression that evolves through two measures of elaboration on the dominant-seventh chord. More expansive still is the deceptive chromatic harmony of mm. 9–12, which robs the binary form of its full contrastive significance. Just before the *A* section ends, the music works its way around to a cadence on the dominant, as if to anticipate a dominant opening to the *B* section. But the *B* section begins with a surprise approach to the subdominant, F, and goes on to evolve a cadential progression in F major. The new key is really F, then—except that it is not a new key at all. The cadential progression no sooner touches on the supposedly tonicized F-major triad than the music dissolves back into C major, a process that occupies only a single beat. C major has been the basic harmony all along, as Beethoven has in effect told us already by his way of forming the dominant seventh of F. Given first with its root omitted (a common procedure), the chord is completed under its prolonged upper notes by a bare fifth in the bass that spells out the tonic: C–G.

With C major so luminously persistent, the new texture at mm. 17–20 does not so much clarify as merely simplify it. The brightness and fullness of the pure tonic sonority borders on excess—a slight discontinuity, a shade of overstatement. In the same vein, the closing passage does not release the tensions accumulated through earlier harmonic indirections, but heightens them. As the music quickens in pace, an ascending scale in thirds carries it into a two-and-a-half measure elaboration of the dominant-seventh chord (mm. 18–20, expanding and destabilizing mm. 3–4). The continuous dissonance draws added force from the details of rhythm and voice-leading, especially from a series of four major-second clashes in the upper voices (mm. 18–19). The high point of harmonic tension coincides with the last of these, which decorates two statements of the dominant-seventh chord by interposing a further dissonance, v^7/ii, a process anticipated at the juncture of mm. 18–19. This conjunction of harmonies condenses and intensifies the broad dominant cadence that closes the binary *A* section, and it compels a reinforced dominant preparation for the final cadence to C major.

Beethoven's lyric miniature, then, depends on an understated, almost casual antithesis in which the opposed elements—oblique and direct harmonic textures—reverse their usual expressive roles. The music is embryonically dialectical; its structural rhythm consists of a single statement of its dialectical possibilities, which are then left in suspension. The piece is, as I said, utterly relaxed; the fullness of its ease is its dialectical laziness.

The Hölderlin poem has a structural rhythm virtually identical to that of the bagatelle. Here again there are two parts—two sentences of unequal length—which again seem to be set in a conventional relationship. The first part pictures a landscape; the second provides a kind of inscription for it, on the model of an epitaph or votive epigram. The genre, as Geoffrey Hartman has shown, is a familiar one.[18] Yet here, too, there is a catch. The poem wants to move from nature, embodied in the forest and flower imagery, to history, embodied in the monumental stones that record the Robert Bruce-like refuge of Duke Ulrich of Würtemberg, a Swabian national hero. On the face of it, this move is a decline as well as an homage; it exchanges the clarity of organic form in nature for the mystification of an unidentified "great destiny," something that acts as a spirit of place only by right of intrusion. Yet the sentence by which Hölderlin describes the natural landscape is almost unintelligible. Its syntax is so snarled as to border on the perverse; its imagery deliberately blurs the actual (the leaves and the forest) into the metaphorical (the valley as a flower in bloom); and the last phrase, "not quite inarticulate," is an enigma until the poem is over. The natural scene, moreover, is not altogether as tranquil as it is supposed to be. The description of the leaves hanging inward like buds registers a slight uneasiness. It is as if time were moving backwards, undoing the organic fullness embodied by the "blooming" of the landscape.

[18] Geoffrey Hartman, "Wordsworth, Inscriptions, and Romantic Nature Poetry," in his *Beyond Formalism*, pp. 42–60.

In the second half of the poem, history appears as an agent of clarification. The quasi-phantasmal forest scene is rationalized, pinpointed, as the site of Ulrich's nook, and Hölderlin puts it on the map in language that is perfectly straightforward, even blunt. It is the stony monumentality of history, moreover, that supplies the organic serenity that nature could not quite sustain. Although obscure, the "great destiny" that haunts the nook is "prepared," fully grown. Its "meditation" constitutes a reassuring presence that fills in the absences suggested by the footprints and the "left-over" quality of the place, in oblique contrast to the "sinking" forest and the involuted, retrogressive leaves. Nature and history thus exchange their conventional roles, just as the harmonic styles do in the Beethoven bagatelle. And the poem, like the composition, unfolds by embracing a pair of dialectical possibilities and then leaving them in an embryonic state. Both works become serene by declining to reconcile the antithesis that shapes them.

V

The high degree of convergence in these works of Beethoven and Hölderlin is, of course, specific to their cultural situation. The possibility of convergence is a function of cultural history; there is nothing necessary about it at any time. If we now ask where and why it arises, the answer will lead to the territory mapped out by my title: the nineteenth century and after.

Broadly speaking, the relationship between music and poetry has undergone two major transformations since the Middle Ages. The first and best-known change evolves during the Renaissance along with the momentous shift from linear counterpoint to simultaneous harmony as the basis of composition; it is marked by the development of text-sensitive styles of vocal composition, most notably in the early Italian opera, the Italian madrigal, and the English air. Music during the Renaissance learns to become responsive to poetry, establishing an unprecedented intimacy with the poetic expression of feeling. As a result, music—and not just vocal music—expands its connotative range by supporting itself on poetic imagery. In return, sixteenth- and seventeenth-century poetry often associates the voice of the poetic speaker with the singing voice by imitating the expressive effects of certain vocal styles. Milton's "Lycidas," for instance, is identified as a "Monody," and its famous injunction to the Muses to "somewhat loudly sweep the string" points to an imitation of the declamatory intensity of Italian song.

The second large-scale realignment of music and poetry is more elusive, almost subliminal, unaffiliated with any given style. Appearing around the turn of the nineteenth century, it belongs as much to instrumental as to vocal music, and as much to poetry as to either. From a theoretical point of view, this new realignment is the rise of convergence itself—the dissemination of structural rhythms from work to work. From the standpoint of cultural history, it might best be described as a conviction that music and poetry have the same preconscious sources, that they differ only in the means of representing a primary condition of imagination. Thus Beethoven could say that his musical ideas were "incited by moods, which are translated by the poet into words, by me into tones that sound"; Schumann could praise Brahms for writing "lieder whose poetry one could understand without knowing the words"; and Whitman could identify his imagination in the act of writing with both the instrument and the "capricious tunes" of a disembodied musician:

> Thy song expands my numb'd imbonded spirit,
>   thou freest, launchest me,
> Floating and basking upon heaven's lake.
> . . . .
> O trumpeter, methinks I am myself the instrument thou playest.
>   ("The Mystic Trumpeter")

Wallace Stevens put it most bluntly: "The music [we heard] was a communication of emotion. It would not have been different if it had been the music of poetry."[19]

The basis of this reciprocity is the appearance of a radically new model for completeness in a gestural work. Avant-garde experiments aside, virtually all works of music or poetry move toward closure by referring to a normative pattern. The composition or poem, to use Barbara Smith's formula, is kept going in some intelligible way and brought to a satisfying close—concluded, not merely stopped—with a relevant gesture.[20] Prior to the nineteenth century, norms for completeness were ordinarily based on some concept of rationality and modeled on forms of discourse that could be accepted as self-evidently coherent. As a rule, these discursive models of completeness produce structural rhythms that function as expressions of a coherent "statement." A lyric poem might accordingly unfold as a logical argument, an extended description, the development of an analogy, the elaboration of a distinction, or the presentation of a problem and its solution. A composition would similarly unfold as an instance of a harmonically or contrapuntally determined form—the fugue, the *da capo* aria, a dance form, or one of the sonata forms, among others. Moreover, a discursively based poem or composition would ordinarily identify its periodic features with the subdivisions appropriate to presenting its statement, to articulating its form. A Renaissance sonnet amalgamates units of thought and units of verse by sub-

---

[19] Wallace Stevens, *The Necessary Angel: Essays on Reality and the Imagination* (New York: Vintage Books, 1951), p. 126.

[20] Smith, *Poetic Closure*, pp. 1–2.

division into quatrain and couplet, octave and sestet. The second theme of a Classical sonata-allegro movement affirms the tonic-dominant polarity on which the whole depends—a functional role so important that the theme itself may be melodically negligible.

A work based on a discursive model can admit discontinuities and perplexities of all sorts without risking its formal coherence. Donne's more fantastic conceits test this proposition to the limit and always vindicate it; so do the puzzle canons of Bach's *Musical Offering*, especially the one marked "Seek and ye shall find," with its inverted and retrograded subject admitting of four possible solutions. Discursive works, we might say, are invulnerably meaningful. Like the "classic texts" imagined by Roland Barthes, they limit the constructive or deconstructive freedom of their interpreters by preempting a complete "mastery over meaning" for the artist. Barthes, with typical fondness for a rhetorical neologism, calls this mastery "a veritable semiurgism," and sees a claim to quasi-divine power in it. The artist's conception originates the work and becomes embedded in it; meaning is understood as a kind of overflow "from content to form, from idea to text, from passion to expression"—in general, from signified to signifier.[21]

For the "semiurgic" power of a discursive work to sustain itself, the route from the signified to the signifier has to be kept open. The sequence of passages from content to form must be transparent, self-explanatory, at least in retrospect. This demand can be met only if the signified is able to rationalize any play of signifiers, no matter how intricate or bizarre, that might be animated by it. Rationally enough, therefore, both poetry and music assign the role of the discursive signified to whatever general term organizes their explicit features. The "content" of a discursive poem is an idea or a passion; the "form" is an adequate statement of the content; and the work unfolds by incorporating the mingled play of connotation and tacitly realized sonority into the "overflow" from content to form. Analogously, the content of a discursive composition is a set of tonal relationships; the form is their dynamic, periodic projection through time; and the work unfolds by incorporating the mingled play of combinatory tension and tacitly realized feeling into the semiurgic overflow.

The discursive models, then, produce structural rhythms that are firmly tied to the incommensurate properties of poetry and music—predicative language and harmony. As a result, the styles based on such models, which were pre-eminent until the end of the Enlightenment, tend to exaggerate the semiotic asymmetry between the two arts. What this means in turn is that discursive poems and compositions are not likely to converge in significant ways; their structural rhythms can only confront each other across the locked gate of semiotic difference. Gestural relationships in "classical" pe-

---

[21] Roland Barthes, *S/Z*, translated by Richard Howard (New York: Hill and Wang, 1974), p. 174.

riods, therefore, will generally be limited to the congruities of style that emerge when cultural circumstances prompt the two arts to adopt similar criteria for coherence. Pope and Handel, for instance, might plausibly be paired on the basis of an analogy between the Baroque sequence and the heroic couplet. But though Pope may praise Handel's power "to stir, to rouze, to shake the soul" (*Dunciad* IV, 67), a Handel *Allegro* and a Pope character assassination are not good candidates for a tandem interpretation.

At the turn of the nineteenth century, a non-discursive model of completeness appears in both music and poetry and makes convergence accessible to the two arts. Announced at first in works that are almost aggressively experimental—Wordsworth's and Coleridge's *Lyrical Ballads*, for instance, or Beethoven's Opus 27 piano sonatas *quasi una fantasia*—this new model quickly naturalizes itself into a position of dominance. Its basis is a historical shift in what might be called the identity of consciousness; broadly speaking, it rests on a surrender of the integration of human inwardness in favor of ontological primacy. A change of such magnitude cannot be compassed by a single description, and I can only try to be suggestive. One thing to call it is the recognition (or constitution) of the ego as one of the activities of a transcendental subject; another is the discovery of consciousness as an independent entity, a dynamic force set over against both the objects and the subject of which it becomes conscious. The discovery of consciousness in this sense is one of the great tasks of post-Enlightenment philosophy and poetry, as Marshall Brown has demonstrated.[22] By drawing on that discovery, both music and poetry could and did develop a structural model in which the criterion of completeness is the full working-out of a process in the mind, the expression of a rhythm within the dynamics of consciousness. The presence of such a model is fully evident even in the little Beethoven and Hölderlin works we have looked at, where the structural rhythm embodies a deliberately detached and indolent review of dialectical tensions. But signs of the consciousness model are hard not to see. Wordsworth's *The Prelude* and Goethe's *Faust*, with their complex ego-psychologies, Beethoven's Ninth Symphony, with its explicit proposal that music is a psychodrama whose resolution at the point of impasse is song—these are only the seminal members of a vast series of works that stretches into the present. At its inception, the consciousness model rested largely on the expressive theories of art and the valorization of organic processes that were culturally ascendant around 1800.[23] Theoretical associations of music and poetry with dynamic elements in consciousness also provided support—the philosophical identification of music with pre-verbal or intuitive consciousness, or what Hegel

[22] Marshall Brown, "The Pre-Romantic Discovery of Consciousness," *Studies in Romanticism* 17 (1978): 387–412.

[23] For a discussion of these theories, see M. H. Abrams, *The Mirror and the Lamp: Romantic Theory and the Critical Tradition* (New York: Norton, 1953).

called "subjective inwardness," and the referral of poetry to a primary creative faculty, Coleridge's "shaping spirit of Imagination." But the model has long outlasted its background, displacing itself through an endless series of reinterpretations. Only the most extreme avant-garde works of recent decades have managed to work free of it, and often at a very high price.

The use of the consciousness model for completeness does not mean that discursive patterns are eliminated, though it is true that the impression of self-evident coherence erodes steadily in both music and poetry until the early twentieth century, and vanishes entirely in works like Schoenberg's *Erwartung* and Eliot's *The Waste Land*. There are no norms here, but in most cases a structural rhythm based on the consciousness model is superimposed on a discursive structure and acts as a kind of subtext to it, a subliminal, "subjectified" flow of tension and resolution that thrusts into the foreground in displaced forms. Our Beethoven bagatelle and Hölderlin lyric both depend on such superimposed structures. Each work uses its "subliminal" structural rhythm to put a conventional discursive pattern out of focus, and each marks its point of departure from discursive control with a slight incoherence, a small touch of thoughtlessness. The bagatelle subverts the poise of binary form by awkwardly balancing seventeen chromatic measures against four diatonic ones; the poem makes the sequence of landscape and inscription irrational by importing the history-centered phrase, "nicht gar unmündig," into its first, nature-centered sentence. The result, in each case, is that the dialectical subtext of the work is translated into a curiously heightened air of casualness.

The nature of a structural rhythm that unfolds, so to speak, below the surface can best be described—perhaps surprisingly—by calling the rhythm cathectic. Cathexis is the process, described by psychoanalysis, by which a subject invests a portion of its psychic energy in an object and thereby makes the object meaningful for itself. Freud's German term, *Besetzung*, means both "occupation" and "electric charge." The exact interpretation of how a subject becomes "occupied" with an object by "charging" it psychologically is a problematical issue in contemporary psychoanalysis, but it is not relevant here.[24] The term can be elucidated very rewardingly with some simple phenomenology.

---

[24] As my argument makes clear, I believe that the concept of cathexis can be interpreted without relying on a reification of "psychic energy"; its essential concern is with the way in which the world of our experience is differentially saturated with affective value. On the general problem, see Roy Shafer, *Language and Insight: The Sigmund Freud Lectures at University College, London* (New Haven: Yale University Press, 1978).

Another problem with cathexis is the term itself. As many commentators have pointed out, "cathexis" is a falsely learned translation of Freud's ordinary German. In this single instance, however, there may be no better alternative. No English word is available with the punning connections of Freud's "*Besetzung*"—electrical charge, investment (of concern), occupation with, occupation of (as in a militaty occupation)—and perhaps the closest English terms, "investment" and "occupation," are the poorest translations because

A bit of scene-setting has to come first. Suppose that I am standing by an open window, overlooking a path that ends some distance away under a low-hanging tree; the tree partially obscures the street beyond the path. I am expecting the approach of someone important to me, though I do not necessarily tell myself that I am looking for the person. Under these circumstances, certain features of the scene before me will take on an extra significance that does not depend on my awareness of them. They will be bathed in a nonperceptual intensity that infiltrates the scene as a whole and subverts its integration. If a bird alights on the lawn, or a car passes, or the sun slips behind a cloud, I will observe these things normally, perhaps even with momentary interest; in a sense, they represent a kind of discursive structure, the process of watching the day go by. But if the low-hanging branches of the tree rustle, as if brushed by someone, or I hear footsteps, or see someone half-hidden by the tree walk up the street, I will instantly concentrate all my attention on that sight or sound. What is more, I have been ready to do so at every moment. What happens at the intersection of tree, street, and path continuously affects me more than anything else in the scene, even though I am watching the day go by all the time. The rhythm of my experience is determined by the space that is crucial to me and consummated by the arrival that I am waiting for. I have "cathected" that spot at the end of the path.

Most of the structural rhythms dealt with below are cathectic in the phenomenological sense. Their relationship to the discursive "surfaces" that they support is concretely unpredictable and always discontinuous. They may disrupt the surface, intertwine with it, alter its focus, or virtually obliterate it—but in one way or another the surface is always marked, perhaps always marred. Here again the expressive imbalances in Beethoven's bagatelle and Hölderlin's lyric are typical. Cathectic rhythms always open a breach in the framework of discourse, as if to posit a place where the dynamics of a consciousness—with itself, with the world, with its unconscious—cannot be contained by an external coherence.

We might describe this effect by one more recourse to a psychoanalytic phenomenology. Wherever the discursive rhythm of a work appears as a breakable surface rather than as a solid foundation, its cathectic subtext takes on the role of an unconscious impulse (more exactly: a train of primary-process thought), though not necessarily the content of one. As Wallace Stevens put it, describing a related kind of "irrational moment,"

> These are not things transformed,
> Yet we are shaken by them as if they were.
> We reason about them with a later reason.
> ("Notes Toward A Supreme Fiction")

---

of their unavoidable connotations of finance and labor. "Cathexis" has also acquired the side-benefit of signifying the interpretive involvement of psychoanalysis itself. For better or worse, we seem to be stuck with it.

The work thus replicates and so to speak de-neuroticizes the intrapsychic tension that invests discontinuities in conscious processes with the intensity of unconscious desire. The insistent subjective thrust of the cathectic rhythm achieves expression through a decrease in discursive lucidity—the classic analytic combination of concealment and disclosure that mediates an unconscious idea. The work, we might say, borrows the power of the dynamic unconscious while demanding nothing more radical than a pre-conscious realization of its cathectic rhythm.

As a result of this "compromise formation," the temporality of a cathectic rhythm is always felt as the function of an ego. The cathectic rhythm itself, moreover, will always take on a tangible form in a qualitative feature of the work—the surplus of relaxation in our Beethoven and Hölderlin examples—that supports the expressive life of the whole. Through the mediation of its cathectic rhythm, the work is "charged" by both the consciousness that it embodies and the consciousness that is occupied with it.

VI

No one would deny that discursive works can incorporate cathectic elements, even ones that cannot be fully assimilated to the discursive pattern. The finale of Haydn's "Farewell" Symphony, with its disjunctive form and constantly thinning texture, is an obvious example, though also a telling one because the work is an unrepeatable experiment. Milton's "Lycidas," taken as a poem about the poet's vocation rather than as an elegy, not only goes even further than the Haydn, but also anticipates the consciousness model. (Only anticipates it, I think, as a comparison with Shelley's "Adonais" should show at once.) Yet cathectic patterns virtually never rival or displace discursive ones as structural rhythms in the absence of the consciousness model. The privileged position of cathexis, and with it the possibility of convergence, is only established when the ego has become dynamic, problematical, and openly constitutive of both inner and outer meaning. In other words, cathectic structural rhythms are a product of Romanticism, and so, consequently, is convergence.

I have held back the term "Romanticism" so far (though it has obviously been waiting in the wings), partly because its musical meaning is nebulous and partly because to identify it as a part of my subject obliges me to spell out my understanding of it. There are mare's nests in those woods. In a famous essay of 1924, A. O. Lovejoy challenged the term, and nervous apologies have dogged it ever since, though no one has stopped using it. My own view is that Romanticism is by now intelligible both as a "closed" phenomenon in the history of the arts—most clearly of literature—and as an "open" phe-

nomenon in the history of consciousness.[25] At least three features are widely
regarded as essential to it; I take these to be neither themes nor ideas, but
structural presuppositions behind works of art and speculative thought.
First, as René Wellek puts it, Romanticism is a "great endeavor to overcome
the split between subject and object, the self and the world, the conscious
and the unconscious."[26] To this we should add several qualifications: that
Romanticism is initially a way of *conceiving* existence as split into antagonistic subjects and objects (a point particularly stressed by Morse Peckham);
that the "great endeavor" of reunification is inherently problematical and
self-questioning; and that subjects and objects are potentially constitutive of
each other.[27] Second, Romanticism is committed, willingly or not, to a
heightening of self-consciousness. Two formulations help pinpoint the consequences: Kierkegaard's "Every increase in consciousness is an increase in
despair"; and Geoffrey Hartman's "[Romanticism] seeks to draw the anti-
dote to self-consciousness from consciousness itself."[28] Finally, Romanticism supports a historical process in which subjects come to occupy the cultural or metaphysical place formerly occupied by objects. Both Jacques
Derrida and M. H. Abrams, antithetical thinkers in most respects, identify
this apotheosis of the subject—Derrida as a shift in the focus of "logocentric" metaphysics from divinity to consciousness, Abrams as the seculariz-
ing and internalizing of the structures of traditional religion.[29]

My treatment of Romanticism in the chapters that follow is fairly cautious about historical boundaries. Each chapter deals with roughly contem-
poraneous figures and more than half the book is concerned with the Romantic period, loosely defined to accommodate both musical and literary
usage. Chronology is not history, however, and I assume without apology
that Romanticism is a historically continuous phenomenon, however problematical its continuity may be. The chronological arrangement here is only

---

[25] A. O. Lovejoy, "On the Discrimination of Romanticisms," in his *Essays in the History of Ideas* (Baltimore: Johns Hopkins University Press, 1948), pp. 228–53. History of
consciousness: Geoffrey Hartman, "On the Theory of Romanticism," in his *The Fate of
Reading* (Chicago: University of Chicago Press, 1975), pp. 277–83.

[26] René Wellek, "The Concept of Romanticism in Literary History," in his *Concepts of
Criticism*, edited by Steven G. Nichols, Jr. (New Haven: Yale University Press, 1963), p.
220.

[27] Morse Peckham, *Man's Rage for Chaos: Biology, Behavior, and the Arts* (New York:
Schocken Books, 1967), pp. 291–307.

[28] Geoffrey Hartman, "Romanticism and Anti-Self-Consciousness," in his *Beyond Formalism*, p. 300.

[29] M. H. Abrams, *Natural Supernaturalism: Tradition and Revolt in Romantic Literature* (New York: Norton, 1971). Jacques Derrida: *Of Grammatology*, translated by Gaya-
tri Chakravorty Spivak (Baltimore: Johns Hopkins University Press, 1976).

a convenience; the various convergence paradigms are not meant to form a sequence, but rather a repertoire of structures which is constantly available. Accordingly, my chapters on historically Romantic figures regularly move forward in time to sketch the subsequent development of the structural rhythms I have been considering. The chapters on later music and poetry similarly assume the affiliations of their subjects with the Romantic past.

By Romanticism, then, I mean not a style but an activity, and one that should not be obscured by our habits of labeling. The "Romantic" Schumann is a contemporary of the "Victorian" Browning—whose speaker in the poem "Le Byron De Nos Jours" remarks that "Schumann's our music-maker now . . . / Heine [the man] for songs."[30] In this connection, Beethoven requires a special comment. When I treat him as a Romantic, I do not intend to recycle old clichés or to suggest that his formal affinities are with Liszt and Wagner rather than with Haydn and Mozart. The point is that his development and transformation of the Classical style is guided by the framework of assumptions that constitutes Romanticism.

VII

When a poem and a composition converge, the intertextual link between them can represent two kinds of intimacy. In some cases, the structural rhythm through which various works are affiliated acts like a genre or paradigm, and its characteristic patterns, problems, and phenomenology appear as a kind of impromptu grammar of particulars. Convergence on a paradigm is usually motivated by the cultural strength of Romantic premises independent of influence, homage, or imitation. (Allusions do not guarantee structural parallels in any case. Debussy, for example, presents his piano prelude "Le sons et les parfums tournent dans l'air du soir" as a reflection on Baudelaire's poem "Harmonie du soir," but the prelude is fluid and asymmetrical where the poem is almost perversely rigid.) My two chapters on Wordsworth and Beethoven and the chapters on Shelley and Chopin, Stevens and Ives are devoted to this indirect form of connection, which is most characteristic of instrumental music, though not exclusive to it. The remaining chapters—one on the problem of song, one on John Ashbery and Elliott Carter—take up the second form of intimacy, the direct appropriation of one work by another. As the chapter topics suggest, direct connection ordinarily proceeds from composers writing vocal music, though program music falls within its province and poets—Browning for one—do sometimes attempt it.

---

[30] The full title of the poem is "Dis Aliter Visum; Or, Le Byron de Nos Jours." The text is taken from Browning's *Complete Poetical Works*, edited by Augustine Birrell (New York: Macmillan, 1915).

The actual essays in gestural analysis now await, but one further issue invites comment before we turn to them. Coleridge once wrote of some poetry, "Had I met [these lines] running wild in the deserts of Arabia, I should instantly have screamed out, 'Wordsworth!' "[31] The deserts of Arabia no longer seem like the last place on earth, but we might still like to know if the same trick would work with a wild convergence. The trouble is that convergence does not depend on overt formal similarities between works but on shared ways of organizing change and provoking interpretation; there is really no way to be prescriptive about it. Our theoretical framework, however, does permit a pair of suggestions. First, since the structural rhythms that support convergence must be "mobile," they are nearly always based on such purely formal properties of temporal progression as may also be highly charged with experience—that is, heavily cathected. Repetition, for instance, the subject of the chapter to follow, can be either a formal burden or, in some circumstances, a psychological burden. Beethoven and Wordsworth treat it compellingly as both in the "Appassionata" sonata and "The Thorn." Second, since convergence ordinarily requires a cathectic rather than a discursive rhythm, convergent works tend to share some vital qualitative feature that results from cathectic pressure against the discursive surface. Such features may also be shared by the styles of two artists in the absence of convergence, but in that case it pays to look for convergent works as well. A great many works by Chopin and Shelley, for example, seem to sustain a high degree of expressive intensity independent of both their ostensible feeling-tone and their primary structural tensions. In some cases, this free-floating intensity seems to be allied with an impulse toward fragmentation. These intuitions may not lead us to scream "convergence" or anything else—but they may help us to see similar patterns of self-transformation at work in Chopin's preludes and Shelley's "Ode to the West Wind." In the end, though, such clues are probably less important than a simple recognition of the importance of gestural questions, the value of gestural time. Once a feeling for structural rhythm plays a part in reading and listening, convergences begin to suggest themselves.

[31] Samuel Taylor Coleridge, *Collected Letters,* edited by E. L. Griggs (Oxford: Oxford University Press, 1956), I: 453.

2

Romantic Repetition

No star
Of wildest course but treads back his own steps;
For the spent hurricane the air provides
As fierce a successor; the tide retreats
But to return out of its hiding place
In the great deep; all things have second birth;
The earthquake is not satisfied at once.

(WORDSWORTH, *The Prelude* [1850])

You say I am repeating
Something I have said before. I shall say it again.
Shall I say it again?

(T. S. ELIOT, "East Coker")

Repetition is a basic structural feature of most music and poetry. At the level of metrical pulse and phrase structure, where it is perceived almost subliminally, repetition is largely responsible for the heightened feeling of interwovenness, the tangible sense of continuity and organic relatedness, that sets musical and poetic forms apart from others. On a large scale—as rhyme or stanza forms in poetry; as rondo, sonata, or binary forms in music; as closural recurrence in both—repetition guides the recognition of structure and shapes the perceiver's sense of balance or proportion.[1] Prior to the nineteenth century, however, neither music nor poetry makes much use of uncodified repetition—that is, of repetition not primarily determined by the norms of style or structure followed by a given work. In poetry, uncodified repetition usually appears, when it appears at all, to suggest an excess of emotion; its use is essentially dramatic and its prototype probably King Lear's "Never never never never never." Milton is the master stylist in this mode:

[1] Barbara Herrnstein Smith, *Poetic Closure: A Study of How Poems End* (Chicago: University of Chicago Press, 1968), pp. 38–40.

More safe I sing with mortal voice, unchanged
To hoarse or mute, though fall'n on evil days,
On evil days though fall'n, and evil tongues.

(*Paradise Lost*, VII, 24–26)

O dark, dark, dark, amid the blaze of noon,
Irrecoverably dark, total eclipse
Without all hope of day!

(*Samson Agonistes*, 80–82)

In music, uncodified repetition is often a principle of stability. Haydn uses it that way in certain of his variation movements—the Romanza of the Eighty-fifth Symphony, for instance, where the genial second half of a folk-song theme returns unchanged in each variation, bathing the whole piece in an air of relaxed warmth. Bach does something similar in the opening Prelude of *The Well-Tempered Clavier*, Book I, where a single figuration is tirelessly repeated over a slowly descending bass. The contour of the bass-line anticipates the design of the entire cycle of preludes and fugues and also hints lightly at the epochal range of harmonies to be canvassed. Yet all the while, the music stays securely in the tonic.[2]

Late in the eighteenth century, uncodified repetition begins to appear, though only in a few works, as an element of disruption and dissociation. The first movement of Mozart's D-Major String Quintet, K. 593, ends with a repetition instead of a coda; both the slow introduction and the opening measures of the *Allegro* return unaltered. Haydn's "Drum Roll" Symphony (No. 103) repeats its bleak, harsh opening gesture—a drum roll followed by a gritty unison in the deep bass—as a kind of obstacle between the recapitulation and coda. The effect in both cases, enhanced by minor-key harmony, is unsettling, even a little uncanny. It is as if the music were turning against itself accusingly for a failure to master the tensions that had originated it. In the *Romanza* of Mozart's D-Minor Piano Concerto, K. 466, the sweetly lulling repetitions of the romance theme are dialectically collapsed by the fulminating G-minor middle section; what has seemed to be tranquil immobility is suddenly challenged as anxious self-control.

In poetry, we find Blake using the imagery of mindless, mechanical repetition, particularly the "starry wheels" of the Newtonian universe and the "for-ever restless" sea, to represent the deathly sleep of the human imagina-

---

[2] C major. The climax of the piece comes in m. 22, where the tritone F♯ emerges as the first and only chromatic bass note in the piece. The function of the chord is iv$^{7♭}_{1♯}$; resolution is to the dominant substitute of vii°[7], with F♯ rising to A♭. The only distance intimated is the farthest. It should be noted, incidentally, that some editions print a spurious measure—not found in any of Bach's autographs—that interpolates a G in the bass between the F♯ and A♭.

tion. The echoes of this bondage also infiltrate his language:

> Albion cold lays on his Rock; storms and snows beat round him
> Beneath the Furnaces & the starry Wheels & the Immortal Tomb.
> Howling winds cover him, roaring seas dash furious against him,
> In the deep darkness broad lightnings glare, deep thunder rolls.
> The weeds of death inwrap his hands & feet, blown incessant
> And washd incessant by the for-ever restless sea-waves foaming
> Upon the white Rock.
>
> (*Jerusalem*, Plate 94, 1–7)

In Klopstock's delicately tense lyric, "Das Rosenband," the surplus repetition of words and phrases is associated with unachieved love; the echoes carry from line to line and from stanza to stanza. Only with the last phrase or so does repetition turn to reciprocity, frustration to fulfillment. The final line, "Und um uns ward's Elysium," revises the first, which had located the incipient lovers "Im Frühlingsschatten," and the effect of this relocation is to cancel out the intervening repetitions in the pleasure of what amounts to self-deification. These instances of disruptive repetition, however, powerful though they are, remain isolated effects, tentative ventures into a new area. Their impact on form is relatively localized; their significance is not fully clarified.

Not until the next generation, with Wordsworth and Beethoven, do we find a fully developed version of disruptive uncodified repetition—one that is both lucid in its expressiveness and critical to the large-scale structure that embraces it. In a work with this structural rhythm—we can call it Romantic repetition—the "unnecessary" repetition of a phrase, a gesture, a narrative unit, a sectional unit, or the like, has the status of a mental stammer, a sign that the normal operations of consciousness have been thwarted. Potentially uncontrollable, this stammer cannot be cured by letting it run its course or resolving it into other material. It has to be thwarted itself, decisively, by the arbitrary intrusion of a new structural element. As my language suggests, the feeling carried by this Romantic repetition usually involves distress, disturbance, or turbulence. The state of mind evoked has overtones of abnormality, particularly of obsessiveness, and the release that follows the abrupt curtailment of repetition has a cathartic or therapeutic quality. It might even be said that the therapeutic impulse is what determines the form of the poem or composition.

Intuitively convincing examples of this poetics of repetition are easy to find.[3] Two works steeped in incipient hysteria make a striking pair: the song

---

[3] My use of this term differs from that of Ronald Schleifer, "Wordsworth's Yarrow and the Poetics of Repetition," *Modern Language Quarterly* 38 (1977): 348–66. Schleifer is concerned with Wordsworth's need to re-create the past in the present—something I discuss briefly later on under the term *recurrence*.

"Die liebe Farbe' from Schubert's *Die schöne Müllerin*, where internal repetitions on the phrase "Mein Schatz hat's Grün so gern" (which also allude
to and negate the music of a song placed earlier in the cycle, "Mit dem
grünen Lautenbande") absorb even the strophic form into the "illness" of
repetition; and the lyric "Go Not, Happy Day," from Tennyson's *Maud*,
with its fingerdrumming and, as it turns out, premonitory insistence on red.
Back at the source, there is the "unscheduled" third repetition of the scherzo in Beethoven's String Quartet in E♭ Major, Op. 74. Ferocious when played
on its two normal appearances as an alternation of loud and soft, the music
returns for its encore as a ghostly *diminuendo* from *p* to *ppp*, as if its vexed
harshness were demanding the right to become an ominous undertone to the
variations of the *grazioso* finale. (But Beethoven also provides the exception
that proves the rule: the stammer of transport in the repetitions of the "Pastoral" Symphony.) As to Wordsworth, the double presentation of percep-
tions estranged by vision—a pool, a tower, and a woman—in Book XI of
The Prelude (1805) not only exemplifies Romantic repetition but even
names its surpassing quality, a "visionary dreariness":[4]

> [I] saw
> A naked Pool that lay beneath the hills,
> The Beacon on the summit, and more near,
> A Girl who bore a Pitcher on her head
> And seem'd with difficult steps to force her way
> Against the blowing wind. It was, in truth,
> An ordinary sight; but I should need
> Colours and words that are unknown to man
> To paint the visionary dreariness
> Which, while I look'd all round for my lost guide,
> Did at that time invest the naked Pool,
> The Beacon on the lonely Eminence,
> The Woman, and her garments vex'd and toss'd
> By the stong wind.
>
>   (303–16)

In this chapter, I will look closely at Romantic repetition in two richly
problematical works—Wordsworth's "The Thorn" and Beethoven's Piano
Sonata in F Minor, Op. 57 ("Appassionata"), then offer some general reflections on its compelling and compulsive character.

---

[4] For a full analysis of this passage in terms of estrangement and repetition, see my
" 'That Other Will': The Daemonic in Coleridge and Wordsworth," *Philological Quarterly* 85 (1979): 298–320.

II

"The Thorn" has always been a controversial poem, and one can still find it disparaged as merely feeble and wordy.[5] Since Steven Maxfield Parrish's study, *The Art of the Lyrical Ballads*, however, readers have increasingly come to recognize the power of the poem by taking it as a dramatic monologue that is intent on exposing its narrator's peculiar state of mind.[6] Approached in this way, "The Thorn" might be described as a study in contagious obsession, in which one person's pathological repetitions turn out to be catching when others are exposed to them. At the start of this mad relay, which both enfeebles and galvanizes its victims, stands the figure of Martha Ray—seduced, abandoned, and demented by grief. Martha resorts to the thorn tree "at all hours of the day and night," and her compulsive actions, in a pattern that holds good for all the characters of "The Thorn," is matched and heightened by a compulsive habit of speech. The verbal tic in her case is a repeated cry, a lament that is itself a repetition: "Oh misery! oh misery! / Oh woe is me! oh misery!" Martha is, in fact, never heard to say anything else but this, as if thought and feeling in her have been completely dissolved into her chant-like babble.

The sound of Martha's "pitiless dismay" begins the cycle of contagion in the poem by capturing the psyche of the narrator in a single traumatic moment. Seeking shelter from a storm, the narrator meets Martha unexpectedly by the thorn, tries to turn back, terrified, and is forced to hear her plangent cry. From that moment on, he becomes her double, her shadow, imitating her day-and-night wanderings and adopting her over-involvement with the landscape around the thorn:

> "And this I know, full many a time,
> When she was on the mountain high,
> By day, and in the silent night,
> When all the stars were clear and bright,
> That I have heard her cry,
> 'Oh misery! oh misery!
> Oh woe is me! oh misery!' "
>   (xxii)

As this stanza suggests, the narrator becomes Martha's echo as well as her double, and during the course of the poem he repeats her lament five different times, seemingly both moved and fascinated by it. But the echoing is

---

[5] For instance, by Stephen Prickett, *Wordsworth and Coleridge: The Lyrical Ballads* (London: Arnold, 1975).

[6] Stephen Maxfield Parrish, *The Art of the Lyrical Ballads* (Cambridge, Mass.: Harvard University Press, 1973).

only the most obvious sign of his full predicament, which, like Martha's, alienates all thought and feeling into abnormal language. The narrator is as obsessed by Martha as she is obsessed by the thorn, and to a great degree his identity is reconstructed in her image. The measure of this loss of self is not only that her chant repeats itself in his narration, but that everything he says becomes a kind of chant, in which the details of Martha's obsession—language, thorn, landscape, and the rest—reappear incessantly. The narrator talks a blue streak, but his notorious loquacity is clearly meant as the index of his literal inability to get Martha and her troubles out of his mind—with the result that he himself is very nearly out of it:

> "Some say, if to the pond you go,
> And fix on it a steady view,
> The shadow of a babe you trace,
> A baby and a baby's face,
> And that it looks at you;
> Whene'er you look at it, 'tis plain,
> The baby looks at you again."
>
> (xx)

This is the language of a man under a spell, and Martha, like Coleridge's Ancient Mariner, is just the kind of outcast whose extreme emotional posture is able to cast one. If anything, she is even more efficient at it than the Mariner; unlike the halted Wedding Guest, the narrator of "The Thorn" has no chance to cry protestingly " 'Now wherefore stopp'st thou me?' "—let alone " 'Hold off! unhand me, grey-beard loon!' " Martha's cry throws mental chains around him at the moment he first hears it, while he is still in the act of trying to turn away; and his recollection of that moment is tellingly burdened with two repetitions of the fatal "O misery!" Similarly, the baby's gaze referred to in the stanza just quoted suggests an external binding force, present in another, that *captivates* the observer, who then becomes a link in the chain that starts with Martha's captivation by her lover and betrayer.

A closer look at the narrator's redundancies can help to expose the roots of the spreading pattern of obsession. The details that the narrator repeats tend to be the most painful and lurid aspects of Martha's predicament; they all suggest waste and desolation—the age, stuntedness, and wretchedness of the thorn; the identification of the nearby hill of moss as the grave of Martha's baby; Martha's lament; her scarlet cloak and the sinister red spotting of the moss. Beyond this, the redundant details tend to be topographical, and taken together they intimate an obsession with the *site* dominated by the thorn. These two features, the recurrence of anguish and the recurrence of landscape, can be brought together by observing that they tend to have one thing in common: a concern with the obliteration of self by assimilation to natural objects, and more particularly by a painful blending into the earth.

The thorn is clasped by mosses "So close, you'd say that they are bent / With plain and manifest intent / To drag it to the ground"; the baby is presumed to be buried beside the tree; Martha's characteristic posture is to be sitting on the ground; and the narrator at first sight mistakes her for "a jutting crag." Martha is also said to shudder and make her cry when breezes ruffle the pond, as if she had lost her independent existence and were a part of the landscape itself.

This dislocation of identity suggests itself as the source of the repetitions that overrun the poem. The thorn and its landscape first enter Martha's mental life as projections, half-willed metaphors for her predicament—the thorn, for instance, obviously signifying the barrenness of her love and the wretchedness of her solitude. The distance between the self and its representations, however, barely survives the primitive movement of imagination that creates them. Martha's projections harden, essentially at once, into permanent alienations of identity that virtually fuse her into the barren spot. The narrator grasps this over-objectification in superstitious terms; in his narrative the spot assumes the functions of Martha's ego by "imagining" a baby's face in the pond and by warding off intruders from the beauteous/ sinister hill of moss with a trembling of the ground. It is as if Martha's inner self had abandoned her in imitation of her lover, so that in some sense she has "gone off" with him. More than being simply obsessed with the thorn, pond, and hill, she is captivated—rapt and captured—by them, absorbed both in them and into them through a perverse, erotically tinged surrender to idealization. Her returns to a place and a cry are endless because they are finally the only way she has to be herself, or to be anyone at all. And the same is true for the narrator once he, too, has been captivated.

Taken in these terms, the chain of repetitions that begins with Martha seems based on what Freud called repetition compulsion, the living-over of a painful action in defiance of the pleasure-principle.[7] Freud saw such repetition as a product of the death-instinct, and "The Thorn," a death-haunted poem, can plausibly be said to suggest a "defusion"—a distinct appearance—of an urge to be inanimate that is usually hidden by aggression. Later theorists, however—notably Heinz Lichtenstein—have suggested replacing the death-instinct with an identity principle, a drive to sustain the particularity of the self that takes precedence over everything else in mental life.[8] It is hard to doubt the presence of such a principle, invested with the full primitive fierceness of the id, in the farrago of ritualized actions and redun-

---

[7] Sigmund Freud, *Beyond the Pleasure Principle,* translated by James Strachey (New York: Norton, 1961).

[8] Heinz Lichtenstein, "Identity and Sexuality: A Study of Their Interrelationship in Man," *Journal of the American Psychoanalytic Association* 9 (1961): 179–260. Norman Holland has made specific use of this concept for literary criticism; see his *Five Readers Reading* (New Haven: Yale University Press, 1975).

dant speech that composes "The Thorn." But the principle is grotesquely distorted, as identity, in every character, comes to lodge only in the frantic energies of self-abandonment.

This dissolution of identity into a drive that destroys the ego it is supposed to preserve can also be given a Lacanian reading. Lacan's psychoanalysis posits unconscious repetition as the fate of the ego that is trapped in so-called Imaginary relationships—that is, one that is dependent on imagined or embodied alter-egos.[9] The characters in "The Thorn" suffer from this bondage in an inverted form, in a version of Imaginary identification that articulates the futility of repetition in full, indeed over-full, consciousness. Wordsworth's obsessives are all captivated by a human figure (and not only in "The Thorn"), but not by an image of the self. The self, in fact, is what becomes an image, a mere alter-ego for the figure who captivates it, to whom it also becomes blind. Not the spellbinding other, but the imagery associated with the spell, becomes the locus of identity. The centered human figure is removed from the ego's vision (in both senses of the term) and replaced by a fragmented landscape and fragmentary language. This reduction is obvious in Martha's case; the landscape is centered almost literally on the grave of her desires and her cry is a kind of keening. As for the narrator, his visual difficulties with Martha reflect the fact that her image is fringed for him with an uncertainty that demands incessant, and fruitless, speculation. Besides, he is more compelled by what he hears of her than by what he sees; what he sees most clearly is her landscape.

The pattern of contagion between Martha and the narrator is repeated between the narrator and his interlocutor. And it seems that the original obsession becomes more virulent as it spreads, because where the narrator is victimized by a sudden, face-to-face trauma, the interlocutor succumbs to the mania of repetition merely by hearing the narrator's story. The process is already complete in the interlocutor's first speech, which repeats as a question the stanza in which the narrator has described Martha's presence, in all weathers, by the thorn. The only significant difference between the narrator's statement and the interlocutor's question comes in the last two lines, in which Martha's refrain is replaced by a refrain of the interlocutor's own: "Oh wherefore? wherefore? tell me why / Does she repeat that doleful cry?" (viii). The irony is harshly overt: the interlocutor's questioning is to be his obsession, as Martha's doleful cry is hers. The interlocutor, in fact, does nothing but question, just as Martha does nothing but chant. With his captivation, all the cognitive powers of language seem to have broken down, as

---

[9] For a discussion, see Jacques Lacan, *The Language of the Self: The Function of Language in Psychoanalysis*, translated with commentary by Anthony Wilden (New York: Delta, 1968), pp. 174–75; Fredric Jameson, "Imaginary and Symbolic in Lacan: Marxism, Psychoanalysis, and the Problem of the Subject," *Yale French Studies* 55/56 (1977): 338–95.

asking joins exclamation and narration in the grammar of obsession. The collapse of the interlocutor's selfhood into this mad jumble is confirmed by his final utterance, a furiously demanding and impatient series of questions in which all of the obsessive images of the poem reappear:

> "But what's the thorn? and what the pond?
> And what the hill of moss to her?
> And what the creeping breeze that comes
> The little pond to stir?"
>
> (xix)

By this point, well before the end, the verbal and visual design of Martha's madness has become a metaphor for the condition of everyone who comes into contact with it—a group that potentially includes the reader.

As the recipient of narration, the interlocutor is a fairly overt substitute for the reader, or more exactly for that aspect of the reader which is susceptible to the disease of the poem. By tugging at that susceptibility, the interlocutor acts as a fatal lure, a "carrier." But he also acts as a scapegoat, and his idiot questioning stands as a warning sign, a monitory epitaph marking the death of an ego. By captivating him, the chain of repetitions enters the area of self-consciousness or even Romantic irony; it begins to look like a self-mocking or self-accusing reflection by the poem on its own senselessness. A certain feeling of vertigo naturally follows as the poem seems to tear itself apart, but the point of this dissociative gesture is therapeutic.

"The Thorn" provides no exit from the echolalic maze of its repetitions except the implicit one of its own status as a fiction. Among Wordsworth's contributions to *Lyrical Ballads*, there are only two poems that never allude to the poet or that feature narrators who are completely separate from him; "The Thorn" is one of these.[10] In context, this throws unusual emphasis on the poem as an exercise, a fabrication, a text; and this, in turn, offers a kind of shelter from the storm of redundancies. Taken as an artifact, the poem negates the principle of contagion that shapes it; the fictional structure of interlocking monologues becomes the privileged form by which contagious obsession can be contained and brought to an end. Nothing within the fictive world described by the poem is of any help in checking its repetitions; the "cure," which is really a cure of the reader from participation in the poem's nightmare, comes from without. The reader, in effect, cures himself of the poem by adopting an authorial attitude of Romantic irony. (This, by the way, can make the poem itself look absurd. The seesaw reputation of "The Thorn" seems to suggest that the cure can work too well.)

Perhaps the best way to describe the reader's "therapeutic" attitude is to identify it with the experience of normal time. The characters in "The

---

[10] The other is "Complaint of a Forsaken Indian Woman."

Thorn" all live in a time that fails to move forward, that remains hopelessly stuck to the origin of obsession. The language of the poem continually alludes to time in circular terms, and continually "tells" time by describing the landscape or weather around the thorn:

> "Now wherefore, thus, by day and night,
> In rain, in tempest, and in snow,
> Thus to the dreary mountain-top
> Does this poor Woman go?"
> (viii)

All time in the poem is deformed into an echo of Martha's subjective time, degraded by the endless chanting rhythms, and captivated, like language and identity, by the landscape. Only once does the poem allow a time to be fixed uniquely, free of all vicious circles, and the time in question is one that never arrives: the morning of Martha's wedding (xii). The reader alone, by adopting the poet's detachment from the fiction, can experience time in a way that negates this unnerving stasis. Felt in detachment, the simple forward motion of reading itself takes on a curative power. Wordsworth seems to have counted on an effect of this kind, as his note to the poem suggests: "It was necessary that the Poem, to be natural, should in reality move slowly; yet I hoped, that, by the aid of the metre, to those who should at all enter into the spirit of the poem, it would appear to move quickly" (*PW* 701). It has to be added, though, that to enter into the spirit of the poem is to decline entering into the spirit of its characters.

Significantly, there is nothing in the poem that specifically provokes the reader's affirmation of time. In fact, the poem actively attacks the reader's time-sense; it deforms time unremittingly to the very end. Moving in an ominous circle, "The Thorn" both begins and ends with a telltale image of the stunted tree bent under dragging moss, a return which, like Martha's, like the narrator's and the interlocutor's, is indefinitely repeatable. The point is underlined by the closing lines of the poem, which are a repetition of Martha's lament: closure, here, is displaced by the principle of enchainment, release by the litany of captivation. The reader, invited by the poem to a kind of participatory hypnosis, is required to free himself arbitrarily, in an act of autonomous selfhood. Repetition can neither be escaped nor transcended; it has to be severed.

III

Turning to the "Appassionata," we find a less relentless pattern of Romantic repetition than the one in "The Thorn," but also a more subtle and disturbing one. Unlike Wordsworth, Beethoven does not create a texture of spurting and furious repetition from the outset. Instead, he holds one in reserve and intrudes it shockingly on a fulfilled developmental pattern—a perverse gesture, far less tractable than Wordsworth's, which deliberately breaks the sonata in half and threatens its ultimate coherence. The first two movements, usually understood to suggest turbulent emotion and a contrasting calm, are actually joined in a continuous design that culminates in a prolonged moment of blended "tumult and peace." As it would almost have to be, the formal principle involved is the antithesis of Romantic repetition: an uncodified non-repetition that exalts continuous change. Within the limits of Beethoven's expressive language in 1804, the music is an outpouring of pure dynamism, or what Elliott Carter, speaking of his own work, calls "the poetry of change, transformation, reorientation of feelings and thoughts."[11] The opening movement, *Allegro assai*, expresses its dynamic impulse by reformulating the structure of tension and release basic to Classical sonata form. The following *Andante con moto* does the same thing by shifting the focus of Classical variation form from contrast to singularity. What happens then is perhaps best described by Wordsworth:

> But, as it sometimes chanceth, from the might
> Of joy in minds that can no further go,
> As high as we have mounted in delight
> In our dejection do we sink as low.
> ("Resolution and Independence," iv)

By the close of the *Andante*, the poetry of change has gone as far as it can, and the finale, *Allegro ma non troppo*, bursts on the scene, mournful and savage by turns, with a totally disorienting barrage of repetitions.

The plan of the first movement depends on a coalescence of large-scale rhythmic structure with a revision of the sectional and harmonic relationships that constitute sonata form. The overall pattern of tension and release in a Classical sonata-allegro movement ordinarily depends on two things: an exposition that establishes the tonic with reasonable stability, then produces harmonic tension with a move to the dominant or its substitute, and a recapitulation that discharges the accumulated tension with a stable return to the tonic. The *Allegro assai* of the "Appassionata" lacks both of these features. The opening subject, in the tonic F minor, is followed immediately by a complete restatement in the Neapolitan area—i.e., a semitone higher; harmonic tension begins in expanded form almost before the home key can be recognized with any assurance. After this, F minor receives a substantial elaboration on its dominant, where still more Neapolitan dissonance emerges; no cadence to the tonic triad appears for many measures, and when one does finally arrive it requires a staggering vehemence to establish itself (Ex. 2). As to the recapitulation, it does not constitute a release of tension

---

[11] Elliott Carter, jacket notes to his Concerto for Orchestra (Columbia M 30112).

but the reverse; it brings the tonic back only over sixteen measures of throbbing pedal point on the dominant and the dominant of the Neapolitan (C and D♭), with a spectral transitional measure of B♮–F tritones added to heighten the sense of dislocation. This celebrated passage forms a large-scale dissonance, both harmonically, as a huge expansion of the tonic triad in its one unstable form, the second inversion, and motivically, as an equally broad expansion of the troublesome, omnipresent rhythmic motive ♪♪♩|♩ with its characteristic descent from D♭ to C.[12] There is no Archi-

EXAMPLE 2. Beethoven, "Appassionata" Sonata, first movement, exposition.

medean point in this music on which its tensions can pivot. The recapitulation as a whole never escapes the shadow of its opening, and Neapolitan inflections persist throughout the coda until the closing measures. Tension is pent up until the last possible moment, and then not so much released as detonated by a violent, cathartic spell of tonic-dominant harmony, the most agitated passage in a very agitated movement (Ex. 3). The sonata form achieves closure only by reaching a point of exhaustion, dissolving away *diminuendo* under a prolonged murmur.

EXAMPLE 3. Beethoven, "Appassionata" Sonata, first movement, coda.

[12] For some other vicissitudes of this motive, see Charles Rosen, *Sonata Forms* (New York: Norton, 1980), pp. 190–94. As Rosen notes, the D♭–C is not fully resolved until midway through the coda.

The animating will to that exhaustion is formally realized by a heightened continuity that excludes true repetition. Beethoven motivates this design decisively by omitting the repeat of the exposition—the first such omission in any of his piano sonatas. With the repeat missing, the movement does not fall into two balanced halves but into an "open" form, an evolving sequence of four broadly parallel sections: exposition-development-recapitulation-coda. To steep the music even further in a sense of dynamism, each section is given a harmonic instability and an associated jaggedness of texture that assimilates it to the model of a development. As the distinctions among the sections are eroded, almost erased, their articulation of a crisis and resolution within the sonata form gives way to a large-scale periodicity, an immense pulsation of form. Though clearly delineated, the four "periods" are blurred at the edges by fluid *diminuendos*, charged with anticipation; the end of one period overlaps the beginning of another. By interweaving them so fully, the movement telescopes its sonata form into a continuous forward surge.[13]

The critical moment in this pattern, its formal and emotional rationale, comes at the close of the exposition. The *Allegro assai* follows the normal procedure for minor-key sonata movements and states its second theme in the relative major, A♭, though only after a fairly extended passage in A♭ minor. What ought to follow is a closing theme that cadences firmly on A♭ major; what follows instead, heralded by a dramatic F♭, is a queasy descent into sixteen more measures of A♭ minor (Ex. 4). It is often said that the remote-

[13] In *The Classical Style: Haydn, Mozart, Beethoven* (New York: Norton, 1972), p. 400, Rosen interprets the sectional structure of this movement as an "unyielding" frame, but to my ear the sections, though "clear"—as in any Beethoven sonata form of this period—are not *distinct*, and the parallels among them only serve to reinforce their interwovenness. The parallelism is also a vehicle for a large-scale organic rhythmic pattern; see below, pp. 38–41. No two measures of the *Allegro assai* are identical.

ness of this key determines the deletion of the exposition repeat, but Beethoven calls for a repeat in the Bb-Major String Quartet, Op. 130, where the exposition closes in the flat submediant, a key as remote as you please. What

EXAMPLE 4. Beethoven, "Appassionata" Sonata, first movement, transition to closing theme of exposition.

propels this music forward is the *behavior* of its tonality: the restless, unqualified shift of mode and the aggressive harmonic activity that it precipitates. Beethoven takes great pains to show that the closing passage *precludes* a repeat because it breaks away from, even breaks down, the tonic/substitute-dominant axis of the exposition.

The passage germinates from an Ab dominant-seventh chord that builds up enormous tension with three measures of trilling on its fifth and root (Ex. 4). In terms of chord progression, the dissonance finally resolves as an Ab-minor scale emerges—again through the sensitive Fb—and descends in a hush from one end of the keyboard to the other. In terms of large-scale structure, though, this is a resolution that adds more tension than it takes away. By resolving the trills with the minor mode, Beethoven dramatically strips the Ab tonality of its dominant quality (only major keys can function as dominants in Classical harmony) and sends the music forward into undiscovered countries. The earlier spell of Ab minor, linked to this one by a pair of stabbing Fb's, turns out to have been a portent.

Once under way, the agitated closing theme systematically expands on the Neapolitan-dominant tensions that shape the opening measures of the sonata. The theme has hardly begun before it is pouncing *fortissimo* on its own root-position Neapolitan triads and resolving them to its dominant (Ex. 5). Like the dissonant restatement that yokes itself to the first theme, but on a larger structural scale, the Ab minor of the exposition forms a dissociated, volatized version of a primary element—in this case of the tonic as we first hear it realized. Beethoven honors the propulsive, outwardly spiraling quality of this music by refusing to pretend that the process of development has not started long before the exposition is over.

The other source of the supple urgency, the heightened continuity, of the

EXAMPLE 5. Beethoven, "Appassionata" Sonata, first movement, closing theme of exposition.

Allegro assai is a structural use of rhythm unprecedented in its long-range coherence. Most obviously, the rhythm is a germinal element. The figure ♩♪♩│♩ draws together the first and second themes and several subsidiary motives, while the figure ♪♪♪│♩ is a foreshortened form of the numerous urgent pedal points and also a feature of the closing theme. More importantly, the music is saturated by shifts of rhythmic orientation. Syncopation is basic to the texture, and its point of attack is continually varied. Rearticulations of pulse occur every few measures; the impulse to rhythmic change matches the impetus of the "through-composed" sonata form. Sometimes insistent, sometimes obscured, the basic unit of the ¹²⁄₈ time is felt variously as a dotted quarter-note, an eighth-note triplet, the two superimposed, or a fluctuation among these forms within the phrase. All four possibilities occur before the exposition is over without exhausting their variations within the movement; by contrast, the entire § movement that opens the Second "Rasumovsky" Quartet, Opus 59, No. 2, relies on a basic dotted-quarter feeling alone. Throughout the *Allegro assai*, the subtlest discriminations of speed and accent are called for. In the development, for instance, a climactic emphasis on the Neapolitan tone G♭ is articulated by a slight quickening in the accompaniment from ♪♪♪♪ (5:6) to ♪♪♪♪♪♪ —a change more felt than heard, but electrifying.

As a rhythmic whole, the *Allegro assai* also has a distinctive contour that mirrors its constant accumulation of harmonic tension. Through a series of careful gradations, the music swings back and forth between a prevalence of strong downbeats and a prevalence of weak ones. The pattern is set by the exposition. After the firm articulation of the first theme, syncopated accents begin to appear as ominous touches on the third beat brought on by the

♪♪♩|♩ figure. The next syncopations are more disruptive: explosive *fortissimo* chords played off the beat at the weakest points of the measure. An agitated, improvisatory feeling attaches to the accents that then follow in pairs, again off the beat, on the sixth and ninth eighth-notes (Ex. 6). The arrival of the second theme restores a firmly articulated downbeat, but the reviving stability is short-lived. The theme ends with a weak-beat *sforzando*,

EXAMPLE 6. Beethoven, "Appassionata" Sonata, first movement, syncopation pattern of exposition.

and the closing theme that ensues resumes the erosion of the downbeat with more *sforzandos*, ending with a sequence of accented upbeats (Ex. 7).

In the coda, this large-scale pulsation is climactically compressed into the span of a few measures, where it merges with the deferred release of harmonic tension. A sudden *diminuendo* and *ritardando* on the ♪♪♩|♩ figure charges the air with anticipation, obscuring both the downbeat and—with a semitonal pedal blur—the harmony. Then the tempo quickens and the second theme reappears in a striking new F-minor form that reinforces the downbeat with *sforzandos* and *crescendos* (Ex. 8). The new episode is a harmonic precis of the whole movement, for the sequence of accented notes

EXAMPLE 7. Beethoven, "Appassionata" Sonata, first movement, closing theme of exposition.

is Gb–F–Gb–F, a resolving alternation of the tones of the Neapolitan and the tonic. In the next moment, however, a rhythmic riot breaks out, all violent syncopations and metric modulations (compressions of the ¹²⁄₈ measure into the time of ⁴⁄₄). Thus the strongest downbeats in the movement abut directly on the weakest. The explosive confrontation intensifies the resolving force of the harmony—the accented chords are all tonic triads and dominant sevenths—but defers a rhythmic resolution to the very last measures and their spent *pianissimo* murmuring.

I am not convinced that comparisons between musical and poetic rhythm mean very much, but a juxtaposition of the relentless sing-song beat of "The Thorn" and the endlessly varied pulse of this *Allegro assai* is at least suggestive. Wordsworth exaggerates the rhythmic squareness of the ballad to evoke a rigid temporality that epitomizes the psychic rigidity of Romantic repetition. By contrast, Beethoven's dissolution of square-cut rhythms turns time into a phantasmagoria, similar in feeling to certain hauntings of the mind that Wordsworth remembered from early childhood:

EXAMPLE 8. Beethoven, "Appassionata" Sonata, first movement, coda.

> huge and mighty forms, that do not live
> Like living men, moved slowly through my mind
> By day, and were a trouble to my dreams.
> (*Prelude* (1850), I, 399–400)

Wordsworth's approaches to a similar temporal freedom in adulthood are celebrations of "higher minds" at their rare visionary best:

> they build up greatest things
> From least suggestions; ever on the watch,
> Willing to work and to be wrought upon,
> They need not extraordinary calls
> To rouse them; in a world of life they live.
> (*Prelude* (1850), XIV, 101–5)

In the fullness of its power, the imaginative mind "feeds upon infinity"; it choreographs the movement of time into an image of eternal presence. Romantic repetition is a "fallen" form of the same activity, a degradation of endlessness to a compulsive's ceremonial. Beethoven, too, regarded Romantic repetition as a travesty on continuous, fluent time-feeling; the "Appassionata" is condemned to end in a struggle with just that.

IV

The emotional harshness of the *Allegro assai* is hard to distinguish from a sweep and energy that is exhilarating in its ultimate cathartic force. The harshness remains disturbing, but it "disturbs . . . with the joy of elevated thoughts" that, as in similar harsh moments in Wordsworth, testify to the power of the imagination even more than to its "deep and genuine sadness." The extraordinary slow movement of the "Appassionata," the *Andante con moto*, translates that power beyond any hint of lament. Charles Rosen succinctly describes its basic features and shows how they grant to the essentially additive form of the classical variations the dynamic unity of sonata form:

> The complete stillness of the . . . theme makes the slightest increase in motion deeply felt: its static harmony—almost an upper pedal on A flat—gives the least chromatic motion the larger significance of a modulation. Most important, perhaps, is [a] restriction of register within each variation: [a] successive rise step by step from the low bass to the treble is the clearest articulation of the form. [A]cceleration of note-values and . . . increased syncopations are the main vehicle of expression and build the most powerful of climaxes, so that the return of the theme in the low register comes to seem not like a da capo but like a true sonata recapitulation.[14]

The three variations of this movement are conceived organically; they form parts of an almost Kantian process in which every part entails the whole. Beethoven creates an impression of continuous unfolding—a heightened form of the continuity in the *Allegro assai*—by dovetailing increases in motion (speed of figuration) with changes in register and dynamics. The variations make up an old-fashioned set of "doubles": each one preserves the outline and harmony of the theme, and each doubles the prevailing motion of the music that precedes it. A purely ornamental pattern, then—except that the concept of ornamentation soon loses its meaning here. Each variation also dwells within a limited registral area that is roughly an octave higher than its predecessor's. At the same time, each variation individually traces a gradual ascent through its own upper octave, reaching a climax on its high A♭ at the peak of a *crescendo*. The climactic note then becomes the starting point for the octave ascent of the next variation, which follows seamlessly after a brief codetta. Change in this music is more than strongly directed; it flourishes at every moment. The generative process ends only after all the registers have been exhausted, with a series of rapturous attacks on the brilliant A♭ at the top of Beethoven's piano. A long descending *diminuendo* then vaporizes the rapture, apparently to end the movement.

One hears this exquisitely graduated design as a single prolonged gesture,

---

[14] Rosen, *Classical Style*, p. 438.

a steady, pulsing, arc–like movement of mounting intensity. As in the *Allegro assai*, the differentiated sections here are so interwoven with each other that difference begins to recede into the impression of continuity. But even more crucial than the fact of this continuity is its nature. Ordinarily, a kind of figure-ground relationship obtains between the elements of musical structure that define tonality—melody and harmony—and the non-tonal elements of motion, register, texture, and tone-color. What Beethoven does here is to reverse that relationship. As the movement progresses, melody and harmony recede further into the background. The weakly contoured theme grows more skeletal, more abstract, with each variation (pianists who try to emphasize its changes trivialize the music); the D♭–major tonality—placid, transparent, devoid of modulation—is a deliberate blank. Meanwhile, the increases in motion and brilliance glitter into the foreground, periodically enhanced by quickenings within cadential phrases and accelerations of registral movement during *crescendo*s. By the third variation, the music represents the ornamentation of a theme far less than it does an epiphany of pure acceleration and pure intensification of color. Consummated at the final *crescendo*, where the theme all but evaporates in the outpouring of sound, this effect has the primitive plenitude of a Wordsworthian "spot of time." It can only be described as the closest possible approach to an evocation of absolute change, of change as such, purified of the objects to which it happens. The transforming impulse that has driven the whole sonata is now no longer a principle, but a presence.

Beethoven presents this climax as an extension of the first movement by his treatment of variation form. The *Allegro assai* has powered its irresistible dynamic thrust by deleting an expected repeat; the *Andante con moto* recreates and intensifies the gesture. Classical variation form calls for the repetition of each half of the theme, and of each half of the ensuing variations. Beethoven follows this format until the third variation, then drops it; variation is suddenly substituted for repetition, and the feeling of sectional structure gradually dissipates. This move marks an important moment of drama in many of Beethoven's variations—the slow movement of the "Kreutzer" Sonata is an especially effective instance—but its purpose is usually to enhance the feeling of distance from the theme, which is a measure of how far the theme itself has been enhanced. What the "Appassionata" enhances is the radical identification of form with change. In the *Allegro assai*, the music has expelled repetition with a sharp rise in harmonic tension. In the *Andante con moto*, repetition falls away spontaneously in the virtual absence of harmonic tension, and this at the very moment when the music quickens—impulsively, in mid-measure—into its most ecstatic passage. The moment is a leap into plenitude—not a disjunction, but an *acceleration* of continuity.

The texture of the *Andante con moto* at its climax is a combination of overwhelming energy and perfect tranquility. The notes run in cascades; the treble tone-color rises piercingly through a series of *crescendos*; syncopation is almost constant. Yet the underlying structure imposes a feeling of suspension—in part because its harmony is unchanging, in part because the rhythmic emphasis on its cadential pattern dwindles as the music intensifies. As in a fountain, the yield of incessant motion is a stasis. Earlier, I borrowed a phrase from *The Prelude* to refer to this moment, and if there is a musical equivalent to Wordsworth's vision of the Ravine of Gondo, with its apocalyptic fusion of motion and stillness, "Tumult and peace, the darkness and the light," then this passage of Beethoven's is it. Purely as music, the gesture is almost unparalleled. Only the *Arietta* from Beethoven's Piano Sonata, Opus 111, with its slow growth into climactic trills, defines a sublimity in the same way, as a stillness in motion; but its vastly expanded time-scale makes it less immediate, though more richly consummatory, than the music here.

When the theme returns after this, it sounds like a transfiguration of its former self, reverberating with the process of the whole movement as each of its phrases appears in a new register. But a curious problem arises at this point. With the return of the theme, every tension in the sonata has been resolved, all passion spent. The piece, in cathectic terms, ought to be over, as Opus 111 is over when an ecstatic variations movement has transfigured a turbulent sonata-allegro. But the proportions in the earlier work are all wrong for that, and worse yet the music is stranded in D♭ major; the cathectic closure has no formal foundation. Beethoven's response to this contradiction is a gesture of complete negation, almost a display of disappointed anger. Denying the *Andante con moto* its closing V–I cadence, he "resolves" the movement into a sickening discord and then plunges violently into the manic territory of repetition occupied by "The Thorn."

Harsh and abrupt though it is, this move has been carefully prepared. The theme of the *Andante* has only a single chromatic dissonance, an unaccented dominant seventh of D major that adds piquancy to the music without creating tension. (D major is the Neapolitan of the movement's D♭; the chord is a subtle link to the Neapolitan-haunted first movement. Its soft-edged quality comes from its other identity—indicated by its spelling—as a German sixth of D♭.) With each variation, the dissonant tones of this chord make brief appearances, a process subdued in the first two variations and heightened in the third. The result is that the chromatic coloring blends increasingly into the enraptured dynamism of the music, until the sense of dissonance is almost completely suspended. At the last minute, however, Beethoven intrudes a diminished-seventh chord derived from the "vaporized" dissonance of the theme by the shift of a semitone. Dragged out through a hushed arpeggio, this disorienting chord is immediately attacked again *fortissimo*; then the music is suddenly a finale, which begins by hammering out the same diminished-seventh thirteen times. A sinking motive enters, and swells obsessively to a *crescendo* in pounding bass octaves. Romantic repetition has arrived with a vengeance, in a form hard to distinguish from noise.

The finale of the "Appassionata" is designed as a specific undoing of the opening *Allegro assai*, a destructive outburst of repetition at every structural level that threatens to invalidate the earlier exaltation of change. The music is pervaded by its initial *moto perpetuo* figure, which appears now as theme, now as accompaniment; the rest of the thematic material consists of impassioned, insistently repeated motives that are built around repeated melody notes. These motives represent a flattening out of the strongly contoured themes that sweep upward and downward through the first movement. Most of them consist of a repetition followed by a falling note or figure; the climactic one, an expansion of the ♩♩♩|♩ motive of the first movement into a more strident, much-harped-on ♩|♩♩♩♩|♩ , eliminates the falling close and is pure repetition. (The feeling of a damaging revision is specific: the earlier motive ended with a falling semitone.) At the same time, the rhythmic suppleness of the first movement is replaced by a rigid feeling of insistence, alternately mournful and vehement, that comes primarily from an exaggeration of the downbeat; for most of the movement, the most conspicuous rhythmic feature is the downbeat *sforzando*.

Most important of all, the sonata structure of the finale is a treacherously ironic reversal of the one in the first movement. Once again there is no exposition repeat, but the omission here is no liberating inevitability; it is a convention for last-movement sonata form, and it leads to a demonic joke. Instead of transforming the sonata design with a strongly motivated non-repetition, the finale *de*-forms it with an unmotivated repetition on the largest possible scale: a reprise of the entire sequence of development and recapitulation. The result is a grotesquely unbalanced structure that is unique in the literature. The second half of a sonata movement is sometimes repeated together with the first half—the Piano Sonata, Op. 78, and the String Quartets, Op. 18, No. 6 and Op. 59, No. 2, are all instances in Beethoven—but no other major work by Mozart, Haydn, or Beethoven repeats the second half alone.[15] The varied parallelism that weaves the four sections of the *Allegro assai* together is degraded by this move into a crude identification. The feeling of a large-scale pulse becomes metronomic, not dynamic; the repeated sections become expanded, exacerbated forms of the repeated notes that define the melodic texture. The structure of entrapment in "The Thorn," where the obsessed characters repeat each other's repetitions, is painfully similar.

To move the orderliness of form even closer to the rigidity of obsession, the finale structures its development section to add extra levels of redundancy to this doubled-up sonata form. As if to undo its counterpart in the *Allegro assai*, the development acts out a jarring failure of dynamism. It begins by recalling the opening measures of the exposition, with a deep bass *dimin-*

---

[15] Cf. Rosen, *Classical Style*, pp. 99, 99n.

uendo leading to two statements of the *moto perpetuo* theme, so that each of the five sections preceding the coda begins with the same gesture. The overinsistent feeling that results is intensified by the underlying harmony, which begins with a stammer and keeps pretty well within the tonal compass of the exposition. The theme tries to launch the development in the subdominant, but twice changes its mind in mid-phrase and manages only to ornament V^7/iv with tonic coloration. A third attempt succeeds better, but by the time a subdominant cadence arrives we are already nine measures into the section. In effect, the tonic inflections arise here to resist the development, to make the music falter over its own basic sonority. In so doing, they give the tonic an anxious, involuntary cast—something that intensifies as the development reaches its mid-point with a massive tonic cadence, and that carries over into the normal tonic beginning of the recapitulation.

And as with beginnings, so with endings. The climax of the development replicates that of the exposition in every way short of literal repetition. Both passages are blunt, harsh affirmations of the dominant; both appear just before the music explodes into disruptive harmonies that lead to a closing *diminuendo*; and both consist of four attacks on an overinsistent, rhythmically violent motive (Ex. 9). The sheer violence with which the climax of the development is pounded out might even suggest an attempt to shatter the dominant framework that ties it to the exposition. The impression is borne out by the harsh *fortissimo* gesture that curtails the passage: a series of dissonant arpeggios that begins abruptly with the remotest possible triad, G♭. The chords at this point (N^6 [$=G♭^6$]-V^7-vii°^{7}) are all tonic sonorities, all heralds of the recapitulation to follow. And all in vain—of course: tonic or no tonic, the identical climax is doomed to return by the recapitulation itself, which stumbles into a first ending that repeats, even intensifies, the explosive interrupted cadence (Ex. 9a) that closes the exposition. From that point, the only way to take a step forward is to take two steps back.[16]

With its epicycles of repetition and its stammering texture, the finale of the "Appassionata" intimates a passion that feeds self-consciously on its own turbulence: "A tempest, a redundant energy, / Vexing its own creation" (*Prelude* (1850),I: 37–38). For Beethoven as for Wordsworth, the psychic cost of this ingrown intensity is a form of appalling second birth. Between the development and the recapitulation, the finale seems to collapse in exhaustion. The dynamic level drops, the harmony stops moving, and the music sinks slowly to rest on a sustained single note in the low bass. Then a

---

[16] Compare the harmonically restless development in the opening movement of Beethoven's String Quartet, Op. 59, No. 2, where the repeat of the development and recapitulation is motivated by the use of the tonic minor for the recapitulation. The repeat defines this tonality as inadequate for closure in the wake of the development; the tonic major saves the situation the second time around with a long coda. This double repeat may be one of Beethoven's rare miscalculations: the recapitulation is problematical enough without it. The music sounds better as an "ordinary" sonata form.

dominant-seventh chord of F sounds softly, rises and falls through a precisely measured fourfold restatement, and conjures up the repetitive frenzy of
the movement from the illusory moment of depletion or release. The cycle

EXAMPLE 9.   Beethoven, "Appassionata" Sonata, finale.

a. climax of exposition

b. climax of development

of repetitions is incapable of exhausting itself; it tries to twice and fails. Like
the reversions to the withered tree that dominate Wordsworth's poem, the
do-over ceremonial of this finale is endlessly repeatable.

Fortunately, Beethoven does not choose to repeat it endlessly. But in order
to stop it he needs an arbitrary gesture, because—again as in "The Thorn"—
there is no element in his structure, not even tonic harmony, that can cure
its repetitions or evolve a closure from them. As the second recapitulation

ends, the music breaks into a heightened, indeed maddening repetition of the ♪ | ♩♩♩♩ | ♩ motive on the dominant-seventh chord. Just as this episode is about to become unbearable, it bursts into a passage that is both aggressively banal and completely unconnected with the thematic material of the movement (Ex. 10). This is the musical equivalent of banging one's fist on the table to shut someone up, and it makes so much noise that it works. The presence of an alien element—and a crude, impatient one at that—frees

EXAMPLE 10. Beethoven, "Appassionata" Sonata, finale, transition to coda.

the movement from the burden of obsessive circularity and allows it a brief, immensely powerful, and cathartic coda. It is worth noting, by the way, that the intruded material is in two parts, both of which are repeated, as if to burlesque the Romantic repetition being exorcised. The whole passage is so grotesque that it suggests Kierkegaard's "rotation method," except that Beethoven exposes the desperation that Kierkegaard's seducer tries to conceal:

> It is extremely wholesome thus to let the realities of life split upon an arbitrary interest. You transform something accidental into the absolute, and, as such, into the object of your admiration.[17]

The impact of Beethoven's coda, the "therapeutic" close to the "Appassionata," is primarily rhythmic. The finale, as I noted earlier, has an obses-

[17] Sören Kierkegaard, *Either/Or*, translated by David F. Swenson and Lillian Marvin Swenson, with revisions by Howard A. Johnson (Garden City, N.Y.: Doubleday, 1959), I: 296.

sive downbeat, and part of the sense of entrapment that haunts the music comes from a series of failed attempts to break up the exaggerated square- ness of the rhythm, and so to return to the rhythmic territory of the first movement. Two of the three attempts are failures because they end up by strengthening the downbeat; all are failures because their rhythmic novelty is cancelled out by a heightening of motivic repetition. The 𝄞 ♩♩♩ | ♩ that arrives at the climax of the exposition is striking for its *sforzando* up- beat, but also for its two strong downbeats, its reiteration as a motive, and the unrelenting repetition of its melody notes. Midway through the devel- opment, *sforzando* syncopations on the weak second eighth note try to es- tablish a new rhythm. But the passage works too well; the primary pulse be- comes imperceptible almost at once, so that no feeling of syncopation is possible. There is simply a sharp jerk, a metric displacement, and the music goes on presenting its repetitive motivic material in a secondary ¾ time with *sforzando* downbeats (Ex. 11). The only episode before the coda to achieve a genuine cross-rhythm is the eight-measure dominant climax of the develop- ment, where accents on the second half of each eighth note are syncopated against a clear ¾ pulse (Ex. 9). But this passage is also the high point of note-

EXAMPLE 11. Beethoven, "Appassionata" Sonata, finale, development.

by-note repetition in the movement; it consists of reiterated C octaves over an ostinato bass. The octaves climb from the low to the high registers, as if in an accelerated version of the ecstatic ascent in the slow movement, but the moment suggests only frenzy—*plus ça change.*

The chain of failures is broken only in the coda, where for sixteen mea- sures a *sforzando* on the second beat is syncopated against unbroken ¾ figu- ration (Ex. 12). Together with a dynamic movement of the harmony, which encapsulates the tensions of the entire sonata with the progression I–N^6– V^7–I, this sustained polyrhythm brings on a visceral feeling of release un- precedented in its day and not matched since. Continued intermittently un- til the last few seconds, it reanimates the principle of continuous difference that had given life to the music until the mad mechanism of the finale

EXAMPLE 12. Beethoven, "Appassionata" Sonata, finale, coda.

whirled into play. Beethoven, though as hard on his listeners as Wordsworth in "The Thorn" is on his readers, is kinder at the close.

V

The poetics of repetition displayed in "The Thorn" and the "Appassionata" takes its most immediate significance as an affirmation of temporality. More exactly, the treatment of Romantic repetition in both works affirms time in its so-called *ec-stasis*, its irrevocable forward movement, felt not as a natural fact but as a subjective necessity. To resist the flow of time, in both works, is to lose being, nothing less. In turn, at least in the "Appassionata," to enhance the flow of time is to attain ecstasy in the familiar sense. The creation of these values is a way of endorsing the restlessness of consciousness which is so central a feature in Romantic texts. The mind's demand for change, for an always new horizon of significance, becomes in this light the Romantic definition of health, challenging Goethe's famous equation of Romanticism with sickness. Sickness, in turn, is the impulse that Blake satirized as the will to achieve "a solid without fluctuation": the mind's entropic tendency to invest too much of itself in single objects or single moments. Perhaps the gloss most pertinent here is Wordsworth's majestic insistence that the imaginative mind thrives on incompletion and deferral, that its instinctive movement is an inner appropriation of the relentless "ec-stasis" of time:

> Our destiny, our being's heart and home,
> Is with infinitude, and only there;
> With hope it is, hope that can never die,

> Effort, and expectation, and desire,
> And something evermore about to be.
> Under such banners militant, the soul
> Seeks for no trophies, struggles for no spoils
> That may attest her prowess, blest in thoughts
> That are their own perfection and reward,
> Strong in herself and in beatitude.
>   (*Prelude* (1850), VI, 604–13)

Beethoven, in his later work, suggests a similar position in several ways: by his increasing reliance on the two musical forms in which transformation is most constant, fugue and variation; by his increasing compression of sonata form and discarding of repeats; and by such magnificent later instances of the poetics of repetition as the scherzos to the String Quartets, Opp. 132 and 135.

Similar stances toward time show up everywhere in the Romantic tradition. Rilke, who perhaps exalted ec-stasis more fully than anyone else, was able to compress the urgency of its imperative into three words: "Wolle die Wandlung." Yet works that specifically involve Romantic repetition are set apart from others by a certain extremity, something that often appears as a courting of the chaotic, the absurd, the destructive. They are haunted by the abyss of indefinite duration established by the outbreak of repetition, and they return to a liveable time—if they do—by an act of negation or illogic. Wordsworth and Beethoven, in the works we have been dealing with, throw candid emphasis on this side of things. In "The Thorn," Wordsworth takes pains to single out the grotesque extremity of the landscape in both space and time. The thorn tree is "High on a mountain's highest ridge," and buffeted by melodramatically awful weather; likewise, its age is so extreme "you'd find it hard to say / How it could ever have been young." Even more harsh than this is Beethoven's basic design for the "Appassionata": the creation and obliteration of a transfigured time that is restored, briefly, not as an ecstasy but only as a therapy. At its least destructive, Romantic repetition creates an effect of something ineffably disquieting or uncanny, like the sight of the woman with her pitcher in the *Prelude* passage I quoted earlier, or the middle-voice ostinato of Chopin's Prelude in D♭, which paradoxically disturbs the music and sustains its harmony.

Romantic repetition may retain its inevitably unsettling quality primarily because of the effect of the pattern on identity. Wherever it appears, repetition of this kind involves the projection and fixation of identity into an alien place, a process necessarily bound up with anxiety. The object that assumes the alienated identity becomes, as it does so, "captivating," in the ambivalent sense I have tried to give that term. In poetry, this captivating quality often expresses itself in supernatural terms, appearing in a kind of visitation. A look at some major instances suggests a pattern in which a human or personified figure, imbued with a transcendental otherness and burdened by emotional extremity, captivates and usually immobilizes the observer. The captivating figure usually suggests either an excess of suffering or an excess of eroticism; often, the observer is forced to recapitulate the figure's experience.[18] The Leech Gatherer in Wordsworth's "Resolution and Independence," Coleridge's Ancient Mariner, Moneta in Keats's *The Fall of Hyperion*, Rousseau in Shelley's *The Triumph of Life*, the self-replicating spectre in Baudelaire's "Les Sept Viellards," the Young Lament in Rilke's tenth *Duino Elegy*—all participate in repetition-structures of this kind. Bewildering at best, these figures at their worst are profoundly accusatory. They suggest an irremediable flaw in the identities that they threaten, and resemble nothing so much as the phantoms of guilty self-knowledge.

In instrumental music, the identity that is alienated by Romantic repetition belongs to the listener, and the object that captivates it is the composition. Music in this dispensation will have either a mesmeric, hypnotic quality or a riveting, fixating one; it enlists the ear's equivalent to a fascinated gaze. Hypnotic intensity is the lure of Chopin's Prelude in B♭ Minor, a piece that is virtually nothing but a *sotto voce* throbbing—twenty-six slow measures saturated with repeated-note ostinati. Brahms's Piano Quintet in F Minor, Op. 34, fixates attention with music of passionate grimness, steeped in concentrated bursts of repetition that are broken off only to be followed by others. The finale of the "Appassionata," of course, is a *ne plus ultra* of fixation, in part because its repetitions violently occupy every level of musical time, from note-to-note movement to the rhythm of the entire piece, and in part because its abrogation of the linear pattern of the sonata results in an almost unbearably tense demand for release from the texture of repetition. (The tension involved is so great that some performers omit the repeats in the finale, which eases the pressure at the cost of making nonsense of the music.) Berlioz's famous comment that the third movement of Beethoven's Fifth Symphony provokes "that strange emotion you feel when you meet the magnetic gaze of certain persons and find it fixed on you" neatly brings the mesmeric and compulsive qualities together, and so to speak reunites the pattern with the human figure. In the *Symphonie fantastique*, Berlioz puts this reading of Beethoven into practice, linking the captivating figure (the beloved), a captivating motif (the *idée fixe*), and the sick ego (his own, thinly disguised).

Berlioz is not alone in restoring the human figure to music as a motive for captivation. In the song, "Ich hab im Traum geweinet," from *Dichterliebe*, Schumann does much the same, in line with the Heine poem that furnishes his text:

[18] The poles of eroticism and suffering are aligned as a rule with female and male figures, respectively. Wordsworth's Martha Ray touches on both.

Ich hab im Traum geweinet,
mir träumte du lägest im Grab.
Ich wachte auf und die Träne
floss noch von der Wange herab.

Ich hab im Traum geweinet,
mir träumt du verliessest mich.
Ich wachte auf, und ich weinte
noch lange bitterlich.

Ich hab im Traum geweinet,
mir träumte du wärst mir noch gut.
Ich wachte auf, und noch immer
strömt meine Tränen flut.

In my dream I wept,
I dreamt—in your grave you lay.
I woke, and still the tears
Were running down my face.

In my dream I wept,
I dreamt you abandoned me.
I woke, and yet the tears
Fell long and bitterly.

In my dream I wept,
I dreamt you were still true.
I woke, and still the tears
All in a flood still flew.

Heine's dream-sequence represents the defeat of wish-fulfillment by obsession. Each dream creates a less grievous fantasy than the last, yet each awakening proves that the speaker's grief is unabated. The first imagery dominates the rest; the lover is in mourning—not for his beloved, who after all is not dead, but for his own ego, which has been captivated by her fantasy-image.

Schumann's response to this pattern is to saturate his song with repetition. The first two stanzas of text are set to the same music—an unaccompanied vocal line interrupted by "drumbeat" figures on the piano—and the melody for each line of verse begins with several repetitions of a single pitch. The refrain, "Ich hab' im Traum geweinet," is nothing but a series of B♭s inflected by a semitonal "sob" (Ex. 13). Only the music for the eighth line, a diminution of the music for the fourth, varies the rigid pattern, perhaps as a reminder that the strophic repetition is paradoxically through-composed. For the last stanza, Schumann heightens the painful feeling of a slow stammer as far as possible; unlike Heine, he articulates the consuming, self-reinforcing aspect of repetition. What little melody there has been dissolves into a drone; the vocal line, now reinforced by the piano, starts with a

EXAMPLE 13. Schumann, "Ich hab' im Traum geweinet," mm. 1-4.

long, almost unvaried series of B♭s, then moves to an even longer series of D♭s over restless, dissonant harmony marked by a faulty subdominant resolution (Ex. 14). The end of the vocal part is an abrupt descent by half-step to the tonic tone, E♭, over a non-tonic chord, V^7/iv—the very chord that led earlier to the faulty resolution. The accompaniment now corrects the fault with a move to the subdominant, but there it stalls, leaving the iv chord itself to linger unresolved through an extended silence (Ex. 14). The piano closes by returning fixedly to its "drumbeat" figure, falling into another long silence, then repeating the V-i progression—it is scarcely a cadence—with which the drumbeat ends.

The chain of associations found here is much the same as the one that appears in "The Thorn" and in Berlioz's program for the *Symphonie fantastique*: obsession, the figure of the absent other, death, captivation, and curtailment. Something "dangerously" similar, to use Wagner's own term, will reappear in the long undulation of *Tristan* from Prelude to "Liebestod."

A surpassingly grim version of the same pattern appears in the third act of Alban Berg's *Lulu* (the part of the opera suppressed until after the death of the composer's widow), when Lulu is murdered by Jack the Ripper. Berg directs that Jack be played by the same singer who plays the husband Lulu has destroyed, Dr. Schön; and he duplicates this repetition musically by setting Lulu's encounter with Jack to the earlier love-music of Lulu and Schön. Lulu, a "captivating" figure in every possible sense, has dismantled Schön's identity and then killed him. Now the ghost of Schön's selfhood, the negative image of his love for Lulu, returns with its erotic music to do the same for her: to kill the woman for whom men die. Lulu's power, throughout the opera, has been the power of Romantic repetition itself, which she generates as the object of erotic obsessiveness. In the end, that same repetition is her nemesis: it consumes everything, even its own source.

In *Lulu*, the disruptive turbulence present in "The Thorn" and the "Appassionata"—the latent destructiveness of all Romantic repetition—

EXAMPLE 14. Schumann, "Ich hab' im Traum geweinet," mm. 30–36.

reaches a horrifying fulfillment. Beethoven and Wordsworth are, of course, no less sensitive than Berg to the possibility of disaster, and Berg's logic of disaster is not simply the expression of a decadent esthetic. Beethoven and Wordsworth are able to contain the destructiveness of repetition in their work without succumbing to it because they present repetition as the dark aspect of an available transcendence, something that later artists increasingly lacked. Repetition may negate that transcendence, but it is also, inevitably, polarized by it into a dialectic of hope. This stabilizing limitation is often embodied textually in an ambiguous detail—the "beauteous" hill of moss in "The Thorn" that is also a grave, the isolated dissonance in the slow movement of the "Appassionata"—but its most powerful representation is again in the human figure. The solitaries and sufferers who most often cast the spell of Wordsworthian captivation never lose their connection to an enduring value that lies, somehow, simply in being human. Figures like the Leech Gatherer embody that value directly, offering consolation to the exact degree that they perplex and disturb. As to music, I think it is no accident that the most violent single instance of Romantic repetition in Beethoven is relieved, in an arbitrary gesture whose very arbitrariness establishes a new form, by a human voice:

> O Freunde, nicht diese Töne! Sondern lasst uns angenehmere anstimmen, und freudenvollere!

3

Generative Form

In 1807, Beethoven and Wordsworth both brought out works that broke disturbingly with the past and expanded the formal and emotional scale of an inherited form almost beyond recognition. Not entirely by coincidence, both ran into trouble for it. Wordsworth was astonished and a little embarrassed to find that some readers of his "Intimations" Ode took its allusions to Plato's myth of recollection literally and objected to the poem on religious grounds. The difficulty of these "good and pious persons" was on his mind as late as 1843, when he dictated his note on the poem to Isabella Fenwick; his remarks include a disclaimer that the poem ever intended to promote a belief in "so shadowy a notion" as a "prior state of existence."[1] Beethoven, for his part, met with an unusually cool reception for two of his three "Rasumovsky" Quartets. Though he must have been disappointed, he professed not to be surprised, breezily telling Clementi, "Oh, they are not for you, but for a later time." But there is an oddity to the story. The one quartet that was well received was the third, the most dissociative and openly problematical of the group, with a slow introduction so harmonically eccentric that it threatens the tonal frame of reference.

These vagaries of reception are closely connected, though they may not seem alike at first glance. Wordsworth suffered, and Beethoven benefitted, from a failure of recognition. Both the poem and the third quartet situated

---

[1] Quoted by Jack Stillinger in William Wordsworth, *Selected Poems and Prefaces* (Boston: Houghton-Mifflin, 1965), p. 538.

material meant to be problematic, questionable, incommensurable, at critical places, but readers and listeners alike failed to grasp the discontinuity. Part of Wordsworth's audience thought that he was dragging out Platonic— that is, pagan—machinery to contain an experience that Christian mysticism (like Henry Vaughn's in "The Retreat") could contain more truly. Beethoven's audience, assuming them to have assimilated what they heard to what they knew, must have written off his mystifying opening as an ordinary chromatic introduction. Yet Wordsworth invokes Platonic recollection only to dispense with it, to affirm the experience he has described in Platonic language in the very act of questioning the Platonic description:

> . . . those first affections,
> Those shadowy recollections.
> *[Be] they what they may,*
> Are yet the fountain light of all our day.
>   (152–55, italics added)

And Beethoven leaves the murky non-harmonies of his introduction for a hesitant cadenza-like passage that seems almost surprised to find itself in C major. When the more vigorous, and very Classical, first theme breaks forth, the effect is dizzying in the way too much light is blinding—a disorientation brought on by an excess of clarity. To hear well, as to read well, is in this case to be perplexed.

The willed incoherence of these moments is the seminal element in what I take to be a seminal structural rhythm. In the "Intimations" Ode and the Third "Rasumovsky" Quartet, we are confronting works that are based on a tension between two different modes of discourse—incompatible styles, expressive languages, semiotic codes. The split in each case is decisive, even obtrusive, and produces a texture of marked unevenness. What Roland Barthes calls "the site of a loss, the seam, the cut" between discourses yields both the odd misalliance of naturalistic and supernatural language in the ode and the mismatching of Classical and alarmingly post-Classical styles in the quartet.[2] Furthermore, the split in form embraces a split in value; where one discourse is potentially celebratory, the other is ominous and entropic. Beethoven and Wordsworth respond to these bluntly articulated fissures by gradually healing them over. Insisting on the continuity of their works, they alter, bit by bit, the relationship of the antagonistic discourses until what began as a disjunction ends as an organic connection. At the point of resolution, the threatening discourse reappears as an origin, and generates the celebratory discourse as a fulfillment and release. More exactly, the one discourse *re*-generates the other—and itself; the moment of fulfillment is a

---

[2] Roland Barthes, *The Pleasure of the Text,* translated by Richard Miller (New York: Hill and Wang, 1975), pp. 6–7. I take the terms "naturalistic" and "supernatural" from Lionel Trilling (see note 16).

detailed re-creation of the earlier moment of disjunction. The result is a tidal outburst of pent-up energy: in Wordsworth, the rapture of no-longer-innocent affirmation that closes the ode, and in Beethoven the almost delirious fugue-like movement that ends the quartet.

This slow unfolding of coherence, with its strongly organic feeling—this generative form, as it might be called—reflects a basic Romantic commitment. The demand for an autonomous yet organic creation, for an esthetic process that transcends expressive rules (codes, systems) and yet retains the intelligibility of codified expression, is universal during the Romantic period. Wordsworth's critique of poetic diction, Schiller's play theory, Coleridge's *Biographia Literaria*, and Kant's *Critique of Judgment* are only the most seminal treatments of the subject. In general, the demand for organic creation is made on behalf of the consciousness of the artist, not the work of art. A great deal of Romantic criticism willingly embraces the idea that the work is only a secondary phenomenon, the very existence of which signifies the loss of the heightened state of mind that produced it. Shelley is explicit on the matter:

> [W]hen composition begins, inspiration is already on the decline, and the most glorious poetry that has ever been communicated to the world is probably a feeble shadow of the original conception of the Poet.[3]

The same idea, though more implicitly, appears in Wordsworth's most celebrated comment on his art. If all true poetry is the spontaneous overflow of powerful feelings, then all true poetry testifies to an origin that only becomes articulate once it has lapsed. The overflowing wellspring of feeling, the poet's consciousness, remains the locus of value. As for Beethoven, it is difficult to find a relevant comment that is authentic amid a remarkable amount of distortion and even forgery.[4] But Beethoven did once write—impulsively, in a rather slapdash letter—something in the same vein:

> As for me, why, good heavens, my kingdom is in the air. As the wind often does, so do harmonies whirl around me, and so do things often whirl around too in my soul.
>
> (To Count Brunswick, February 13, 1814)

Generative form is central to Romantic poetry and music—early and late, from the "Intimations" Ode and the Third "Rasumovsky" Quartet to Theo-

---

[3] Percy Bysshe Shelley, *Poetry and Prose*, edited by Donald H. Reiman and Sharon B. Powers (New York: Norton, 1977), p. 504.

[4] See Maynard Solomon, "Beethoven's Creative Process: A Two-Part Invention," *Music and Letters* 61 (1980): 272–81.

dore Roethke's *North American Sequence* and Elliott Carter's Double Concerto—because it provides the means to present the organic and re-creative
values of the artist's consciousness directly in the structural rhythm of a
work of art. Its purpose is to externalize the actions of mind and yet—by
remaining problematical, by flirting with incoherence—to avoid losing the
organic suppleness of the Romantic subject in an objective fixity.

The Third "Rasumovsky" Quartet and the "Intimations" Ode—the primary topics of this chapter—associate generative form with a strong sense
of subjective risk and a possibly disintegrative self-consciousness. Or, more
exactly, they propose the form as a means of recuperation from such drastic
self-confrontations. Both, I think, achieve the sense of renewal that they
seek, though that view—not surprisingly, given works that so openly court
collapse—will not stand as simply self-evident.

II

The introduction to Beethoven's Third "Rasumovsky" Quartet is bleak,
painfully slow, and thoroughly devoid of key-feeling (Ex. 15). "Traditional-

EXAMPLE 15. Beethoven, Third "Rasumovsky" Quartet, introduction.

ly," as Joseph Kerman observes, "a sonata-form slow introduction will begin in or near the tonic key and then work its way to an extended dominant ... [But] the listener is left completely in a fog at the start of the [C-major Quartet] for many bars, an effect that is carefully compounded by melodic and rhythmic vaguenesses to go along with the harmonic obfuscation."[5] There is much to be said about the harmonic obfuscation, but in large structural terms the most important point about it is that it constitutes a serious effort to approach Classical tonality dialectically, and so to question the status of Beethoven's musical language. The introduction works its way to a not-very-extended dominant only in the most tenuous, not to say spurious, of terms. More critically, it does not lead on from there to a cadence on the tonic, or even prepare for one; the glassy, undifferentiated texture of the music denies the very possibility of a cadence from start to finish. The tonic has no recourse but to enter the work as an isolated, secondary element, which it does by splitting off abruptly from the fog of indeterminate sonority in the form of the cadenza theme, a melodic elaboration of the dominant-seventh chord which is repeated sequentially on v⁷/ii. Trailing clouds of the sonorous void that precedes it, the emergent tonic sounds fabricated, arbitrary, even facile—an effect that constitutes the most drastic harmonic obfuscation of all. Even the long-awaited C major cadence that introduces the main theme is mystified, prepared through an ambiguous swelling chord that sounds like v⁷/IV but is interpreted otherwise, and with a specific allusion to mm. 16–17 of the introduction (Ex. 16). The structure of the Quartet as a whole is directed towards rehabilitating the decentered, destabilized tonality of this opening, and it will take nothing less than the whole quartet to accomplish the task.

The dialectical questioning that Beethoven sets up in the introduction incorporates both negative and constructive elements. The negation is based on a sustained antithesis between sonority and structure, something already implicit in the very first chord—a diminished seventh that, having no con-

⁵ Joseph Kerman, *The Beethoven Quartets* (New York: Norton, 1966), p. 134.

EXAMPLE 16. Beethoven, Third "Rasumovsky" Quartet, first movement.

text, has no meaning, and so simply fades into silence. The harmonic vocabulary of the introduction is entirely that of Classical tonality, though
with a reversal of emphasis; it consists of a few triads and a great many seventh chords. But the musical syntax is deranged. The Classical procedures of
tonal definition and coherent chord-progression disappear almost completely; the few lingering traces of them only enlarge the pervasive sense of their
absence. Tonal continuity appears only in an openly false or at least fictive
form, the vestigial use of stepwise voice-leading to connect unrelated harmonies. Even the C-minor triad, which can be analyzed as the latent tonic
chord of the passage, is neutralized. When the chord turns up in m. 17, it
does not even have a tonal function, let alone a tonic one.

These dissociative features establish the relationship between Beethoven's introduction and the Classical slow introduction as a form of serious
travesty, a radical exaggeration that has the impact of a critique. The central
tonal area of the quartet is not evolved from a peripheral one; it is juxtaposed with a tangle of meaningless and yet ordinary chords. The materials of
a tonal organization are gathered together in the introduction but they are

left, so to speak, disassembled. The music continually seems to approach a tonal clarification that it continually postpones—all at a glacial pace; the result is a diffuse, non-specific harmonic tension that can become almost unbearable. Tonality is both omnipresent and chimerical. The feeling of a fantastic extremity is probably at its height during the three wrenching trills that, spaced almost evenly, give the introduction its only trace of periodic rhythm. A trill of any duration increases harmonic tension, which it normally resolves in behalf of the principal note. Here, the trills are pure surges of intensity with no access to harmonic release. Their dissonances subside, but do not resolve; they can only move by (false) step into further mystification.

The constructive side of Beethoven's dialectic depends on the presence of a harmonic organization that is independent of Classical tonality and, in this context, antithetical to it. In order to expose the relativity of his tonal language, to abolish its Classical naturalness and self-evidence, Beethoven provides the introduction with a consistent harmonic system—call it a "non-tonical" harmony—that is uniquely its own.[6] A small group of principles is put together to govern the succession of chords without reference to a tonal center. Chord-type rather than chord-function becomes the main determinant of musical motion; harmonic progression is replaced by a circular pattern based on the recurrence of functionless diminished-seventh chords. In particular:

1. Diminished-seventh chords normally lead to dominant-seventh chords. On the two occasions when this does not happen (mm. 13–14, 20–21), the deviant chords are treated as dissonances that resolve to the diminished-seventh–dominant-seventh pairing. It is worth noting that both of these non-tonical dissonances suggest sonorities of F minor; the choice foreshadows the large-scale harmonic structure of the quartet.

2. Dominant-seventh chords do not require resolution and may lead to any triad or half-diminished-seventh chord (diminished triad with major third added). This denaturing of the dominant seventh is certainly the most radical element in Beethoven's dialectic. The most strongly directed of all Classical sonorities is converted into the most "open," most undirected, sonority in non-tonical chord-succession. And the paralyzing grip of non-tonicity on the music is broken only with (and by) the restoration of the dominant-seventh function.

---

[6] For a discussion of such independent relationships in post-Classical music, see my "The Mirror of Tonality: Transitional Features of Nineteenth-Century Harmony," *19th-Century Music* 4 (1981): 191–208.

Taken together, the functionless diminished– and dominant-seventh chords define the underlying formal contour of the introduction. The music is based on the abstraction of the familiar dominant progression vii°⁷-V⁷ from any tonal basis; it is the large-scale expansion of a defamiliarized fragment of tonal syntax.

3. Triads normally appear in inversion and lead either to dominant-seventh or diminished-seventh chords.

4. Half-diminished-seventh chords lead to diminished-seventh chords. The half-diminished chords are non-functional, but their content suggests supertonic sonorities of C minor and F minor.

The austere rigor of this design represents Beethoven's response to the art of harmonic levitation as practiced by Mozart in the introduction to his "Dissonant" Quartet in C Major, K. 465. (The coincidence of keys is no accident.) Mozart's phantasmal opening is intensely, even bizarrely chromatic, but it never breaks its connection with C major—indeed, is remarkable for sustaining it. As Charles Rosen notes, "the chord of C major will appear always as the stable point around which every other chord in these measures revolves."[7] Mozart, we might say, conjures up a very good illusion of nontonicity. Beethoven, who wants to outdo him—to take greater risks, to grasp Classical tonality as a subjective choice rather than as an objective fact— plunges deep into the real thing.[8]

At this point, the harmony of the introduction might seem completely immune to tonal affiliations. If it were, however, the basic problem of the quartet would be unsolvable. Some thread of continuity must run between the introduction and what follows it; otherwise, no tonal progression in the piece could escape being compromised by the mists lurking behind it. Beethoven therefore takes a cue from Mozart and creates an illusion; he composes a fiction of C minor. A spectral sort of C minor must have been what his first audiences heard. Nothing else was available for them to hear—nor

---

[7] Charles Rosen, *The Classical Style* (New York: Norton, 1972), p. 186.

[8] The *Adagio* introduction to the finale of Beethoven's B♭-Major String Quartet, Op. 18, No. 6, should also be mentioned here. This remarkable *Adagio* is evasive, even radically evasive, in its harmony, and it also incorporates harmonic patterns that move independently of tonality. (For an analysis, see my "Mirror of Tonality," pp. 198–203, and Joseph Kerman's discussion in *The Beethoven Quartets*, pp. 76–81.) Compared to Mozart's, the tonality of this music is problematical. Nevertheless, the *Adagio* is definitely in B♭, and it assures that key as a point of reference by beginning with the tonic triad. Beethoven's writing here is tonally eccentric; in the introduction to Op. 59, No. 3, it is effectively pretonal. What appears in the earlier work as a feeling of mystery turns, in the later one, to the twilight of alienation.

is there for us. But we can no longer hear it naïvely. The tonality sounds—faintly—only in tension against the non-tonicity of the music; one system of discourse is pressing against the other, implacably.

In harmonically fuzzy contexts, melody is often a primary clue to tonality. There is no melody in this marginally contoured introduction—shape and rhythm have been stripped away like ornaments that hide some kind of Ur-music—but Beethoven does compensate for his hopelessly indeterminate chord progressions by individualizing the movement of the instrumental voices. Two of these are especially important: the cello line, which sinks steadily by step and half step from $F\sharp^1$ in the first measure to its low C at measure 21, and the first violin line, which rises with slight hesitations in a scale-like pattern from d^2 to c^3 between measures 7 and 21. These complementary patterns are highlighted by the increasing registral separation of the outer voices and by the gray neutrality of the inner voices, which remain cramped in register and aimless in motion. As the violin and cello continue to draw apart in slow-motion antiphony, the music takes on a mounting but always obscure sense of direction. Then, at m. 21, a destination appears as the outer voices simultaneously attack the same note, C. This is the only doubling of its kind in the whole introduction, and its climactic appearance, spanning four octaves against a background of tied inner voices, invests the doubled tone with the structural significance of a tonality. Beethoven carefully calls for a down-bow on the resonant open C-string of the cello to establish the moment as a firm structural downbeat.[9]

The harmony at this point is an F-minor triad that poises itself ambiguously between the clashing harmonic systems of the introduction; it can be taken either as a non-tonical dissonance (the chord-sequence is dim 7th-f$\natural$) or as a tonal landmark. Because the doubled C that frames it is so supercharged, this triad does not suggest the tonic of F minor but the subdominant of C minor, and the suggestion is reinforced by a resolving half-step, B–C, in the first violin—the corrected version of a B♭–C step in mm. 16–17 which leads to the functionless C-minor triad there. At long last, the music seems to affirm a tonality, gingerly enough, but audibly. Yet the implied C minor is very far from being a genuine tonal area, a key with referential power and dominant support. It is only the fiction of a key, a projected form of the ear's desire for tonal meaning. From the standpoint of non-tonicity, the meaning of the crucial F-minor triad is indifferent; its harmony resembles a tonal function the way Hamlet's cloud resembles a whale. Beethoven proves the point by giving the triad a non-tonical resolution to a diminished-seventh/dominant-seventh pair. The *Allegro vivace* is about to insist that

---

[9] The term "structural downbeat" is taken from Edward T. Cone's *Musical Form and Musical Performance* (New York: Norton, 1968); for an explanation, see the first chapter. Briefly: a structural downbeat is a large-scale point of arrival that discharges accumulated tension.

these two chords have secretly been functioning as dominants of C major, but as Beethoven drags out the diminished seventh to excruciating lengths (mm. 22–24, 25–28, with a silence between), it sounds much more like an icy blank, a harmonic place-holder, than like a functional sonority.

As we know, the structural rhythm of the quartet as a whole is directed toward the release of tonal discourse from the quicksand of non-tonicity. Beethoven addresses this task in exemplary fashion. If the music is clouded by a sense of dissociation, then the sense of dissociation will have to become illluminating. The C-major tonality of the quartet is at its weakest during the transition from the introduction to the *Allegro vivace*; the naked juxta-position of tonality and non-tonicity across the sectional boundary seems to denature the tonic, at once to enfeeble it and lay bare its contingency. The music responds to this rent in its fabric by letting the echoes of disjunction reverberate continually. Until the finale, the major sectional divisions with-in and between movements are virtually all problematical in some way. Strange, disruptive, or startling, the sectional junctures are a little too ex-posed, too highly sensitized to the conflict of languages that goes on beneath the surface. The texture produced by these musical "sore spots" is ambiva-lent. On the one hand, the music is haunted by its troubled beginnings. An-tithetical, almost antiphonal styles clash across sectional lines, recalling the disparity between the bleak anonymity of the Introduction and the unmis-takably Classical cut of the *Allegro*. Classical forms take on peculiar shapes, reminding us that to weaken a harmonic language is to erode the style that it supports. On the other hand, the recurrent defamiliarization of transitional moments produces a large-scale rhythm that is organic in feeling and ulti-mately generative in effect. Its presence prepares for a transition to C major that can rehabilitate both the tonal language of the quartet and its Classical form.

In the first movement, strange goings-on begin as early as the first ending of the exposition, which consists of four unexpected measures on F minor—probably an allusion to both the f♮ at m. 21 of the introduction and the false V^7/F that leads to the first tonic cadence. When this passage returns the sec-ond time around, the development takes it as a cue to repeat the opening measures of exposition yet again, this time in E♭ (a key that will grow in sig-nificance as the quartet proceeds); the music seems unable to tear itself away from the material of its first few measures, as if it were preoccupied with the moment of its escape from non-tonicity. More quasi-repetition of the open-ing follows, continuing the stalled feeling as E♭ leads back to F—now F ma-jor, which persists for a dozen measures. The development is all but over be-fore any real motivic and harmonic tension emerges, and this through a stuttering canon that feels stalled in its own right. Beginning in the tonic mi-nor, the canon both recalls the harmony of the introduction and represents a brooding spell of Romantic repetition. After harping on the juxtaposition of C minor and F minor, the passage follows a tortuous path onto the dominant, where the pace of the motivic repetition quickens into urgency while the harmony slowly grinds to a halt on the dominant-seventh chord.

The moment of recapitulation that follows from this is blurred and tenuous; it stands to the development as the exposition does to the introduction. After a pair of lengthy trills silence the canon with the requisite arbitrariness, but without budging from its harmony, the first violin breaks unexpectedly into a genial flourish that turns, just as unexpectedly, into the second half of the much-played cadenza theme. As it did at the start of the movement, this theme forms an elaboration of the dominant-seventh chord, which means here that it merely prolongs the expectancy-laden dissonance that first closes and then curtails the canon. A version of the earlier sequential restatement also returns before a cadential progression emerges—and emerges with an agitated backward glance at the close of the introduction (Ex. 17). In effect, then, the harmonic tension of the development is first carried over into the recapitulation and then evaded, elided, more than resolved there; the decisive cadence constitutes only an indirect response to it. What

EXAMPLE 17. Beethoven, Third "Rasumovsky" Quartet, first movement.

Beethoven recapitulates here is not simply an exposition, but specifically an inadequate exposition.

In this setting, we could hardly expect the coda to bring closure, and it emphatically does anything but that. The movement ends as it begins, with a forceful dislocation. A few measures of static harmony are followed by a harsh, accelerated *crescendo* over a dominant pedal, a chromatic ascent that alludes in texture to the F-minor interpolation at the first ending of the exposition. Startlingly brusque and dismissive, this gesture is a kind of self-accusation. It throws into relief both the brittle uncertainty of the sonata form and the latent vulnerability of the final cadence.

When the second movement opens, on a deep cello pizzicato, the abrupt collapse of the *Allegro vivace* is confirmed in its regressive impact. The music has returned to the mysterious otherness (though not the grimness) of the introduction. The hypnotic rise and fall of the A-minor main theme in triplets at once bleak and graceful, the ominous pulse of the pizzicato cello, the restless harmony—all promise a new dissociation of Classical language and form, and perhaps one with an ambivalent allure.

With the appearance of the second theme in C, the relative major, Beethoven begins to keep that promise. In minor-key movements, the relative major acts as a dominant substitute, and the tonal balance that it ought to provide is especially in demand here because the A-minor music is both richly dissonant and chromatically biased towards F minor, to which it eventually leads through the Neapolitan sonority of B♭ minor. Yet the balance is not forthcoming. The C-major theme seems to mimic the rise and fall of its fascinating A-minor opposite in a pleasant-enough but teasingly exaggerated Classical style, all ornamental staccato scale-work and stereotyped gracefulness. The suspicion of enervation is hard to resist, and it falls equally on the tonality of the theme. Already compromised as a tonic (both long- and short-term) in the first movement, C major makes its appearance here with elementary simplicity, as if to overcompensate for the prevailing harmonic restlessness with a willed naïveté. But Beethoven approaches the key from the F-minor/C-minor axis that has troubled the quartet from the start, and the C-major theme responds by sinking into a static, uneasy cadential passage that is colored insistently by the subdominant-minor third, F-A♭. (An earlier "sore spot," the canon of the first movement, hovers allusively behind this close, as the cadenza theme does behind the Classical second theme.) In every respect, the relative-major episode confirms what the first movement has intimated: a move into the Classical ambience is the sign of a deteriorating structure. But the sense of fecklessness that results here is dialectically transformed into a feeling of fluidity in the section that follows, a development *quasi una fantasia* that carries the first theme from ♭vi to ♭v and all the way back to i around the circle of fifths.

Later in the movement, the weakness of the second theme proves even more dissociative. After appearing in A major, as if for its long-range resolution, the theme takes an utterly unexpected turn into the remotest possible key, the tritonal E♭. Once there, it achieves a surprising lyric warmth, eventually soaring legato over a subtly heightened accompaniment. An expressiveness latent in the theme seems to be unlocked by a sudden turn of dialectic, as the epitome of demystified Classicism precipitates the most baffling mystification in the movement. The E♭ apotheosis is followed by a gripping transitional passage that leads to a reprise of the first theme in the tonic. The episode is strongly reminiscent of the introduction in its texture, with sustained, slowly-changing chords arching over the cello pizzicato—the cello line falling, then static, just as before (Ex. 18). The harmony, too, turns back

EXAMPLE 18. Beethoven, Third "Rasumovsky" Quartet, second movement, E♭–major—A–minor transition.

to the remote, alienated territory in which the Quartet begins. The resolution, or at least the return, to A minor emerges from the defile of a mysterious diminished-seventh chord and proceeds with a positively mesmerizing strangeness (Ex. 18). Rarely has a diminished seventh been asked to do so much. Despite its symbolization in Ex. 18 as a primary progression in A mi-

nor, the sequence of harmonies here is phantasmagorical as approached from
E♭. The music sounds like a free-associative fabric of expressive voice-leading until the closing resolution of an A-minor six-four chord—a deferred
resolution at that—makes retrospective sense of what has happened. The
earlier passage from E♭ minor to A minor along the circle of fifths is not so
much condensed as abolished, vaporized, by this gesture. The antithetical
E♭-major and A-minor harmonies are not only brought into direct relationship with each other here, but E♭ is also established as a fully tonicized key
with stronger cadential support than the A minor that it produces. The tritone is effectively set in the structural place of the dominant, a procedure
that violates both the letter and the spirit of the Classical style. Harmonic
resolution once again regresses from a palpable release of tensions toward
something that resembles wish-fulfillment. Of necessity, the tonic that returns across this seductively uncanny threshold is dissonant and unstable.
Before the close, the earlier B♭ material returns, resolves, then hauntingly
returns again, as what was once only a Neapolitan inflection becomes an
area of genuine harmonic restlessness. Only slightly less than its counterpart
in the first movement, the tonic of the *Andante* is eroded by a transition that
requires it to emerge from a region too disjunctive to generate it properly.

   With the Minuet, Beethoven restores us to the Classical style, or pretends
to. Music of studied naïveté, this movement is more a confection than a con-
struction; it resembles the minuets of Mozart, Haydn, and the early Beethoven the way a Mahler waltz-tune resembles Johann Strauss, but without the
irony. Joseph Kerman calls it a "rococo vision," a "dreamlike" evocation of
a style remote in feeling if not in time, "abstracted in all senses of the word,
almost affectionate."[10] The Minuet, in short, is a Beethovenian music box, a
reflection of the glaze that hardens over the Classical style once a movement
like the *Andante*, a passage like the introduction, becomes possible. Obviously, the junctures in this music cannot be made too problematical without
breaking the rococo spell, so Beethoven contents himself with making them
rather stilted, a little too wooden and idealized. The sectional nature of the
Classical form is subtly exaggerated, especially in contrast to the smooth
running figuration that pervades the movement, often gliding seamlessly
from instrument to instrument. There is an impression of energy contained
by nostalgia; the finale will set it loose. Meanwhile, one curious element
does make an appearance, with a mildly alienating effect. Contrary to Classical practice, the first strain of the Minuet is not repeated. But it is not exactly missing.

   After the *da capo*, Beethoven clouds the air with a very unclassical passage indeed. Much altered, the "omitted" strain of the Minuet returns as a

---

[10] Kerman, *Beethoven Quartets*, p. 141.

coda in C minor that leads from the Minuet to the finale. This is the transition that is meant to lay the ghost of the introduction. In its overall harmonic movement, it does precisely what the introduction refused to do except as a retrospective illusion: it moves through various vicissitudes of C minor to a dominant seventh of C from which C major is set to emerge. Nor is the resemblance only general. In its middle measures, the coda gloomily indulges itself in diminished-supertonic harmonies emphasized by gawky tritonal leaps from A♭ to D (Ex. 19). Toward the close, two quiet measures in

EXAMPLE 19. Beethoven, Third "Rasumovsky" Quartet, coda to minuet.

slow-moving chords recall the texture of the introduction and allude to its harmonic problems with a tortuous dominant resolution. These and other details—especially F-minor details—make the coda seem like an entropic sigh, a sinking-away into formal and tonal inadequacy. Yet there is also a growing implication of recovery as the passage evolves from a cadence on E♭

that raises the spectre of the *Andante* (mm. 3–4) to emphatic, even overstated tonic-dominant harmony (mm. 11–14). The turning point is dramatized by an Ab–G resolution in octaves that both anticipates a critical unison-octave passage in the coda of the finale (discussed below) and constitutes a large-scale clarification the Ab–G step that closes the introduction with tonal intent, but under a non-tonical shadow (Ex 19; cf. Ex. 17). Taken as a whole, the music gives an uneven, indecisive impression, as if it were not so much exerting a dominant pull over its dissonances as vacillating nervously between tonal strength and weakness. The issue is brought to a crisis in the final measure. Extended by a fermata and sounded *diminuendo*, the closing dominant-seventh chord creates a tense, indefinite duration, recalling the close of the introduction. The effect is heightened by the dropping away of the root and third of the chord, so that the final sound is a whispered, mysterious minor third, D–F. But this time, as the finale is about to prove, the mystery is regenerative.

The emergence of the finale alludes to that of the *Allegro vivace* in considerable detail. In both passages, the quickening of tempo is marked with a metrical shift from a disintegrating ¾ to a vigorous, square ¼; the emergent tonic postpones a cadence for some time—in the *Allegro vivace* until the arrival of the main theme, in the finale until the last fugal entry; and the *forte* statement of the deferred cadence sends the first violin soaring until it reaches its top G and A over more tonic harmony. The first fugal entry, necessarily a solo, even sounds a little like a more spirited version of the cadenza that opens the earlier *Allegro*. Most of the uneasiness that has haunted the music vanishes with this revisiting, or revision, of its origins. The feeling of change is strongest in the effect produced by deferring the cadence: in the *Allegro* a sense of hesitancy and alienation, in the finale an exciting accumulation of energy. The organic relationship between the emergent tonic and the dubious music that precedes it makes all the difference.

Overall, the finale can be said to satisfy three purposes. It makes an emphatic demonstration of the organizing, centralizing power of tonality; it gives a precis of the harmonic tensions that prevail earlier in the work and at the same time resolves them by integrating them into a coherent Classical structure; and it rehabilitates transition as an organic principle.

The first purpose is served by an extreme tightness of tonal organization that also works as an underlying principle of rationality to set bounds on the furious release of energy. As Kerman points out, the finale emphasizes the supertonic, "the sound of D minor in the context of C major."[11] This emphasis has powerful long-range consequences, beginning with an emphasis on the supertonic of the dominant during the statement of the second theme. The first half of the development is ruled by supertonic relationships. Starting in Eb, the development proceeds to F minor and to Db major/minor,

[11] Kerman, *Beethoven Quartets*, p. 142.

which is respelled as C♯ minor. F minor is the supertonic of E♭; E♭ is the supertonic major of D♭. From C♯ minor, the music moves to D minor, the supertonic of the movement as a whole.

At this point a new area of harmonic tension intervenes. Throughout its course, the finale maintains the sonority of the lowered leading-tone as a strong independent dissonance. From D minor, the development moves to the key of the lowered leading-tone, B♭; the transition is perfectly smooth, because B♭ is approached diatonically within D minor and sounds at first like a local submediant. The establishment of B♭ (IV/IV) suggests an approach to the tonic from the subdominant direction, and that is just what follows, with F minor leading through C minor to C major. Some strong supertonic coloration at the close of the section is also worth noting as a reminder of large-scale harmonic relationships.

Later, just before the coda begins its final whirl, the two chief sources of tension in the movement are condensed, juxtaposed, and once more organically integrated with each other and with the whole. After a silence, there is a unison fortissimo B♭. Another silence follows; then the dissonance resolves down a half-step into a unison A, which asserts the fifth degree of the supertonic triad and leads to D via a scalewise descent that dramatically expands the unison into octaves. After still another silence, the F of D minor passes through F♯ onto the dominant tone G, and the coda resumes by elaborating the dominant triad. The strong, smooth movement from B♭ to D and down the circle of fifths reverses the resolving direction of the development (from D to B♭ and up the circle of fifths) and anticipates a group of ii–V–I progressions to follow in the rush to a final cadence. Similar cadential descents from the supertonic are prominent throughout the movement, and in the largest structural terms they can be thought of as reversals of the all-too-airy V^7-V^7/ii sequence with which the cadenza theme begins the exposition and recapitulation of the first movement.

With the same passion for long-range integration, the finale both recapitulates and resolves the harmonic tensions that thread the quartet as a whole. The focal point for this process is the B♭ sonority, which first comes to prominence in the finale as the top note of a ferocious, marginally functional diminished-seventh chord. During the development, B♭ acts both as a key area (IV/iv) and as the dissonant tone of V^7/iv to guide the subdominant minor towards the tonic. This process, perhaps the single most extended harmonic action in the finale, constitutes the resolution of that long-range tension we have heard so much about—and of: the clash between the sonorities of F minor and C major/minor, which surfaces in the introduction, intrudes on the exposition and development of the opening *Allegro*, reaches its height in the tonal design of the *Andante*, and even mocks the F-major Trio of the Minuet with F-minor echoes in the coda. The link to the *Andante* is particularly firm. There, F minor emerges from B♭ minor and leads through C minor to a C major that is the focal point of Classical inadequacy, a lame dominant substitute that quickly collapses back into the very B♭–F nexus that generated it. Here, F minor acts as a primary source of stability as it arises from B♭ major and leads again through C minor to a climactic and wholly adequate C major. The force of the resolution intensifies when we remember that F minor first appears in the finale near the start of the development as a derivative of E♭ major, the formidable tritone of the *Andante*.

Finally, there is the principle of transition. With its emphasis on the supertonic, the finale redoubles its organic connection to the coda of the Minuet. The coda, as we know, ends with the sustained third, D–F, that forms a continuation of its concluding dominant-seventh chord. At the same time, however, the D–F third anticipates the supertonic chord of the finale, and there is a specific sense in which the finale's supertonic saturation can be understood as an expansion of this transitional sonority. The bare D–F mediates between the disruptive ii° chords that are prominent in the coda and the cadentially oriented ii chords that proliferate in the finale. The significance of this connection emerges only in the very final moments of the quartet, when Beethoven dramatically diminishes a number of supertonic harmonies en route to the dominant. The result is to echo once again the A♭–G step-resolution that seems so problematical at the close of the introduction—and to vindicate it decisively (Ex. 20).

EXAMPLE 20. Beethoven, Third "Rasumovsky" Quartet, coda to finale.

An equally important stress on transition as continuation first, disjunction second, comes with the entry of the finale's fugal counter-theme at the start of the recapitulation. The theme is initially stated as C–C♯–D–G, and thus constitutes a melodic precis of the chief harmonic features of the movement: the tonic, the most remote tonality (C♯ minor), the most prominent tonality (D minor, approached from C♯ minor in the development), and the dominant. The feeling of connectedness, of musical shape compelled by an overpowering centripetal energy, is almost physical in its impact, and it takes on a sense of inexhaustibility from the steady yet urgent pace of the quarter-note motion.

Together with this recovery of tonal vitality, the finale also provides the long-sought recuperation of Classical form, and with a vengeance. The music is hyperbolical; it offers not one, but a combination of fully three Classical forms. There is the fugal finale, like those of Haydn's "Sun" Quartets, Op. 20, and Mozart's Quartet in G, K. 387 (a probable model); there is the *moto perpetuo* finale, like the one in Haydn's "Lark" Quartet, Op. 65, No. 5; and there is the ubiquitous sonata finale. The immense energy of the movement derives primarily from the tensions among these forms. For instance, the fact that the fugue subject is also a *moto perpetuo* theme makes it long and loose, even gawky. Spun out through the four-voice fugue texture, the sprawling subject proceeds to crowd the sonata exposition and disturb its balance of tonic and dominant. The music has been criticized for these features, but their point is the vindication of the harmonic unity that is resuscitated here and given free rein at long last.[12] The forms unmistakably strain against each other, so that the movement is constantly about to burst at the seams. Yet the coherence of its tonal relationships holds everything—barely—together, in a *tour de force* of harmonic organization that breaks the shivery grasp of the introduction. Beethoven seems to anticipate a formula of Wallace Stevens's:

> It is not enough to cover the rock with leaves.
> We must be cured of it by a cure of the ground
> Or a cure of ourselves, that is equal to a cure
>
> Of the ground, a cure beyond forgetfulness.
> ("The Rock")

It is the cure beyond forgetfulness that brings an exhilarating sense of closure to the final measures, as the music sweeps to a cadence with repeated attacks on the tones of the C-major triad.

III

At first glance, the risk that Wordsworth takes with myth in the "Intimations" Ode might seem insignificant beside Beethoven's protracted gamble with tonality. Nothing so very vital seems to hinge on the use and discarding of a "shadowy notion" that has long lost its cultural sanction, and certainly Wordsworth's achievement here has other sources. Yet the Platonic stanzas are very important to the ode, more so than we like to acknowledge. They

---

[12] Kerman, *Beethoven Quartets*, p. 142.

take up a sizeable portion of the text, for one thing; for another, they represent Wordsworth's means of continuing the poem two years after the fourth stanza had brought him to a halt. Even so, we will find this material intractable and confining if we repeat, only more subtly, the mistake of its early readers by missing its sheer oddity and using it as a key to the poem.[13] What the myth of recollection *says* matters surprisingly little to the pattern of tension and resolution in the ode; what matters a great deal is its disjunctive, discontinuous relationship to the poetry around it.

Like a tonality, a myth represents a formal language; it derives from a system of discourse that it exemplifies. Ordinarily, Wordsworth has little use for such "magic lore." In the passage from *Home at Grasmere* that he published as "a kind of *Prospectus*" to his unfinished *magnum opus*, he decisively rejected myth, or systematic metaphor, as a means of embodying the relationship between natural experience and transcendental truth. Both Hebriac and Hellenic mythology pale for him before "the Mind of Man," which he calls "My haunt, and the main region of my song"; the "fair ideal forms" invoked so powerfully by poets like Spenser and Milton, or by Blake and Shelley later, are surpassed by an immediate "Beauty—a living presence of the earth." That Wordsworth in all seriousness resorts to myth in the ode is a measure of crisis. Bewildered by loss, the poet props his failing ego on the mythical framework that he once dismissed, until the framework fails him—and in so doing frees him to regain his strength.

Ultimately, the issue raised by this pattern is the value of transcendental knowledge. Both before and after its Platonic section, the ode presents the light that Wordsworth has lost as an intimate and all-but-ineffable presence, something felt rather than understood. Displaced continually around a circle of synonyms that fail to clarify one another—"celestial light," "visionary gleam," "glory," "dream," "radiance," "splendour," "something that is gone"—the light constantly teases us out of thought. Only under the pressure of Wordsworth's Platonizing does it behave itself as if it were knowable, at which point the poem schematizes it with a disconcerting minuteness. Taken in these terms, the ode seems every bit as risky as the Third "Rasumovsky" Quartet; its mythical imagery does nothing less than divide being from consciousness. Unlike Beethoven's shadowy music, however, Wordsworth's "shadowy notion" is not meant to point to the Emperor's clothes but to wear them.

---

[13] Cleanth Brooks ("Wordsworth and the Paradox of the Imagination," in his *The Well-Wrought Urn* [New York: Harcourt, Brace, 1947], pp. 124–50) recognizes the problem of the incongruities but—still taking the poem "straight"—judges them to be signs of failure.

As a large structure, the "Intimations" Ode is generally acknowledged to consist of three events.[14] In stanzas I-IV, the poet asks where the "visionary gleam" of his childhood has gone; in stanzas V-VIII, the Platonic stanzas, he gives a mythical answer, a move that ends in blank despair; and in stanzas IX-XI he abruptly answers again with his own memories of vision, releasing a great surge of joy. This rhythm is to some extent progressive, a matter of "growing up," as Lionel Trilling says; and it is to some extent therapeutic, the restoration of an elemental joy in nature that the poet fears has been blighted.[15] Even more, though, the rhythm of the ode is a circle that involves a process of mourning as Freud understood it, the work of painful retrospection that the ego performs to detach itself from what it has lost.[16] The poem begins with a sensation of loss that turns to joy prematurely amid "the gladness of the May." What Freud called "the absorbing work of mourning" then takes over, a painfully detailed anatomy of separation from the light which culminates in the image of a ground-frost, the antithesis of the May festivities:

> Full soon thy Soul shall have her earthly freight,
> And custom lie upon thee with a weight,
> Heavy as frost, and deep almost as life!
> (127–29)

From this nadir, both joy and the May come back, but only in association with the ego's willingness to loosen its ties with the lost light.

Wordsworth identifies this circle of emotions with the passage from intuitive to mythical discourse and back again. And to make the linkage concrete, he gives each discourse a characteristic figurative structure.

The dominant trope in the intuitive sections of the ode is metonymy, and its purpose is to confront the speaker with the lost visionary gleam through the mediation of the objects that the gleam once "appareled." One possible result is a nagging disquiet, a sense that no natural object is really present to consciousness because the light of vision is absent:

> The Rainbow comes and goes,
> And lovely is the Rose,
> . . . .

---

[14] Variously described. See Lionel Trilling, "The Immortality Ode," in his *The Liberal Imagination* (1942: repr. Garden City, N.Y.: Doubleday, 1953), pp. 129–53.

[15] "Restoration": see Geoffrey Hartman, *Wordsworth's Poetry, 1787–1814* (New Haven: Yale University Press, 1964), pp. 273–77.

[16] Sigmund Freud, "Mourning and Melancholia," in his *General Psychological Theory*, edited by Philip Rieff and translated by Joan Riviere (New York: Collier Books, 1963), pp. 164–80.

But yet I know, where'er I go,
That there hath passed away a glory from the earth.
(10–18)

Elsewhere, blissful fragments of "the glory and the dream" will produce a moment of reunion, a movement, at once ecstatic and imperfect, from emptiness to fullness, from exclusion to participation:

Oh, evil day! if I were sullen
While Earth herself is adorning
   This sweet May morning,
And the children are culling
   On every side,
In a thousand valleys far and wide,
Fresh flowers; while the sun shines warm,
And the Babe leaps up on his Mother's arm.
(42–49)

Moments of this second type—"uneasy bursts of exultation" that condense an overflow of reviving feelings into a series of metonyms—arguably represent the most privileged imaginative structure in Wordsworth, the poet for whom "a stone, a tree, a withered leaf" bespeak an eye that can "find no surface where its power might sleep" (*Prelude* (1850), III, 162–66).

The celestial light that glimmers behind the festival of "blessed Creatures" takes on an idyllic immediacy from Wordsworth's pastoral images, but the fragmentary, associative nature of metonymy constantly removes it again to a kind of middle distance. As the gradual success of mourning shifts the emphasis from imperfect ecstasy to an ecstatic imperfection, the distancing effect redoubles; the reunion continues by feeding on the encroachments of absence, the loosening of the metonymic threads:

I love the Brooks that down their channels fret
Even more than when I tripped lightly as they.
(193–94)

In its outer sections, the ode is faithfully anti-conceptual about the object of its visionary intuitions. At times, its language is close to pure gesture, insistently tenuous in referential force as it speaks of "the fields of sleep," of "High instincts before which our mortal Nature / Did tremble," of "the hour / Of splendour in the grass, of glory in the flower." Throughout, the prevailing fusion of immediacy and remoteness is enhanced by an undulation in the meaning of the key word "glory." As a term of celebration, "glory" suggests a sublimity that is conventionally alien to the pastoral setting of the ode. As a visual term, it harmonizes the sublimity by interpreting it as a ring of light. But an aureole cannot encompass the all-pervasive radiance that the poet is mourning; it is another metonym, another gracious substitute, this time presented as a visual memory. The failure of precise evocation confesses that the vocabulary of light cannot finally interpret, or even identify, the visionary gleam, but only acknowledge it.

The Platonic section of the poem cuts across the figurative texture that surrounds it with an air at once impassioned and pedagogical, if not pedantic. Unable to master the ambivalence of his metonyms, the speaker invents defensive substitutes for them. The dominant trope in his myth of recollection is metaphor, in particular allegorical metaphor, and its function is to cut off the human subject from the sphere of transcendence. The severance begins emphatically with the first Platonic line, "Our birth is but a sleep and a forgetting." As it does in Beethoven's quartet, the displacement of one discourse by another disturbs a sectional juncture with a dialectical shock. The first mythic metaphor identifies birth with an oblivious sleep just a moment after intuitive metonym, at an impasse, has turned longingly to the waking "glory and . . . dream" of early childhood. What one discourse exalts, the other degrades. An overflowing of being into consciousness suddenly turns into a primal swoon; and where intuition takes "the fields of sleep" as a source of reviving joy, myth intrudes a sadly demystified sleep as an image of joylessness and exile.

Exile, indeed, is the constant burden of myth in the ode. Even the mythical metaphor for the visionary radiance is really an image of alienation, a covert depiction of emptying-out and the failure of participation: "not in utter nakedness, / But trailing clouds of glory do we come" (62–63). The undoing of metonymic fullness is close to systematic; a texture thickly woven with metaphors of departure, solitary journeying, and toil displaces the reunitive scene in which the solitary self joins others at a festival or holiday. All of the mythical motifs involve a sense of widening distance and the deferral of pleasure. They suggest an anti-pastoral impulse that erodes the idyllic genre of the poem in favor of a more complex, more disintegrative intertextuality. Dissociation increases as the imagery crosses the boundaries of pastoral decorum to include prison-houses, imperial palaces, master-slave relationships, and such exotica as pygmies and Samuel Daniel's *Musophilus*.

Once regimented by myth, Wordsworth's images can only dissemble a sense of transcendence; they become a higher poetic diction, polished to a false sheen of lucidity. Taking over a prefabricated cosmology, the ode portrays the career of vision with a pictorial artifice and labored urbanity that have no organic connection to the "Blank misgivings of a Creature / Moving about in worlds not realized." At times, the poetry seems to recall the eighteenth-century descriptive ode much as the Third "Rasumovsky" Quartet recalls the Classical minuet, as the attractively faded image of a once-viable form:

> The little Actor cons another part;
> Filling from time to time his "humorous stage"
> With all the Persons, down to palsied Age,
> That Life brings with her in her equipage.
>   (103–6)

Passages like this one attempt to mute the pain of mourning by making loss intelligible, or at least by putting on a style that connotes intelligibility.

At its most rigid, Wordsworth's mythmaking radically betrays the visionary core of his poem by forgetting his earlier dictum, "We murder to dissect." In the allegory of stanza V, which meticulously details the fading of the light as the child becomes a man, the image of light itself is covertly degraded. Earlier, the radiance of early childhood has been presented as precious in itself alone; the adult poet's loss is the loss of its simple, enveloping presence, "the glory and the freshness" that once bathed everything. Now, absorbed into a dense figurative system, the same radiance is nothing more than the symbol of something more primary, the "glories" that the soul has known before birth. The poet's loss has become a loss of meaning; the visionary gleam is no longer an indwelling fullness, but an exotic fragment. The sense of exile could scarcely go much further. Merely to be conscious of the light is to be divested of it; even what is lost is a condition of loss.

The result of this deconstruction—what else is it but that?—is a fierce and indignant despair that gradually overwhelms the last Platonic stanza and re-ignites the pain of mourning. Coleridge regarded the crucial transitional passage, where the final flight of allegory represents the child as "haunted for ever by the eternal mind," as "an approximation to what might be called *mental* bombast," in which the "thoughts and images [are] too great for the subject."[17] But the mental bombast is bound up too closely with outbursts of grief and bitterness to be a mere accident of style. Its presence suggests the collapse of the house of cards that is Wordsworth's mythical discourse, a *reductio ad absurdam* of metaphor under the stress of a misery it can neither explain nor confine. Characteristically, a vexed transition is the source of the crisis:

> VIII
> Thou, whose exterior semblance doth belie
>   Thy Soul's immensity
>   . . . .
> Mighty Prophet! Seer blest!
>   On whom those truths do rest
> Which we are toiling all our lives to find,
> In darkness lost, the darkness of the grave.
>   (109–18)

[17] Samuel Taylor Coleridge, *Biographia Literaria*, edited by John Shawcross (London: Oxford University Press, 1907), chapter 22.

"Seer blest" is what Adam, in *Paradise Lost*, calls the Archangel Michael
after learning from him that time will be redeemed. Wordsworth thus places
himself in the position of a fallen Adam who is deaf to the divine message
and immune to the "peace of thought" that it brings. Like the Minuet of the
Third "Rasumovsky" Quartet, only far more drastically, this last Platonic
stanza of the ode translates its inadequacy into a sudden sinking-away—a
sad coda that veers into a featureless void.

The culmination of this entropic movement is the image of heavy frost
that ends Wordsworth's Platonic excursion. Yet this image, like the last measure of Beethoven's coda, is also the threshold of renovation for both feeling
and form, both joy and the system of discourse that sustains it. The transition itself is stunningly abrupt, but it does not feel arbitrary; there is something organic about it, though only latently. Wordsworth presents this
strange moment as a kind of miracle, and I do not want to pretend that it can
be explained away. Nevertheless, it makes sense to regard it as a hyperbo-
lized representation of the end of mourning. In describing the ego's protracted farewell to the "hopes and memories" associated with the object it
has lost, Freud remarks that the extreme painfulness of the process "is hard
to explain in terms of mental economics." He goes on: "It is worth noting
that this pain seems natural to us. The fact is, however, that when the work
of mourning is accomplished the ego becomes free and uninhibited again."[18]
For Wordsworth, mourning seems to end when its pain has gone as far as
possible, "deep almost as life," so that the subject is almost projected onto
the plane of the absent object. What follows is the resurgent moment of dis-
inhibition, immeasurably heightened and prolonged.

Whatever its basis, the structural logic of this transition is impeccable.
The Platonic myth has entered the poem with an association between birth
and forgetting; it exits with a reverse association between rebirth and remembering:

> O joy! that in our embers
> Is something that doth live,
> That nature yet remembers
> What was so fugitive!
> (130–34)

Though a kind of consolation, this joy in embers is no mere consolation-
prize. It is an unqualified blessing, finally indifferent to loss, and the rest of
the poem is devoted to it.

Wordsworth would like to present his grown-up joy as a fullness even
greater than the one he has lost; like "Tintern Abbey," the ode tries to pass
beyond an "abundant recompense" for diminished feeling to a "warmer"
and "holier" love than the past could offer. The medium of this holier love

---

[18] Freud, "Mourning and Melancholia," p. 166.

is a vast cathectic rhythm of "perpetual benediction," and in his last three stanzas Wordsworth acts it out by linking joy to joy in a constantly self-renewing metonymic chain. Every turn of feeling leads to celebration, despite a matching awareness of loss that makes this continuity more precarious all the time—the Ode, as Geoffrey Hartman remarks, being prayer as well as praise:[19]

> And O, ye Fountains, Meadows, Hills, and Groves,
> Forebode not any severing of our loves!
> Yet in my heart of hearts I feel your might;
> . . . .
> The innocent brightness of a newborn Day
>   Is lovely yet;
> The clouds that gather round the setting sun
> Do take a sober colouring from an eye
> That hath kept watch o'er man's mortality;
> Another race hath been, and other palms are won.
>   (188–200)

We can affiliate the sheer emotional ambition of this ending to the giddy impetus of Beethoven's finale, with its similar self-renewing rhythm and its drive to cram as much feeling and as many structures as it can into a single gesture. Apparently, the moment of release into generative relationship is needed so badly that it all but compels hyperbole when it arrives.

The ode, however, has passed through a very dark defile of myth and mourning, and the organic bond between constriction and release needs to be strengthened if the flow of perpetual benediction is to carry a genuine sense of fulfillment, or convey what Trilling calls "a dedication to new powers."[20] Wordsworth's first step in meeting this demand is to link his renewed joy to the very condition that has made him mourn: the dwindling of vision from a presence to a memory.

The passage in which this happens is more than a little enigmatic, though very powerful. Throwing off the burden of myth, with its petrified knowledge, Wordsworth returns to the anti-conceptual language of vision and raises a "song of thanks and praise." But he seems to forget about the visionary gleam, and instead celebrates

> obstinate questionings
> Of sense and outward things,
> Fallings from us, vanishings;
> Blank misgivings of a Creature
> Moving about in worlds not realized.
>   (142–46)

[19] Hartman, *Wordsworth's Poetry*, p. 275.

[20] Trilling, *Liberal Imagination*, p. 127.

The discontinuity is certainly strange, almost bizarre, but it becomes more accessible once we realize that it is tacitly relocating the origin of vision. The first four stanzas of the ode present the visionary gleam as an external phenomenon, a "vividness," as Wordsworth later described it, that specifically "invest[s] objects of sight."[21] But the obstinate questionings rise up explosively from within; they sweep all objects of sight into an "abyss of idealism." Versions of Wordsworth's "spots of time," they yield uncanny moments in which "The mind is lord and master—outward sense / The obedient servant of her will" (*Prelude* (1850), XII, 221–22). These interludes, indeed, seem to be empty of everything but a sense of boundlessness that belongs to the consciousness that produces them. Ecstasy is consumed without a trace; tinges of guilt and aggression are called on, stripped of content, to suggest the antinomian power of raw subjectivity.

Because they are ego-states, Wordsworth's fallings and vanishings cannot be lost like a radiance that rests upon objects. Concealed under the "earthly freight" of adulthood, they nevertheless constitute a dynamic element of the psyche. It is this that allows the poem to recall them with no tinge of the nostalgia that informs its memories of the visionary gleam; the remembering is a partial reliving. The abyssal memories are accepted, even passionately desired, as the mere after-images of a lost presence because they confirm a persistence of vision that can "uphold" and "cherish" the adult mind.

But the renewal of psychic integration is no more than a turning-point. Wordsworth now seizes on his abyssal memories to reinterpret the loss of the visionary gleam as the incorporation of the gleam into the ego. With a kind of metonymic delirium, he first conflates the falling away of sense and outward things with the "first affections" inspired by the gleam, then identifies all such early ego-states—"be they what they may"—as "the fountain light of all our day," "a master light of all our seeing" (151–52). Geoffrey Hartman sees this as a willful confusion, but I prefer to take it as psychodynamic literalism.[22] It can be read as such if we realize that "seeing" here does not mean merely looking, but looking without a "sullen" grief that wrongs both the eye and the object. Before he surrenders his longing for the visual glory of his childhood, Wordsworth is unable to see anything at all without a pang:

> The sunshine is a glorious birth;
> But yet I know, where'er I go,
> That there hath passed away a glory from the earth.
> (16–18)

---

[21] Wordsworth, *Selected Poems and Prefaces* (Stillinger), p. 537.

[22] Hartman, *Wordsworth's Poetry*, p. 276.

In stanzas III and IV, sight is continually warded off. Hearing acts as a defensive substitute for it; the glad *sights* of the May are *heard* with joy:

> the sun shines warm
> And the Babe leaps up on its Mother's arm—
> I hear, I hear, with joy I hear!
> (47–49)[23]

The cry, "Shout round me, let me hear thy shouts, thou happy / Shepherd boy!" is almost a direct appeal for a protective envelope around seeing. But when the ego, its mourning done, yields its attachment to the gleam in favor of abyssal memories, the capacity to see freely is renewed. It is this healed visual power that the poem represents as an introjected "master light" in the eye. The gleam that was once the primal object now becomes the impulse by which the ego displaces it with new objects in an endlessly proliferating chain. When the adult Wordsworth finally looks with benediction at his pastoral surroundings, he sees *with* the light of vision that he can no longer see. Originally consecrated by the light, "The earth, and every common sight" are now consecrated by his consciousness.

Before acting it out, Wordsworth gives his renovated sight a brief mythical expression, as if to throw organic filaments between the two discourses of his poem. Perhaps it would be more accurate to call the relevant passage an anti-myth. Wordsworth severs its language from the need for precise Platonic interpretation by referring to our "shadowy recollections" with the skeptical "be they what they may," and his images are more evocative than allusive—mock tropes that read like metaphors but lack the rigorous denotative force that governs stanzas V–VIII. The shadowy recollections

> have power to make
> Our noisy years seem moments in the being
> Of the eternal silence;
> (154–56)

they lead us to moments of reunion in which

> Our Souls have sight of that immortal sea
> Which brought us hither,
> Can in a moment travel thither,
> And see the children sport upon the shore,
> And hear the mighty waters rolling evermore.
> (164–68)

[23] Harold Bloom, *The Visionary Company* (Garden City, N.Y.: Doubleday, 1961), p. 88, notes that the speaker in the first four stanzas "fails to see what he hears."

No doubt the "immortal sea" can be linked to the "eternal deep" of stanza VIII, though the deep is an image of divine truth and the sea of what the Neoplatonists used to call the defluction of the soul. It seems more fruitful, and more faithful to the emotional weight of the passage, to note the intuitional play of willed incoherence between the sound of mighty waters, a Biblical image of revelation, and the eternal silence, an ecstatic image of denied knowledge. The real affiliation of the vision by the shore, however, is with the earlier May pastoral, which it re-creates in a dreamlike, fantasy-tinged setting. In the re-creation, the poem both reaches an emotional watershed and prepares for the transition that will consummate its generative form.

At the juncture of stanzas IX and X, Wordsworth re-enacts his move from myth to renewed intuition, from figurative transcendence to the immediacy of perpetual benediction, in an explicitly organic form. His means for this—what I cannot help calling his modulatory pivot, though I am supposed to avoid musical metaphors—is the "anti-mythical" image of the sporting children. The sight of the children on the shore heals a psychic wound that has worsened steadily since the May pastoral collapsed, seemingly to evaporate, at the end of stanza IV. During the Platonic phase of the ode, Wordsworth increasingly comes to see children, condensed into an allegorical Child, across "a mighty gulf of separation" that finally moves him to bitter envy and outrage:

> Thou little Child, yet glorious in the might
> Of heaven-born freedom on thy being's height,
> Why with such earnest pains dost thou provoke
> The years to bring the inevitable yoke,
> Thus blindly with thy blessedness at strife?
> (122–26)

As the anti-myth reaches its close, children return in place of the overgrown Child and their presence revives as a source of joy. This enables Wordsworth to recover his failed earlier moment of rapture—to resume it where it broke off—with what Blake might call a cleansing of perception. As stanza IX becomes stanza X, the dreamlike displacement of the May festival dissolves into the actual May morning, where the poet is once more linked to the "blessed Creatures" in a bond of "jollity." Hearing, free now of defensiveness, is the first sense to revive with the season, but it modulates at once into Wordsworth's long-lost power of joyous looking:

> Then sing, ye Birds, sing, sing a joyous song,
>   And let the young Lambs bound
>   As to the tabor's sound.
> We in thought will join your throng,
>   Ye that pipe and ye that play,

> Ye that through your hearts today
> Feel the gladness of the May!
> (169–74)

By unveiling a *scene*, the ebbing of mythical thought becomes a flow of plenitude. In response, the (literally) enlightened eye re-creates and enlarges the landscape of bliss—now a bliss without transcendence. This healing return to a damaged moment unfolds in the same way that Beethoven's quartet does in the passage from Minuet to finale. From a moment of strangeness, a transition that is at last organic recuperates both a failed beginning and a threatened language.[24]

Only one thing remains to be done. In the premythical phase of the ode, Wordsworth is initially able to rejoice in spite of his loss, but the loss still blinds him and makes him "sullen." In the postmythical phase, this ambivalence is transformed into the recognition that the loss and the joy are inseparable, and finally indistinguishable. With the completion of mourning—marked slightly earlier by Wordsworth's almost over-generous surrender of the visionary gleam, "What though the radiance that was once so bright / Be now forever taken from my sight . . . / We will grieve not" (176–80)—joy becomes a form of loss, and loss itself a form of joy. This union is consummated in the closing image of the ode, a final metonym that is linked both to loss and joy, division and reunion:

> To me the meanest flower that blows can give
> Thoughts that do often lie too deep for tears.
> (203–204)

---

[24] It is interesting to note that Wordsworth's later revisiting of the great ode, the poem "Composed Upon an Evening of Extraordinary Splendour and Beauty," employs a reverse pattern of mythical and intuitive discourse. The poem both begins and ends with a mythical language drawn from Biblical and Miltonic sources; with this it tries to explain a brief, perplexing return of the visionary gleam. The mythical discourse distances what it explains, but this time the distance is what Wordsworth wants; he no longer trusts (or can no longer bear the indefiniteness of) intuitional language. Such a language does try to break forth at the opening of the second stanza:

> No sound is uttered—but a deep
> And solemn harmony pervades
> The hollow vale from steep to steep
> And penetrates the glades.
> Far-distant images draw nigh,
> Called forth by wondrous potency
> Of beamy radiance, that imbues,
> Whate'er it strikes, with gem-like hues!

Wordsworth, however, quickly stifles the cognitive insecurity of these lines with a mythic reinterpretation of what they describe, and the grip of this mystification is sustained until the close. The poem is not generative but defensive, as if the speaker were reluctant to risk a hope of renewed vitality; the moment of intuition is treated as an intrusion.

The flower invoked here quietly sums up the generative rhythm of the whole. The premythical phase of the poem closes when a common pansy compels a surge of grief and a shift to myth; the Platonic phase closes with an image of killing frost. Both earlier images are repealed by this last flower, yet both, too, are recalled by it—as thoughts too deep for tears.

IV

What are the hallmarks of the generative form articulated by Wordsworth's ode and Beethoven's quartet? The most obvious of them is the use of heterogeneous discourses as the basis of a continuous design. In general, a generative work will establish a large-scale tension along a sort of dialectical fault-line. The entire work is usually needed to develop a resolution, and *not* by dialectical means; eventually, one of the discourses will take on a privileged status and supplant the other by recasting it as an organically conceived origin. The privileged discourse is not itself revised in the process, not subjected to a dialectical change; on the contrary, its last appearance leaves it blissfully immune to dialectic. A strong closure naturally follows, often with an outburst of passion or energy so extreme that it seems indifferent to its own credibility. Such episodes can suggest a self-transcendentalizing of the ego—the giddy and dangerous state of heightened self-projection that Ludwig Binswanger called *"Verstiegenheit,"* "climbing past return."[25]

Though the threat of incoherence is basic to it, this structural rhythm does not require Wordsworth's or Beethoven's reckless questioning of primary languages. In Mahler's Second Symphony, for example, the formal tension arises between irony and rapture, as articulated by clashing styles. One of these is dissociative: disjunct in gesture, vulnerable to self-parody and grotesquerie, steeped in an allusiveness that subverts the spiritual ambition of the music, especially in reference to Beethoven's Ninth. The other is continuous in gesture and expression, freed from self-deprecating allusiveness by the consoling poetry that Mahler sets on Beethoven's own model—first for solo voice, then for soloists and chorus. The discontinuity first appears in the exaggerated contrast between the traumatic ritual music and lyrical second subject of the opening *Allegro maestoso.* Contrast intensifies to the point of formal and emotional crisis at the juncture between the scherzo and the "Urlicht" movement—the one a grotesque and parodistic instrumental fantasy on Mahler's satirical song "St. Anthony of Padua's Fish Sermon"; the other an ecstatic alto setting of a naïve religious folk poem. After this the split between styles widens into a gulf. The finale, marked *Wild herausfahrend,* breaks out with a hideous burlesque of the "wild" opening of Beetho-

---

[25] Ludwig Binswanger, *Being-in-the-World: Selected Papers,* translated by Jacob Needleman (New York: Harper and Row, 1967), pp. 324–49.

ven's finale in the Ninth. It is just this cacophony, however, that develops into the generative core of the music. After a silence, "as many horns as possible" intone a fanfare that Mahler himself called apocalyptic; then the unaccompanied chorus, almost inaudible, begins the Mahlerian "Ode to Joy" that will close the symphony with a variant of the lyrical melody of the first movement. It is worth noting that the closing melody transposes its precursor from E major, a key distant from the tonic C minor, to E♭, the relative major. Mahler certainly felt that this music was rooted in a profound personal crisis, so perhaps he saw an affinity between its generative form and intensity of risk. But in purely musical terms, he is far from staking as much as Beethoven did, even though the feeling of crisis in the Third "Rasumovsky" is far less plangent.

Nevertheless, some element of crisis seems intrinsic to the generative rhythm, and I suspect that it comes from the excessive strength of Romantic consciousness. The often jerky texture of generative works, their transitional awkwardness, their allusiveness and self-reflexiveness, and above all their willfully schizoid character—these features suggest an unusually restless subject at work, one both extravagant and ambivalent. In other words, they point to the archetypal Romantic subject: a volatile inner self that can constitute and threaten to displace much of the outer world. It is fair to speculate that this subject may seek generative form as a curb on its own imaginative power in order to sustain a relationship of mutuality with language and reality; the form would express a reluctance over what Keats called "the egotistical sublime." Perhaps that is why dialectic, which is the expression of a detached consciousness, must begin but not end the generative process. In this context, generative form suggests a kind of mirror-reversal or inside-out version of Romantic irony.[26] Where the Romantic ironist makes his ego "transcendental" by exposing its dominance over a text, the Romantic generativist exposes the vulnerability and contingency of his ego by exposing the dominance of a discourse. The subject only re-acquires its privilege in the labor of privileging the discourse that supports it. A heightened sense of self must coincide with the organic working-through of form; only in the at-last-justified language can one say, with Yeats at the end of "The Tower," "Now shall I make my soul."

The quality of working-through inevitably suggests growth, and the medium of growth is, of course, time. Generative works always involve a heightened sense of time, and usually find imaginative freedom in the fullness of time, not in a suspension of it; that may be why they are often longer examples of their genres. So emphatic is the temporal pressure that nothing in a generative rhythm can be fully valuable until it is delayed, immersed in the

[26] For a discussion of Romantic irony in Beethoven, see Rey M. Longyear, "Beethoven and Romantic Irony," in *The Creative World of Beethoven*, edited by Paul Henry Lang (New York: Norton, 1971), pp. 145–62.

creative agency of long-range rhythm, extended duration, purposive movement. True acts of creation, as a result, are paradoxically identified as moments of re-creation.

The palpable presence of time moving forward is a specialty of Beethoven, but it is perhaps especially forceful in the Third "Rasumovsky," which is framed by the near-immobility of the introduction and the headlong rush of a finale meant to be played as fast as possible. The two tempos face each other in the C-minor coda to the Minuet, which is written to convey a sense of slowing down and closes with such telling reluctance. Given the entropic quality of this music, the slackening of speed feels like a lingering resistance to organic form. As to the "Intimations" Ode, its marking of time is almost obsessive, and this is not entirely a matter of its theme. Wordsworth enhances the overall rhythmic pulse by giving too many precise time-signals. Temporal relationships are mapped out with unusual complexity to bring time into the foreground; the shifting play of verb-tenses has the volatility of Beethoven's rhythm in the first movement of the "Appassionata." It is no accident that the opening words of the poem are "There was a time."

Perhaps the best way to sum up generative form is to ask how it sums itself up. Central to both the "Intimations" Ode and the Third "Rasumovsky" Quartet is an interval of indefiniteness, both of duration and form. Attributes of ambivalence, misgiving, and estrangement attach to it; in relation to its surroundings, it appears as a sheer incommensurateness that is both threatening and somehow fecund. I am thinking here of the obstinate questionings and blank misgivings of vision as Wordsworth praises them, of the sustained chords interwoven with trills and turns of Beethoven's introduction, and of the fall towards immobility in both introduction and coda. Other examples are easy to think of. From Wordsworth, the "fixed, abysmal, gloomy breathing-place" that opens on Mount Snowdon in *The Prelude*; from Beethoven, the inchoate, partly unbarred introduction to the fugue-finale of the "Hammerklavier" sonata; from Berg, the *pianissimo* haze of percussion that begins and ends the first of his Three Pieces for Orchestra; from Whitman, the penultimate moment of "When Lilacs Last in the Dooryard Bloomed," with its double vision of "passing" as both an enduring and a releasing:

Passing the visions, passing the night,
Passing, unloosing the hold of my comrades' hands,
Passing the song of the hermit bird and the tallying song of my soul,
Victorious song, death's outlet song, yet ever-varying ever-altering song,
As low and wailing, yet clear the notes, rising and falling, flooding the night,
Sadly sinking and fainting, as warning and warning, and yet again bursting with
    joy,
Covering the earth and filling the spread of the heaven,
As that powerful psalm in the night I heard from recesses,

Passing, I leave thee lilac with heart-shaped leaves,
I leave thee there in the door-yard, blooming, returning with spring.
(185–194)

Whether disruptive or re-creative, these generative intervals demand a formal response that identifies radical change not with discontinuity but with an erasure of discontinuity. Perhaps, at bottom, they are figures for a fundamental mystery: the inchoate, brooding potentiality from which all creative acts fluently and inexplicably emerge.

4

The Transit of Identity

Even the drifting of the curtains,
Slight as it is, disturbs me. I did not know

That such ferocities could tear
One self from another, as these peaches do.
(STEVENS, "A Dish of Peaches in Russia")

Une dentelle s'abolit . . . .
(MALLARMÉ, "Triptyque")

Why should the drifting of a curtain radiate "ferocities" sharp enough to abolish either the curtain itself or the ego that observes it? One context, if not an answer, for the question is that the Romanticism of poets like Stevens and Mallarmé takes the category of identity to be inherently dynamic and unstable. The Romantic "*A is A*" asserts being only as a form of transience, even of volatility. As Proust puts it near the beginning of *Swann's Way*:

> Perhaps the immobility of the things that surround us is forced upon them by our conviction that they are themselves, and not anything else, and by the immobility of our conceptions of them. For it always happened that when I awoke . . . and my mind struggled in an unsuccessful attempt to discover where I was, everything would be moving around me through the darkness: things, places, years.[1]

Evidently, the illusion of immobility did not much trouble the major artists of the early nineteenth century. Disappearance, in their work, is often a heightened version of presence. Wordsworth, only a little less than Freud, sees the adult ego as a fragment of something earlier, and his most privileged spots of time are disturbances of its boundaries: "fallings from us, vanish-

---

[1] Marcel Proust, *Swann's Way*, translated by C. K. Scott Moncrieff (New York: Vintage Books, 1956), p. 7.

ings." Nor is this kind of transcendental fluidity confined to the subject. Objects, too, undergo passages; not only the ego, but also what it cathects, may exchange one self for another:

> all the distant grove
> That rises to the summit of the steep
> Shows like a mountain built of silver light!
> See yonder the same pageant, and again
> Behold the universal imagery
> Inverted, all its sun-bright features touched
> As with the varnish and the gloss of dreams;
> Dreamlike the blending also of the whole
> Harmonious Landscape, all along the shore
> The boundary lost—the line invisible
> That parts the image from reality;
> And the clear hills, as high as they ascend
> Heavenward, so deep piercing the lake below.
> (*Home at Grasmere*, 567–569)

Objects in Turner seascapes similarly dissolve into great washes of light, though always in vibrant, violent colors. Beethoven, meanwhile, writes two early sonatas in the form of fantasies, identifies an amorphous eleven-measure passage as a "movement" of his Op. 131 String Quartet, and uses introductory passages in two other quartets to let Classical tonality, like Mallarmé's lace curtain, abolish itself.

The movement from Classicism to Romanticism, then, renders the identity of both things and persons fundamentally insecure, and perhaps uncontrollable. Especially in the first Romantic generations, the arts seem quick to sanction Rilke's demanding principle that "staying is nowhere." In a Classical composition or poem, ambiguity and near-incoherence can take over the foreground, as any number of passages in Haydn or Pope will bear out, but no Classical work is ontologically open. Only after the 1790s is identity something that can undulate, fade away, explode. Let me begin with an example.

Chopin's Prelude in B♭ Major is a piece that unfolds by dissociating the texture of its opening. Bit by bit, the broad *cantabile* phrases of its first measures break down into the agitated chains of intervals that make up the accompaniment. The music seems to aim at a feeling of deliquescence as it moves toward a stabbing climax; its lyrical gestures increasingly seem to precipitate their own dissolution. Most of the details that contribute to this pattern are rhythmic and textural, but in the passage that precedes the climactic *crescendo*, Chopin combines these with a harmonic effect that concentrates the self-consuming quality of the music into the sound of an oddly deadened chord.

The harmonic materials involved are nothing special in themselves: a chain of lowered-submediant (Gb) triads, a pair of appoggiaturas—the second one climactic—and a busy accompaniment with dissonant inflections (Ex. 21). What is special about this episode is its articulation. Chopin directs the six *forte* measures 19–24 to be played with continuous pedal. Pianists do

EXAMPLE 21. Chopin, Prelude in Bb Major, mm. 19–27.

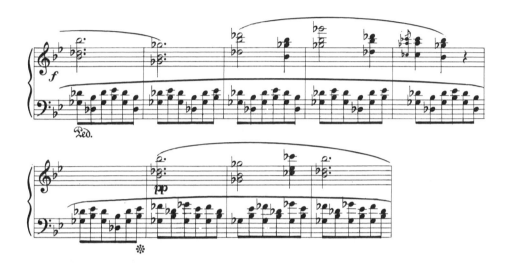

not always play it that way, but the effect is a considered one—is, in fact, a revision of the original pedalling, which called for a release at m. 22. If the pedal instructions are followed, as they should be—pedalling always has a structural meaning in the Preludes—the result is a dissonant resonance that envelops the resolving consonance and persists through the end of the passage. To describe this expressive gesture in the obvious way, as a blurring of a climactic discord into its resolution, is not enough to encompass it.

The four measures following the onset of the pedal at m. 19 unobtrusively distort the sound of the lowered-submediant chord. The aural haze produced by the pedal is a kind of prolonged braiding of normally innocuous dissonances into the harmony. With the forceful appoggiatura at m. 23, the background sonority brims over and bVI, the chord of resolution, seems to be muted by a gauze of lingering discords. Chopin takes real pains to subdue this final consonance, and so to mystify the entire passage. The climactic appoggiatura makes an inspired extra appearance as an ornamental upbeat to itself, so that the resonance captured by the pedal is not just sustained but redoubled, self-reinforced (Ex. 21). The enhanced sonority is supported by concentrated harmonic tension as the appoggiatura both echoes and heightens the dissonance of its counterpart in m. 18. So borne down, the resolving

♭VI chord is not merely blurred by Chopin's pedalling, but destabilized; its very identity erodes as triadic clarity succumbs to a curious muffled jangle.[2] The chord, we might say, cannot be heard as a fully realized form, but only heard in embryo; it appears in the process of becoming itself by resisting or expelling the alien harmonies that have been worked into it.

The music responds to this flight of identity by trying to undo it, to make it "unhappen" in the listening ear. The whole problematical passage is repeated as soon as it concludes, but with the destabilizing elements deleted. This time, the music sounds *pianissimo* and without pedal, so that the blending of sonorities is minimized and the harmonic resolution is luminously clear. The tones of the ornamental upbeat to the appoggiatura are even altered so that they belong to the chord of resolution. But the music cannot finally contain its volatility, and the effort at undoing is carried too far. By adding a persistent F♭ to the accompaniment, Chopin substitutes one flight of identity for another: he turns the now stabilized chord of resolution from a lowered-submediant triad to a German sixth (Ex. 21)—a chord that, while built on the lowered submediant, is not technically a submediant sonority. The music, then, is changing direction even as it seems to be repeating itself; the right-hand chord that resolves the appoggiatura takes exactly the same form as it did before, but it no longer has the same harmonic function. Any lingering illusion of continuity is soon swept aside by the abrupt beginning of the *crescendo* that leads to the climax of the prelude: two measures of violent *fortissimo* pounding in which the mercurial tone G♭ is once again braided subversively into a chromatic neighbor by the pedal (Ex. 22).

EXAMPLE 22. Chopin, Prelude in B♭ Major, mm. 39–40.

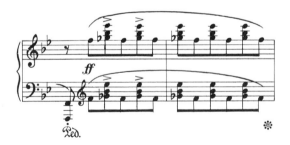

I would like to describe the erosion and reconstruction of identity, the shimmer of metamorphosis, that appears in this prelude as a *transit*. The terms refers both generally to a passage or crossing and specifically to the

---

[2] Compare the D♭–C pedal blur in the coda of the first movement of the "Appassionata": the resolution, to C, is articulated by the release of the pedal.

movement of a star or planet across a meridian—the broaching of a boundary. Such transits compose what might be called the vanishing act of Romanticism, a willed heightening of the intrinsic insecurity and inadequacy that haunts all subject-object relationships. My chapter began by alluding to some seminal instances, and others are easy to find. They range from the pedal-blending of tonic and dominant in the finale of the "Waldstein" sonata; to Rimbaud's pronouncement "*Je* est un autre"; to Rilke's curious habit of addressing his poems to a "Du" who is both himself and his reader; to Schoenberg's subliminal transformation of chord-colors in his Five Pieces for Orchestra. In order to explore this structural rhythm, I will focus here on Chopin's preludes and on the work of another shaper of intensities whose formal power is often underestimated, Shelley.

II

Not altogether by coincidence, Shelley tends to associate the transit of identity with music. The self-transfiguration that closes the "Ode to the West Wind" epitomizes both the transitive pattern and Shelley's figurative language for it:

> Make me thy lyre, even as the forest is:
> What though my leaves are falling like its own!
> The tumult of thy mighty harmonies
>
> Will take from both a deep, autumnal tone,
> Sweet though in sadness. Be thou, Spirit fierce,
> My spirit! Be thou me, impetuous one!
> (57–62)

To be made the West Wind's lyre is to become, both literally and figuratively, the "instrument" of transcendental power. For this to happen, two seemingly contradictory things are required. First, the wind must pass through the self as through the strings of the lyre. The wind both remains apart from the subject and transfigures its identity. (I should add that the lyre Shelley refers to is not the ancient instrument but an Æolian lyre, a stringed sounding-box set in a window and "played" by the wind. Hence the passing-through.) The human subject, again in a double sense, loses possession of itself and becomes the possession of the wind: its lyre. Yet the identity gained is, paradoxically, the same as the identity lost; the one is merely a heightened version of the other. As the wind's lyre, Shelley remains what he has been throughout the poem, the expressive voice of "autumnal" sadness. His identity has been disturbed only to be re-created, like the smooth surface of a pool after a stone has been dropped into it. The transforming agent itself is marked by this underlying consistency, and takes on, in the "deep autumnal tone," the distinctive feature of the poet's voice. Ontologically, the self moves in a circle: *A* returns upon *A.*

Set against this cyclical rhythm is a transit in which the wind enters into the self and is incorporated by it. Here, the self is not the possession of the wind, but its possessor, and a genuinely new identity replaces the old one. If the wind answers the plea for a fusion of spirits, the self will move along an ontological line. *A* will cross over to not-*A;* the sad poet will become a prophet of apocalypse. The poem symbolizes this radical transit by rhetorically interpolating the wind within the prayer that delineates the dawning identity: "Be thou, Spirit fierce, / My spirit." And this sentence immediately "closes up" as if to anticipate—to compel?—the responsive in-spiration that must come from the wind. The vocative is elided so that self and other are juxtaposed, and the prayer becomes an imperative: "Be thou me!"

The contradiction between the cyclical and the radical movements of identity in Shelley's text seems to reflect competing interpretations of the same process. The cyclical movement concedes that the barrier between self and non-self is ultimately impassable: to cease to be what one *is* is to cease to be at all. It is impossible for the poet to become the West Wind, if only because the West Wind is bodiless; only as a child can one think that to "outstrip [its] skiey speed / Scarce seem[s] a vision." What *is* possible is an image of transfiguration, the self as lyre; the human subject can imagine itself as an object seized briefly by a transcendental subject. Opposing this concession, however, is a will to absolute transcendence that does not acknowledge limitations on either the self's transitivity or its desire. One might identify this will with undiluted imagination, or what Geoffrey Hartman has called apocalyptic imagination: a force of subjectivity blind to any suggestion that the mastery-over-being implied in the command "Be thou me!" might be an illusion.[3]

It is not hard to associate the cyclical and radical aspects of transit with the interwoven appoggiatura and resolution of Chopin's B♭ Major Prelude. To the extent that it is deadened by absorbing the appoggiatura, the resolving chord is an incipient non-tonal sonority. Its latent breach of tonality, in fact, is what motivates the *secco* reprise of the over-pedalled material; the transit is resolved like a dissonance. Nonetheless, the listener has been exposed to a defamiliarized harmony and has felt its tonal inadequacy; for an instant, at least, the giddy abyss of a radical transit has opened up. The original chord can no more be un-heard than the wind can un-blow. The sonority that it distorts cannot even be repeated in pristine form. Otherness has

---

[3] On apocalyptic imagination, see Geoffrey Hartman, *Wordsworth's Poetry, 1787–1817* (New Haven: Yale University Press, 1964), p. 17–18.

marked the place where identity has shifted, and nothing can entirely remove it.

Chopin's "braided" harmony and Shelley's metaphors of the self take on
much of their volatility by participating in a cathectic rhythm so forceful
that it can momentarily obliterate the fixities of discursive form—boundaries, definitions, the whole paraphernalia of secondary-process thinking. It
is just such cathectic intensity that, in general, allows musical and poetic
form to take ego-activity as a model and to converge as a result. Transitivity,
however, often gives a special impression of white heat, and it is worth paus-
ing to ask why. The answer may help to explain, and perhaps to validate,
Shelley's apparent feeling that the transit of identity is an inherently musical
phenomenon.

As I noted at the outset of this chapter, both subjects and objects may undergo transit. The poetic evidence, however, indicates that the subject- and
object-transit are not entirely separable. In the "Ode to the West Wind," the
poet's transit occurs in tandem with that of the forest, which also becomes
the West Wind's lyre. In fact, when we hear that the wind "Will take from
both a deep, autumnal tone," there is a suggestion that the forest-lyre alone
cannot alter the wind's "mighty harmonies." For the wind to be changed the
object-lyre must find its echo in the subject-lyre. Earlier, the wind has been
harsh, sublime, terrifying, not "Sweet though in sadness"; the "tone-color"
called for requires the presence of a feeling subject. Shelley does discard the
landscape when he cries out for a radical transit, but the openness of natural
objects to radical change is established very early in the poem, and with explicitly apocalyptic imagery. The "winged seeds" are driven by the wind to
lie "each like a corpse within its grave" until the spring wind

> shall blow
> Her clarion o'er the dreaming earth, and fill
> (Driving sweet buds like flocks to feed in air)
> With living hues and odours plain and hill.
> (9–12)

Subjects and objects are opposed by definition, but they are also linked by
definition, and neither is meaningful without the other. A transit of identity
for either is always a moment that collapses their polarity, an episode
steeped in the "blank misgivings of a Creature / Moving about in worlds not
realized." In the mythographic vocabulary of Hölderlin, the experience of

such a transit, not only but especially in an object, intimates the return of the gods.[4]

The relationship between a subject and an object-in-transit, or an object and a subject-in-transit, is one of intermingling, a mixing or weaving-together of identities. In Shelley's ode, the poet's self is mingled figuratively with the forest and the falling leaves just at the moment when both he and they begin to be transfigured: "Make me thy lyre, even as the forest is!"[5] A moment later, his first paraphrase of the climactic cry "Be thou me!" explicitly confirms both the mingling of identities and its link to a renewal of being: "Drive my dead thoughts over the universe / Like withered leaves to quicken a new birth!" (63–64). Shelley's figures here are precisely those that mingle but do not identify subject and object: similes, not metaphors. Full identification with the subject must be purely reflexive, confined to the wind that is the destination of change: "Be thou me!"

Intermingling of this sort may well suggest the act of listening to music as a prototype for transitivity. Musical "objects"—chords, themes, rhythms, and so on—are always realized for the listener by a process of mixing-in. What I hear, unlike what I see or touch, is not set over against me; it is set *into* my consciousness, mixed into my reflexive awareness of my own presence. Edward T. Cone has described something like this resonation of the ego as the listener's identification with the persona of the composer, but it has to be added that the composer's persona is only constituted in and through the more primary identification with the music.[6] These basic phenomenological circumstances, which are not far from simple acoustic fact, take on psychological value because of the receptivity I bring to the music I

---

[4] Compare these lines from Hölderlin's "Greece" (third version; "God" refers to Æther):

> But silver
> On clear days
> Is the light. The earth
> Blue-violet, betokening love.
> To small things, too,
> Can come a great beginning.
> Everyday but wonderful, for man's sake,
> God puts a garment on.
> And hides his face from the knowing
> And clothes the winds with art.
> (19–28)

[5] As Harold Bloom has argued (*The Visionary Company* [Garden City, N.Y.: Doubleday, 1961], p. 315–16), the fourth stanza of the ode is a misconceived plea for a kind of transfiguration that cannot be granted. The line quoted, which begins the fifth stanza, is a sudden turn modeled on the break between stanzas viii and ix of Wordsworth's "Intimations" Ode.

[6] Edward T. Cone, *The Composer's Voice* (Berkeley: University of California Press, 1974), pp. 20–40.

willingly hear. One might say that music, if it moves me, becomes what psychoanalysis calls a transitional object: something situated neither in my mind nor in the world, and which I perceive only in terms of this neither-nor.[7] The availability of transitional objects is associated with a heightened sense of life, with intensity of experience, with a sense of supreme value. Recognizing the power of music to initiate and—even more—to prolong the transitional neither-nor may help to explain why hyperbole is so often the key figure in statements about the value of music, from Nietzsche's "Without music, life would be a mistake," to Jean-François Leseuer's response to Beethoven's Fifth: "When I tried to put on my hat, I could not find my head!" In any case, the involvement of the subject in a musical object-in-transit is a virtual certainty, and at moments of high intensity the musical transit is likely to become a transit-in-tandem like the one described in Shelley's ode. It is no accident that the most radical transfiguration in all of Shelley's work is represented in just these terms, as a response to a song. Asia, in *Prometheus Unbound*, undergoes an apotheosis into the "Life of Life," as she herself learns from a disembodied singing voice. Her reply identifies the movement of her identity with the movement of the song:

> My soul is an enchanted Boat,
> Which, like a sleeping swan, doth float
> Upon the silver waves of thy sweet singing.
> (II,v,72–74)

The sense of being held and carried, felt paradoxically as perfect freedom, is used here to signify both a rapt response to music and an ascent on the scale of being.

III

Chopin's collection of preludes is a profound study of transit at every level of structure, from the individual chord to the work as a whole. Since a chord started us off, let me go to the other extreme and consider the work. In order to do that, I must immediately raise the question of whether the preludes actually constitute a single work, and if so, in what sense. The question is not an innocent one. Chopin's design ensures that once it is asked, it must be asked again interminably—that every yes implies a no, and vice versa. The diverse pieces published together as Opus 28 radically question what it means for various segments of music to constitute an opus, a work.

The most immediately striking features of the preludes are those that undermine their coherence as a group. Chopin does not link the different pieces motivically, as Schumann does in suites like *Carnaval*, and he does

---

[7] See D. W. Winnicott, *Playing and Reality* (New York: Basic Books, 1971), pp. 1–26.

not arrange them on the basis of any dramatic or expressive logic. Consistencies that do appear are teasing; they break down as the sequence proceeds. The first six preludes, for instance, seem to establish a large-scale rhythm in which the alternation of major and relative-minor keys is aligned with a contrast between very fast and very slow tempos, but the little seventh prelude, the A-major *Andantino* associated with *Les Sylphides*, disrupts the pattern. A reversal seems to be promised as a *Molto Agitato* in F♯ minor leads to an E-major *Largo*, but the hint of mirror symmetry is brushed aside by three very fast pieces in C♯ minor, B major, and G♯ minor. The up-tempo series vaporizes all feeling of a gestural pattern and spells out the instability latent in the oscillation of extreme speeds. One realizes in retrospect that the initial consistency has been an accident, or rather a deliberate imitation of one: a pattern tossed up by chance like stones strewn on a path in geometrical designs. Taken as a gestural sequence, the twenty-eight preludes sound like an exaltation of juxtaposition, of parataxis, of random association. Combined with the brevity of the pieces and with Chopin's chromatic, incessantly active piano sonority, this willed incoherence creates an impression at once darting, restless, shimmering, and troubled. It is as if whimsy were being promoted to the rank of the sublime. The effect is unprecedented, perhaps prefigured only by Beethoven's experiments with the disjunctive two-movement sonata (Opp. 78, 90), though Beethoven leaves as a shock the discontinuity that Chopin elevates into a principle. From this perspective the preludes are not a work at all, but simply an aggregation of what Schumann called "sketches, beginnings of Etudes, or, so to speak, ruins, eagles' wings, a wild motley of pieces."[8]

Set against the wild motley, however, is the most orderly set of harmonic relationships in all of Chopin, an experiment in rationality as radical, in its way, as the wildly dissociative key-sequence of the Op. 25 Etudes. Like its model, *The Well-Tempered Clavier*, the sequence of preludes is defined as a traversal of the twenty-four major and minor keys. Bach's harmonic arrangement of his pieces is designed to emphasize the chromatic possibilities of equal temperament: each group of preludes and fugues leads from a given major/minor area to the area a semitone higher. If one listens to this sequence with an ear to its harmonic effect, the shock built into the semitonal movement quickly dissipates. It is impossible to hear each new group as a flat supertonic of its predecessor, at least more than once or twice; the relationship is too distant, too much like non-relationship, to have any tonal reality. The effect of Bach's traversal is, as he intended it to be, didactic, not

    [8] Robert Schumann, in the *Neue Zeitschrift für Musik*, no. 41 (Nov. 19, 1839): 163, translated by Edward Lowinsky and reprinted in Frederic Chopin, *Preludes, Opus 28: An Authoritative Score, Historical Background, Analysis, Views and Comment*, edited by Thomas Higgins (New York: Norton, 1973), p. 91.

dramatic—a fact particularly highlighted by the absence of any closural feeling at the end of either series of preludes and fugues.

Chopin, by contrast, arranges his preludes so that their key-relationships form a strongly foregrounded pattern. In its essentials, the harmonic plan of Op. 28 is well-known: each major key is paired with its relative minor around a double circle of fifths. The beauty of this arrangement is that, unlike Bach's, it continuously interweaves one harmonic unit with another; every key is audibly linked not only to its relative major or minor within a pair, but also to its dominant or dominant minor in the subsequent pair. As the sequence of pairings is spelled out, the relationships inherent in it superimpose a more forceful harmonic rhythm based on the movement from each major key through its relative (submediant) minor to its dominant. The move from a major key to its relative minor is a dramatic and unstable one, so that the articulation of each major/minor pair produces a harmonic tension. A partial resolution follows as each new major key takes its place on the circle of fifths. Applied recursively throughout the preludes, this harmonic grouping produces a large-scale analogue to a cycle of step-progressions or modulations:

$$I \quad vi \quad V$$

$$I \quad vi \quad V$$

$$I \quad vi \quad V \quad [etc.]$$

The minor keys lead to the major ones as structural upbeats to structural downbeats. Their role is to establish the overall harmonic rhythm as an expansion of the diatonic relationship between vi and V: the affinity of submediant sonority for the dominant. As a melodic step, the sixth scale-degree tends to resolve to the fifth; as harmonies, the various forms of the submediant tend to lead to the dominant as a chord of resolution. The I-vi-V rhythm of the preludes functions on the model of these melodic and harmonic tendencies. Felt almost as if it were a metrical pulse, it gives the work a compelling sense of direction that promises closure when the cycle of keys has been exhausted.

The harmony of the individual preludes repeatedly echoes this large-scale harmonic process. In their closing measures, most of the pieces introduce a prominent submediant-dominant relationship, sometimes melodic, sometimes harmonic. By turns aggressive and relaxed—and sometimes miss-

ing—these allusions show the same wild variety as the pieces themselves.[9]
The effect of one of them near the end of a given prelude is to prefigure, in a
general way, an impending step in the large I-vi-V rhythm. At the mid-point
of the cycle, this prefigurative function is heightened from a general harmonic parallelism to a specific functional relationship. The Prelude in F♯
Major (No. 13) is the only piece in Op. 28 to have a middle section in a new
tempo. This section begins on vi and moves to V, then establishes IV and
returns to I. The penultimate measure of the prelude compresses this progression to vi-I, and the closing emphasis on the sound of vi, D♯ minor, prepares for the key of the prelude to follow, the enharmonically equivalent E♭
minor. The final prelude, in D minor, both sums up the prefigurative process and brings it to a resolution. After seizing on the submediant tone B♭ to
frame a massive *crescendo*, the closing measures make dramatic use of it to
form a German sixth—here as in the B♭-Major Prelude a punning allusion to
true submediant sonority—which then resolves straight to the tonic to end
the cycle.

It is the harmony of the preludes that permits a listener to respond to
twenty-four disconnected short pieces with no lapse in consistency-building, even though the sense of continuity that results is under constant attack. Every piece in the sequence is embedded in a vivid mosaic of tonal relationships which contradicts the expressive contingency of the music with
harmonic necessity. The sustained interplay of fixity and flux even comes to
approximate a deep structure, a Schenker-like background, for the work. By
means of the primary I-vi-V rhythm, Chopin turns the cycle as a whole into a
macrocosmic image that heightens the latent continuity among its seemingly dissociative pieces. Most of the individual preludes are built from the repetitions of an invariant rhythmic or melodic shape that undergoes fluctuations in harmony. The full cycle turns this common Romantic format
inside-out by assigning invariance to harmonic movement and fluctuation

---

[9] There are both direct progressions from the submediant to the dominant (Preludes in
B Major, B Minor, C♯ Minor, and F Minor) and indirect progressions through the supertonic and flat supertonic (Preludes in A Major, C Minor). The B♭-Major Prelude moves
from vi (a long-term resolution of the problematical ♭VI) to I through vii°, a dominant
substitute. The A-Minor Prelude introduces the submediant as part of a prolongation of a
cadential six-four chord; the G-Major uses it as a decoration of IV en route to V. The G-
Minor Prelude turns a vi-V⁷ progression into an extended deceptive cadence by returning
to vi through vii°⁷ for three measures. The G♯-Major also turns near the close to deceptive cadences, which are remembered in the melodic 6–5 resolutions of its final measures; the B♭-Minor precedes its turn to a closing full cadence with a deceptive cadence
from V⁷ to vi of the Neapolitan. The Prelude in E Major even offers the basic harmonic
model warped down a semitone: ♭VI-♭II-♭V. The melodic resolutions are especially effective where exchanges of major and minor appear. The D-Major emphasizes the melodic
resolution of the lowered-sixth degree, while the F♯-Minor moves from resolutions of the
lowered-sixth to resolutions of the raised-sixth degree. The D♭-Major also makes a pointed contribution to the melodic pattern when—at virtually the last moment—it crosses
parts to turn an inner-voice dominant-seventh resolution of B♭ into a melodic clash.

to the expressive shapes of rhythm and melody. Where the individual preludes frame an often volatile harmony with rigid surfaces that isolate one piece from another, the cycle as a whole invests the quasi-improvisatory passage from prelude to prelude with an organic quality derived from the underlying harmonic consistency. I doubt if this essentially subliminal relationship can be felt as anything more than a fringe of stasis around the prevailing volatility, but the vagueness of the feeling goes right to the core of Chopin's design. The point throughout is not to deny structure, but—more radically—to withdraw structure from immediacy, to confine it to a tacit, almost non-perceptual realization. The result is a paradox: the formal unity of the completed work seems to remain a pre-conscious intention.

To hear the Op. 28 Preludes as an integral work, then, requires an interpretive attitude that matches but vastly expands the one applied to the deadened resolving chord of the Prelude in B Flat. The sequence can only appear as an identifiable whole if one sets it against the process of its own dissolution and listens constantly to the whole reinstating its unity after each new fragmentation. Within the limits set by his musical language, Chopin systematically deprives the music of all "surface" continuity in order to tap a more primary integrating force. By performing what amounts to a phenomenological reduction on his work, destroying every feature of large-scale coherence that is subject to destruction, he arrives at a quasi-transcendental "essence": a fixed harmonic shape that recurs like a pulse. To the listener, though, this essence is indistinguishable from the process of destruction that determines it; that is surely why a piece in D minor can offer closure to a cycle that begins in C major. One does not emerge from a performance of Op. 28 grasping its harmonic design as a kind of prize; all one can do is to catch at it in transit.

IV

What holds for the preludes as a cycle also holds for them as individual pieces. With a variety that is both heady and insidious, the Preludes of Op. 28 continually raise the question of what constitutes a musical entity, a complete "piece" of music as opposed to a fragment—a sketch or an eagle's wing. The Prelude in A Major, for instance, consists entirely of one quiet statement of a binary theme; in what sense is that a musical whole? Or what integrates the D-Major Prelude, a fleeting spell of sustained sixteenth-note figuration that at two moments becomes almost melodic before burbling away? In the last analysis, such questions turn out to be focused on time—or more exactly on the relationship of duration to musical form. In tonal music, a symmetrical structure consisting of a statement, a contrastive statement, and a return of the first statement—the ubiquitous *A B A* design— can absorb almost any amount of miniaturization and still remain a whole. The only limitation is that the framing statement must itself be a harmonic whole, that is, it must both establish a tonality and cadence on it. The scherzo of Beethoven's "Spring" Sonata for Violin and Piano, Op. 24, is an *A B A* miniature almost as small as one can be. By contrast, a piece lacking in symmetrical structure requires sufficient duration for a continuous pattern to imply an overall shape, usually through repetition. Fast patterns need to be repeated more often than slow ones, motivic patterns more often than thematic ones, but the basic duration involved varies between the same indefinite limits—say from just under one minute to just over two. Most of Bach's Two– and Three-Part Inventions are miniatures on this model, and so are Chopin's Op. 28 Preludes, only two of which have an *A B A* design.

For the most part, the preludes are intent on exposing a latent antagonism between musical meaning and musical time that most music tries to obscure. The first prelude, fleeting, genial, and rhythmically intricate, candidly raises the question of whether its repeating pattern appears too briefly to create a whole, and most of the other pieces do likewise. (In a nontonal context, the same question is typically Webern's, and his solutions to it are often quite Chopinesque. The contrast between static figuration and melodic fragments with prominent leaps plays much the same role in Webern's six-measure Orchestra Piece, Opus 10, No. 4, and in Chopin's E-Minor Prelude.) Some of the preludes are so brief that they seem to fall into a gap, a vague divide, between piece and non-piece; one can keep their identities from vaporizing only by assimilating them to the model of the preludes in which the duration, though dangerously brief, is still sufficient. The shorter pieces, in effect, maintain their wholeness by becoming metonyms of the longer ones. Thus the D-Major Prelude coheres less on the basis of its own quite marginal contour than through emphasis on a melodic clash between B♭ and B♮ that links it to the durationally more secure pieces on either side of it. The B♮ both recalls the preceding E-Minor Prelude, where the dominant B assumes special melodic prominence, and foreshadows the following B-Minor Prelude, where the tonic B is repeated hypnotically. B♭ takes over at the close, where B♮ is deleted, and again looks forward to the B-Minor Prelude, which supplies the quite insistent B♭ dissonance with a deferred resolution in the form of the missing B♮.

Chopin's most extreme attack on compositional wholeness, the Prelude in E♭ Minor, deserves to be singled out. This little torso of duration reduces integral contour to a bare minimum, and at that to a form of transition. The music is nothing but a rapid modulating sequence, begun without introduction, prolonged without a break, and abruptly stopped (Ex. 23). As if this were not enough, the harmonic coherence of the sequence is relaxed to the point of dissolution, an effect redoubled by a restriction of harmonization to bare octaves. The nineteen-measure *Allegro* touches, sometimes very tenuously, on a dizzy variety of keys; its modulatory movement is eccentric and willfully harsh; and it bristles with tritones and implied chords that are triadically ambiguous. The reward of this recklessness is that when the chro-

EXAMPLE 23. Chopin, Prelude in E♭ Minor.

matic motion of the music is at its height, the tonality ceases to be merely tenuous and breaks into transit. Ambiguity aside, Chopin unravels his perverse sequence far too quickly to support either a definite recognition of for-

eign keys or a sense of tonal direction based on relationships to the tonic.
The key-relationships—and more broadly, tonal harmony itself—are not so
much negated by this as defamiliarized, the way an action is when a film of
it is run too fast. But one could say the same thing for every other aspect of
the music. Every source of integral shape is stopped up; melody is absent,
rhythm is reduced to the repetition of eighth-note triplets, color is muted by
a tessitura that rises no higher than gb^1, and rarely that high. In sum, the
identity of the music seems to depend on almost nothing at all, or as close to
nothing as it can get. At best, one might hear an abstracted, accelerated version of the repeating-pattern contour basic to the preludes, but if so, that
contour, too, is dissociated—indeed, is barely audible.

Chopin's "nothing," though, contains a surprising core of substance. The
harmonic restlessness of this prelude is not equally intense at every point.
The first two measures confine themselves to repeating a progression that
leads, though a bit tortuously, from tonic to dominant, thereby establishing
the tonic with some security. Only with the third measure does Eb minor
leap into the giddy series of harmonic changes that distinguishes the piece.
This harmonic cascade runs on for seven more measures, finally exhausting
itself in a remote region, D minor. Then the first measure returns, followed
by a variant of the second, to reinstate the tonic-dominant oscillation with a
powerful *fortissimo.* This leads directly to another spell of chromatic dizzi-
ness, now condensed into three measures of *crescendo,* followed by four final measures in the tonic. But this pattern, if the alternation of the tonic
passages with what might be called the harmonic glissando is taken as the
unit of form, is a symmetrical one: *A B A B A!* Harmony and form, the most
radically transitive elements in the prelude, have been dissolved only in order to merge seamlessly with each other. And this, paradoxically, allows each
element to re-assume the identity that it has lost. The symmetrical form, superimposed on the "formless" repetition of a phrase-pattern, turns a noisy
fragment into a miniature rondo. At the same time, the presence of a "middle section" in the tonic prevents the heavily emphatic tonic harmony of the
final measures from sounding dismissive or automatic, so that the severely
disrupted tonality of the piece seems recouped by the close, not ironically
reaffirmed by it. All of this, of course, happens very fast, and it can probably
be felt only as one feels a trope—a word or image tangibly charged with the
implication of latent significance. Such things vary with the listener, but I
suspect that in this case the trope is likely to produce a feeling of gratifica-
tion at the dark final sound of $\overline{Eb}$, which is all out of keeping with the gritty
harshness of the piece.

Powerful though it is, the disruption of formal integrity that reaches its
climax in the Eb-Minor Prelude is only the most conspicuous aspect of a
transitive process that the preludes as a whole carry much further. Before
the twenty-four pieces are over, virtually every aspect of music that can carry expressive force has been submitted to a transit of identity, swept up by a

will to exhaustiveness that is sometimes hard to distinguish from a will to exhaustion. More is at stake than the boundaries drawn around a piece; in the long run, Chopin throws his musical language itself into question. Inevitably, the impulse toward so much uncertainty has something explosive and anarchic about it, but what dominates in the preludes is finally a contrary feature: an almost violent sense of purpose, aimed not at detonating musical meaning but at expanding its sources.

Time and again, Chopin makes transitive thrusts that single out a non-harmonic element and invest it with a quasi-harmonic significance. A certain register, a dynamic level, a rhythmic shape—potentially anything at all—is thereby enabled to compete with harmony as a source of structure. Much of the time, this valorizing of elements that more often articulate meaning than constitute it has the effect of diffusing the expectancy and ambiguity that belong to harmonic tension over the whole field of sonority. Such a diffusion may account for the unique, often feverish intensity of these pieces; the music is, so to speak, sensitized, as a body is by fear or desire. In the more extreme cases, the movement of a valorized non-harmonic element may virtually displace harmonic movement as the basis of form, thus effecting a radical change in the conditions of musical intelligibility as Chopin inherited them. The *Klangfarbenmelodie* of Schoenberg's "Farben" and the audible rhythmic serialization in Messiaen's *Quatre études de rythme* have roots in his practice.

The C-Minor Prelude presents Chopin's "cross-harmonic" transit in its simplest and most teasing form. The piece, a *Largo*, is one of those that challenge wholeness by extreme brevity; it consists entirely of a four-measure antecedent clause, *fortissimo*, and a four-measure consequent, *piano*, which is repeated *pianissimo* and rounded off by a single measure of "coda." Though highly colored in detail, the harmony is quite simple in broad outline; without leaving the tonic, its variegated progressions resolve on the last beat of every measure with a docility that provides the music with some part of its doleful charm. What really animates this piece is its peculiar drops in dynamic level. From a harmonic standpoint, there is nothing to motivate the dramatic shift from *fortissimo* to *piano*, no structural tension to articulate by the change. The consequent, like the antecedent, is nothing more than a fourfold repetition of the rhythmic pattern ♩ ♩ ♫ ♩ , with the final beats mapping out an elementary progression in C minor. Is the shift, then, an arbitrary break in the monotony? And what of the second shift from *piano* to *pianissimo*, which needlessly repeats a perfectly adequate cadential movement? These dynamics invest the music with its only genuine tension: what sense do they make?

One answer is that the prelude is meant to evoke a fading echo, presumably in Gothic surroundings; but a slight awkwardness in harmonic rhythm suggests something more. The pattern of resolutions in the antecedent (m. 1–4) is i-VI-i-V; the pattern in the consequent (m. 5–8) is v-V⁷-i-i. Innocent enough in theory, the doubling of cadential tonic triads in mm. 7–8 is made to sound rather stilted by Chopin's rigid alignment of metrical and harmonic units. Measure 7 in particular has a premature feeling about it; its counterpart in the similarly-structured A-Major Prelude, a more elegant piece, forms an extended half-cadence to the dominant-ninth chord. A good way to convince oneself on this point is to play mm. 5–8 of the C-Minor Prelude *fortissimo*; the music sounds absurdly overemphatic at that volume. We might argue, therefore, that the shift from *fortissimo* to *piano* is meant to accommodate the redundant harmony. But since the redundancy is harmonically unnecessary, even pointless, the opposite conclusion seems to be called for. It is actually the shift to *piano* that requires the harmonic doubling, as if the music were indeed a fading echo and needed an extra cadence to leave the impression of its tonality behind it. The key of the consequent is not conceived of as C minor, but as a new and intrinsically weak harmonic area, a sonorous afterimage of C minor. The mysterious second consequent confirms this subversive identification of musical form with acoustic process by falling entropically to an even weaker area, a secondary echo zone, which requires a further redundancy to protect its tonality from fading with its sonority. This "extra" extra is the one-measure coda to the prelude, where the tonic triad that closes m. 12 is repeated in a higher register, even though it has already been enhanced by a small *crescendo*. The final chord is assigned a fermata and marked *decrescendo*, indicating a long fade; the primary tension of the piece, transferred from harmony to dynamics, is resolved as the reinforced tonic envelops the threshold of audibility.

A more disturbing cross-harmonic transit is the impulse that drives the Prelude in F Minor, where the focus is not on audibility but on silence. The essential paradox of musical silence is, of course, well-known. Non-music by definition, silence within the framework of a composition is heard as an integral part of the music.[10] Chopin's furious *Allegro molto* prelude attacks this principle, not by wittily or dramatically prolonging silence in the manner of Haydn or Beethoven but by using it to undermine tonal cohesion.

Piano sonority, shaped by minutely detailed pedalling, plays a primary role in directing the expressive process, which consists here of heightening rhythmic volatility to the breaking point. The prelude is based on the rhythmic contour of its opening, a flurry of sixteenth notes curtailed by a short retarding figure (Ex. 24). The first six measures form a continuous fourfold statement of this pattern; then the sixteenth-note motion accelerates only to break off abruptly on a heavy *forzando* (m. 9, Ex. 25). A sonorous pause follows—an eighth-note's duration without attack, with the pedal down (Ex. 25). This little "nick" in the music precipitates a headlong rush into dis-

---

[10] For a discussion, see Suzanne Langer, *Feeling and Form* (New York: Scribners, 1953), pp. 108–9; Edward T. Cone, *Musical Form and Musical Performance* (New York: Norton, 1968), pp. 12–23.

EXAMPLE 24. Chopin, Prelude in F Minor, m. 1.

EXAMPLE 25. Chopin, Prelude in F Minor, mm. 7–12.

sociation. The basic rhythmic contour is now violated repeatedly; the Prelude in F Minor, like the one in Bb Major, unfolds by destroying the gesture
that originates it. The rapid note-flurries agitatedly take on new forms, now
packed with extra notes (mm. 12–13), now severely abbreviated (m. 15), but
every quickening of motion is abruptly broken off.

From measures 9 through 12, this almost blatantly disintegrative process
depends on a clash between sound and silence. The note-flurries jolt to a
stop in the first beat of the measure and a silent pause—one without the
pedal—intrudes on the texture; then a heavy chord is attacked on the second
beat, and a sonorous pause leads on to the next flurry (Ex. 25). Measures 13–

EXAMPLE 26. Chopin, Prelude in F Minor, mm. 14–21.

17 compress this pattern by eliding the silences (Ex. 26). An urgent yet curiously brittle continuity results as each flurry is joined to the next by the pedal echo of a *forzando*.[11] Disturbingly loud and fast, the overall design suggests that the silences of mm. 9–12 are less a part of the music than a kind of anti-music that threatens to tear holes in the musical fabric. The silences take on the value of unresolvable dissonances. By condensing the rhythmic pattern to exclude them, Chopin implies that the music requires an unbroken continuity of sound to keep from ripping apart.

That implication is confirmed by the extraordinary climax of the prelude (mm. 17–18). A double-octave *fortissimo* C♭, the tritone of F, hammers itself into the final sonorous pause, as if to announce with violent dissonance that pedal effects can no longer draw continuity out of fragmentation. Then a cascade of thirty-second notes leads to a clangorous double trill deep in the bass. The principal note of this trill is F, the tonic, but Chopin approaches it very explicitly as the third of the submediant triad; the F has no cadential value. The function of the trill is not to reorient the harmony but to reclaim the music from silence with a sheer, continuous noise. The noise is, in fact, remarkably satisfying, but there can be no stability in this piece, and the trill

---

[11] As Thomas Higgins points out ("Notes Towards a Performance with References to the Valldemosa Autograph," in his edition of Chopin's *Preludes*, p. 67), Chopin's autograph uses wedge-marks in mm. 14, 15, and 17, where some editions use staccato dots. Only the autograph version makes sense, given the dynamic contour of the piece.

breaks down into a final agitated flurry of sixteenth notes which fall with pungent dissonance to a dominant C♮ and a shocking return of silence (Ex. 26). The silence lasts for a measure and a quarter—five beats—but it seems to last much longer, painfully long. The unvoiced duration is a void opened up in the music that far outdoes anything in the work of John Cage; what it suggests, with epiphanic force, is an utter negativity, the absolute discord. The full cadence that follows, despite its *fff* dynamic (Chopin's loudest[12]), sounds hollow, hopelessly severed from the chromatically overwrought half-cadence that faces it across the emptied, no-longer-musical interval of five quarter notes. The raw openness of the silence has robbed the harmony of its closural power.

But then, the harmonic design of the whole F-Minor Prelude is essentially a reflection of the work's rhythmic and sonorous disintegration. Chord progressions are defined throughout by the harmonies of the breaking points, the retarding figures and *forzando* attacks, and the progressions themselves give substance to this expressive alignment by following an entropic pattern that steadily undermines the dominant. Measures 1–6, which fuse the rhythmic units into a continuous whole, anchor their harmony with pedal points—first dominant, then tonic. The chord over the dominant pedal is ii⁷, while the chord over the tonic pedal is vii°⁷; the result is that the sequence of harmonies suggests a polyphonic presentation of fragments from a cadential progession, ii⁷-vii°⁷-V-i. Measures 9–12, where the rhythmic units split apart, spell out this implicit progression in attenuated form, with the dominant deleted and the tonic carried over into a dissonant elaboration (Ex. 24). Measures 13–17, which attempt to restore rhythmic continuity, also try to expand and stabilize the core progression, and with equally poor success. After dwelling awhile on the mediant, the harmony turns down the circle of fifths from V⁷/VI to VI to ii⁷, only to come to grief on the ever-troublesome supertonic-seventh chord. The roots of VI and ii lie a tritone apart in minor keys, and the supertonic seventh seems bent on expanding this routine tritone relationship into a major structural crisis. Instead of resolving to the dominant, ii⁷ decisively rejects it and descends, with a strident leap in octaves, to the tritone of the work, C♭ (Ex. 26). The hectic return to VI that follows is like a warped deceptive cadence, and as we know it is genuinely deceptive in relation to long-term tonic resolution. The silence that follows in turn is both an acknowledgment of the harmonic impasse and an exposure of its ultimate origin.

With this harsh epiphany, the more radical aspect of cross-harmonic transit makes itself felt, as it does, too, in the final measures of the final prelude, which hammer out the lowest D on the keyboard three times, *fff*, under a pedal haze, a gesture so brutal that the closural effect of the D, which is the tonic note, is all but obliterated by the sheer violence of the sound. Chopin,

---

[12] Higgins, "Notes," p. 67.

however, is less disposed simply to shatter harmonic meaning than he is to replace it with other kinds. Perhaps inevitably, his most frequent substitute is defined rhythmically, on the basis of what might be called a rhythmic tonic.

As I noted earlier, most of the preludes unfold by repeating an invariant or near-invariant rhythmic pattern through a series of changing harmonies. In many cases, the harmonic flux is so constant and so chromatic that shifts in tonal orientation lose their customary power to govern the rise and fall of tension or the emergence of climactic moments. When this happens, the function of managing tension is taken over by the rhythmic contour of the music. Changes in the primary rhythmic pattern become more conspicuous than changes in harmony and acquire the status of expressive dissonances or foreign keys. These, in turn, can resolve or modulate back to the original, or "tonic," pattern—though they are also free to follow a dissociative course, as we have just seen. This technique is so pervasive in the preludes that an extended illustration is not necessary. One strikingly dramatic instance, though, is worth special notice.

In the Bb-Minor Prelude, the rhythmic tonic is the pattern: ♪♪ | ♪♪♪♪ | ♪♪ . Throughout the piece, Chopin raises the level of tension by thickening the texture of this figure at the third eighth note, so that the contour at that point, an upward leap followed by a rest, is thoroughly sensitized. This prepares a climax that arrives when the upward leap abruptly disappears and a series of quarter-note arpeggios begins, stretto, where the subsequent rest should be (Ex. 27). The resulting visceral jolt does not coincide with a moment of harmonic stress, and the climactic passage as a whole

EXAMPLE 27. Chopin, Prelude in Bb Minor, mm. 29–30.

affirms and then ornaments the resolution of a dominant-seventh chord while its rhythmic tension mounts steadily. What counts here is a purely rhythmic dissonance, just as what counts through the overall cacophony of the piece, which "is extreme even on a Pleyel of Chopin's time,"[13] is the pre-

[13] Higgins, "Notes," p. 66.

vailing rhythmic consonance. In the same vein, the passage that follows the climax both achieves a rhythmic resolution and defers a harmonic one. The primary rhythm returns in alliance with a precadential progression (vii°⁷-i) that eventually wanders off on an elaborate Neapolitan tangent; no cadence is forthcoming until the final measure. And when the prelude approaches that cadence with a prolonged sixteenth-note run in octaves, the overpowering force of the close comes not from the harmony—the passage is an unprepared series of broken B♭-minor scales—but from the decisive shattering of the rhythmic pattern that has given the music the formal tension usually based on harmony.

By common consent, the centerpiece of Op. 28 is the longest of the preludes, the so-called "Raindrop" Prelude in D♭ Major, and it is in this piece that Chopin's most extreme cross-harmonic transit takes place. The prelude owes its fame to the hypnotic repeated note that pervades almost every measure as an upper dominant pedal, both as A♭ in the outer sections and as G♯ in the enharmonically related middle section. This pedal is the most complex single entity in Chopin's cycle; it attracts harmonic significance not only to its rhythm but to its tone-color as well. And this is both a reflection of the Romantic repetition that informs the music and a "polyphonic" consummation to the organized volatility that animates all of the preludes.

The double valorizing of the pedal as a primary figure depends on a striking restriction of harmonic movement in the D♭ Prelude, a narrowness that is especially ascetic in the mercurial context of the cycle as a whole. The pedal's expressive monotony finds its structural equivalent in an incessant tonic-dominant alternation; even the underlying sound-texture is static, since the enharmonic middle section changes nothing but the mode of the omnipresent tonic and dominant chords. Of the forty-one D♭ measures in the outer sections, all but nine (mm. 10–18) are entirely devoted to elaborating the movement from V⁷ to I. The plangent middle section in C♯ minor gradually expands the harmonic scope of the work, but only to draw every widening gesture into the unyielding tonic-dominant design. The most prominent enrichments are based on the subdominant and raised submediant; adjacent to the dominant, these lead to it directly, creating an emphasis that signals the large-scale role of the middle section as a structural dominant. (A broad shift from the dominant-seventh chord to dominant and dominant-minor triads has the same implication.) This harmonic astringency, acting here the way heightened fluidity does elsewhere, moves the throbbing pedal into the foreground as a rhythmic tonic, and so invests the tensions of the music in rhythmic dissonances—shifts and brief deletions of the pedal. It has to be noted, though, that the rhythm here is still a harmonic as well as a gestural one: the rhythmic tonic is always the pulsation of the *dominant* pedal.

Unlike its counterpart in the B♭-Minor Prelude, the primary rhythm of the "Raindrop" Prelude works through harmonic relationships rather than against them. Since the A♭ pedal of the outer sections is equally at home in both the tonic triad and the dominant-seventh chord, and since we hear no chords but these outside mm. 10–18, the pedal emerges as the one perfectly stable feature of the harmony. This is a pedal-in-transit: no longer the constructive dissonance familiar from a thousand other pieces, but an enhanced consonance. Supported by its incessant pulsation, the pedal rivals the tonic triad as the core of the work: it literally becomes the sonority to which everything else refers.

The harmonic excursus at mm. 10–18 is designed to confirm this state of affairs. By destabilizing the pedal, the excursus both invests an ordinary Db progression with the kind of dissonance value usually reserved for a new key, and commits that dissonance to a resolution in which the return of the pedal is as essential to the return of the tonic—perhaps even more essential. Measures 10–14 begin the process by repeatedly transposing the pedal in contexts where its Ab would be dissonant; the final transposition, to F, persists from m. 14 through m. 18 and a little beyond. At the same time, the harmony works its way somewhat unsteadily up the circle of fifths to the submediant (Bb-minor) triad, whereupon a resolving movement is mandated by the appearance of V⁷/vi. This chord is stated twice (mm, 15, 17), and the important thing about it is that it contains an A♮, which appears in the registral position of the pedal Ab (Ex. 28). Chord membership aside, the A♮ functions here like a chromatic appoggiatura conceived on a large structural

EXAMPLE 28. Chopin, Prelude in Db Major, mm. 15–21.

scale: the dissonant chords with A♮ must resolve to the submediant, but the dissonant section with A♮ must resolve to the critical tone, Ab. Chopin underlines the point on the second appearance of V⁷/vi, where its A♮-Eb dissonance, muted earlier, is harshly exposed. The resolution of this chord then forms the basis of a transitional gesture that is striking for the way it dramatizes large-scale relationships. For two measures (18–19), the thirds C-E♭ and D♭-F are dangled before us. Theoretically, these intervals continue to imply V⁷/vi and vi, as mandated by the reinforced B♭ in the bass at m. 18. But what if the A♭ pedal were now to return in much the same way as it had departed? Properly managed, the return would transform the teasing intervals into V⁷/ I and I, thereby resolving the entire excursus into the original, all-pervasive oscillation of tonic and dominant harmony—the primary structural consonance of the work. After dwelling uncertainly on D♭-F, measure 19 accomplishes just this resolution (Ex. 28; note the role played by the sustaining pedal). Measure 20 then reconfirms the critical use of the dominant-seventh chord as a structural downbeat by resolving a passing melodic B♭ into the next dominant-seventh chord that we hear. The identical resolution has already occurred in mm. 1–2, but it takes on its full significance only at this point: the B♭-minor harmony on which the excursus turns is a large-scale expansion of the passing B♭ dissonance in m. 1, and its resolution is equivalent.

Turning to the C♯-minor middle section, we find the pedal continuing in its special role, as well as a new development, the establishment of the register of the pedal as a tonic in its own right. Throughout the D♭ section, the pedal remains fixed in register. The stasis that results assures the music of its mesmerizing ambivalence but does not seem to have an effect on structure. In the C♯-minor section, however, the pedal undergoes a series of registral displacements to g¹♯; and when this happens, the demand for resolution to the pedal tone also becomes a demand for its original register. In an extraordinary passage at mm. 35–43, Chopin writes an extended *crescendo* for g♯-g♯¹ octaves in alternate tonic and dominant harmony; as they mount in volume, the octaves sound as harsh as the most chromatic of dissonances. The pedal has been so woven into the texture of the music that even a shift to its octave "equivalent" is disorienting. The passage goes on to heighten the tension thus created by shifting to a new pedal on b-b¹ and simultaneously deleting the tonic from the harmony, which now dwells on the dominant minor (Ex. 29).[14] The natural way to reach a structural downbeat from this point is to cadence on the tonic through the dominant-seventh chord; but instead of this, Chopin proceeds to "cadence" on the dominant pedal and its original register. The double move is shaped quite concretely in m. 42 when the g♯¹ of the dominant-minor triad is altered to f𝄪¹. The sudden rise in expressive intensity that results from this dissonance underlines its structural role, which resembles that of the A♮s in mm. 15 and 17. The f𝄪¹ demands resolution to g♯¹, the upward displacement of the original ped-

---

[14] The shift of the pedal to the mediant of the dominant parallels the earlier shift, in the excursus, to the mediant of the tonic.

EXAMPLE 29. Chopin, Prelude in D♭ Major, mm. 39–43.

al—and g♯¹ in turn demands resolution to the registral tonic, g♯. Voice-lead-ing and dynamics combine to dramatize the shift in register, which follows at once and proceeds directly from the substitute pedal on b¹. With the reap-pearance of g♯¹, the b¹ pedal plunges down a tenth to g♯, and the dynamic level responds by sinking immediately from *ff* to *p*. Resolution arrives not with a harmonic cadence, but with the return of the primary pulse and color, even in emotionally agitated surroundings. The pedal is pointedly unhar-monized upon its return; it resolves the passage not by its dominant func-tion but by its tonic presence.

Further analysis of the "Raindrop" Prelude leads to similar conclusions: the basis of the tension, structure, and closure of this music is the pedal tone in its registral position. Particularly worth noting is the repetition of the tonic-dominant *crescendo* at mm. 51–59, which fails to achieve a structural downbeat because it resolves only to the pitch, and not to the register, of the pedal (m. 59)—a move that precipitates the most dissonant and registrally unstable episode in the piece (mm. 60–74). Also striking is the deferred ap-pearance of the pedal on the metrical downbeat at the same time as it articu-lates a structural downbeat, something that is saved for the final measures in order to create closure (Ex. 30). In sum, though the key of the Prelude is D♭, its true tonic is the multivalent pedal. Barring the basic D♭/C♯ minor divi-sion (which is really an equivalence), the only modulations are not to keys at

EXAMPLE 30. Chopin, Prelude in D♭ Major, mm. 83–85.

all but to key-analogues that might be called textural zones: "near" zones, with the pedal displaced by octave transpositions; remoter zones with the pedal tone displaced by a foreign pitch; and very remote zones that combine transposition and displacement. It is only a small step from this attenuating cross-harmonic transit to a tonic use of pitch and register in the complete absence of tonality. That step was taken by Schoenberg in a piece as radical and as spellbinding as Chopin's D♭ Prelude, the *Klavierstück*, Op. 11, No. 2, which uses an ostinato D–F as its rhythmic/registral tonic and systematical-ly exploits every possibility of zonal modulation. Where Chopin reduces to-nality to the vicissitudes of a tone, Schoenberg reduces it to a mere tonal im-age.

Within the limits of Chopin's musical language, the transitive thrust of the Op. 28 Preludes is an extreme as the later, more obvious thrusts of Liszt and Wagner. Yet Chopin does hold back at one point, does refuse to write in a language so volatile that it destroys itself in the process of utterance. Earli-er, I introduced a distinction between cyclical and radical transits—the first characterized by a return to the identity that has been disrupted, the second by a breakthrough into a new ontological area, a breakthrough propelled by the dynamic otherness that Shelley symbolized as the West Wind. Chopin does share the apocalyptic thrust of Shelley's imagination to a degree, and the preludes do seek and find a genuinely radical transit when they deal with boundaries and raise the question of what marks a musical duration off as a composition. Chopin's cross-harmonic transits, however, are always cycli-cal, sometimes disturbingly so. Many of the pieces do not simply pass back into the formal framework from which they have been dissociated but are actually wrenched back to it. As a rule, the endings of the preludes are abrupt and discontinuous; often, they involve the disintegration or blunt curtailment of the rhythmic pattern from which the music has been built. Closure is arbitrary, and always, with the significant exception of the very last prelude, conventional. Even the "Raindrop" Prelude ends with the fad-ing of its pedal into a sustained tonic chord. In the more vehement or hyp-notic pieces, these hasty, curiously fabricated endings have a defensive in-tensity. Their presence suggests that the rhythmic dynamism of the preludes constantly verges on the captivating uneasiness of Romantic repetition. When they curtail the transitive process, Chopin's endings almost seem to be protecting the music. They may be taken to reflect either an anxiety on the threshold of absolute novelty or a surrender to the intrinsic power of to-nality. Either way, the endings show an impressive candor. Chopin seems to admit through them that transitivity not only raises questions, but is also questionable in itself.

V

Shelley, I think, would not make the same admission. Where Chopin clearly sees transitivity as an outer limit, alluring but dangerous, Shelley seizes on it as an origin, the source from which all imaginative life is disseminated (as in the West Wind's scattering sparks of thought as seeds) or regenerated (as when Prometheus sheds his "wound-worn limbs" for his radiant primal form). One reflection of this difference is the relative position of transitive elements within each man's total output. Although Chopin turns to transitive processes elsewhere—in what the F-Minor Ballade and F-Minor Fantasy do to their nominal key, for instance—the preludes remain unique among his works in their transitive scope and intensity. It is almost as if he were confining unrestricted volatility to a single place in order to defend against its eruption elsewhere. Shelley, by contrast, has no single work as exhaustively centered on transitivity as the preludes, though *Prometheus Unbound* comes close with the insistent heterogeneity of its materials and its threefold apotheosis of Prometheus, Asia, and the Spirit of the Earth. Where Chopin concentrates, Shelley diffuses flights of identity throughout his work, which takes much of its characteristically supercharged intensity from their insistent presence. Asia, in her transfiguration scene, speaks of sailing "by the instinct of sweet music driven," and her paradox of a compulsive sweetness plausibly epitomizes the condition that Shelley seeks by refusing to restrict the variability of identity. Chopin, with a more ambivalent though not a more complex attitude, is willing to open his music to the drive of its "instinct," but he is quite unwilling to surrender the drive of its rationality.

As I suggested earlier, Shelley regards the transit of identity as intrinsically musical, and he consistently gives it musical representation, from the early lyric, "To Constantia, Singing," to the group of poems written to Jane Williams at the end of his life.[15] A basic role of music in his work—probably the primary role—is to provide a concrete middle term between an identity disrupted and an identity revived. Appropriately enough, its own identity in this position is rather volatile. Most often, Shelley's music constitutes the ecstatic, quasi-erotic process of transit itself, the sweetly compulsive movement from one *I* or one *it* to another. Associated with this is a suspension of natural causality; the music seems both to begin the change and to be produced—sung or played—by it. When Asia launches the "enchanted boat" of her soul "Into a sea profound, of ever spreading sound" (II, v, 85), her transfiguration both conjures the music and yields to its prior presence as it carries her "through Death and Birth, to a diviner day" (103). Elsewhere, such

---

[15] Ronald Tetreault, "Shelley at the Opera," *ELH* 48 (1981): 144–71, documents Shelley's knowledge of music in fascinating detail. The comparative aspect of the essay is less successful: the Furies' chorus in Act I of *Prometheus Unbound*, for example, is said to be "balanced by a Chorus of Spirits who enter with a decisive triple rhyme, like a tonic chord in Beethoven" (p. 158).

music as this can become a miraculous interim selfhood, the form assumed by an identity in the midst of transformation. When that happens, the music absorbs, replaces, and yet preserves its listener—Panthea, for instance, who at one point "submerges" herself in a music that then gives her an Aphroditean birth like Asia's:

> I rise as from a bath of sparkling water,
> A bath of azure light, among dark rocks,
> Out of the stream of sound.
> (IV, 503–5)

In its role as an interim self, music frequently takes on the metonymic form of a musical instrument, like the lyre in the "Ode to the West Wind" or the guitar in "With a Guitar, To Jane," which, as a tree, "Died in sleep, and felt no pain, / To live in happier form again" (55–56). (Shelley makes a fine imaginative link here between the tree-guitar and his own persona, Ariel, who is also "born" from a tree [*Tempest*, I, ii, 269–93].[16]) At other places, music as the "middle" self appears as a song that disembodies its singer, who then reappears in the song. When the veiled maid of *Alastor* sings, her heartbeat is "heard to fill / The pauses of her music" while "her breath / Tumultuously accord[s] with those fits / Of intermitted song" (170–72). Similarly, Asia's voice is said to become a "liquid splendour" that "folds [her] from the sight" (II, v, 63–64)—this is a double change that not only dissolves Asia's original self but also transforms her musical middle self into water and light.

In its other dimension, as the palpable form of the transitive process, music tends to ally itself with the primary forces of creation. Whoever hears it is severed from what appears to be reality and lifted to a higher position on the scale of being. In most cases, this pattern of transfiguration is represented as a floating, a buoying up, or a rising, and it tends to blur the boundaries of both body and mind. Asia describes the effects of Prometheus's gifts in these terms, in a passage that also alludes to music as a middle self:

> the harmonious mind
> Poured itself forth in all-prophetic song,
> And music lifted up the listening spirit
> Until it walked, exempt from mortal care,
> Godlike, o'er the clear billows of sweet sound.
> (II, iv, 75–79)

Several ontological changes are woven together here, each supporting the

---

[16] The link helps to defend the poem against Jerome McGann's claim that "Ariel really has no reason for being there": "Secrets of an Elder Day: Shelley After *Hellas*," in *Modern Judgments: Shelley*, edited by R. B. Woodings (Nashville: Aurora, 1970), p. 260.

others. In a self-perpetuating interchange, music as the overflow of mind into reality utters a prophecy that is fulfilled in the moment of utterance by music as the motion of transfigured identity. Like the song heard by Asia, the Promethean music lifts the self and carries it to apotheosis, while at the same time the passive self paradoxically appears as the active origin of its own change, an innately "harmonious" form that turns to music by pouring itself forth. The spirit is literally supported upon the music, yet the music is a forthcoming of the spirit. The outcome of this "concert" is a "Godlike" self whose divinity consists of a permanent transitivity, a resonance or reciprocity of divine natures. The spirit walking on the billows offers a startling interpenetration of the Logos (whether as Christ on the waves or the Spirit over the waters) and Eros (in another re-enactment of Aphroditean birth), both with each other and with human consciousness. This composite divine image fuses Prometheus, the giver of speech and song whose voice is a "music which makes giddy the dim brain / Faint with intoxication of keen joy" (II, i, 66–67), and Asia herself, the primal listener, whose sheer openness compels "sounds i' the air" to "speak the love of all articulate beings" (II, iv, 35–36).

Like the "Raindrop" Prelude, though without its conspicuousness, this moment from *Prometheus Unbound* achieves a consummatory force by the unusual density of its transitive relationships, a plenitude that Shelley will later celebrate in Panthea's vision of

> A sphere, which is as many thousand spheres,
> Solid as chrystal, yet through all its mass
> Flow, as through empty space, music and light:
> Ten thousand orbs involving and involved.
> (IV, 238–41)

By radically changing the conditions of intelligibility, multiplying, displacing, and revising them, both Shelley and Chopin create textures that are too intense or too deliquescent for immediate comprehension. The result is an evocation of the breathless thwarting or bafflement characteristic of Romantic treatments of the sublime.[17] Even more than Chopin, however, Shelley is able to see transitivity apart from sublime contexts, probably for the ironic reason that he was less aware than Chopin of its innate disruptiveness. For Chopin, transit exerts an inevitable pressure toward violence of feeling, and some of his most congenial effects come from resisting that pressure, as in the gracefully scampering Prelude in E♭ Major. Shelley, by contrast, is capa-

---

[17] For a discussion, see Neil Hertz, "The Notion of Blockage in the Literature of the Sublime," in *Psychoanalysis and the Question of the Text*, edited by Geoffrey Hartman (Baltimore: Johns Hopkins University Press, 1978), pp. 62–85; and my "Ocean and Vision: Imaginative Dilemma in Wordsworth, Whitman, and Stevens," *Journal of English and Germanic Philology* 79 (1980): 210–230.

ble of treating transit both fantastically, as in "The Witch of Atlas," or "The Cloud," and with the utmost urbanity, even with playfulness, as in the Jane Williams lyrics:

> Dear Jane [!]
> The guitar was tinkling
> But the notes were not sweet 'till you sung them
> Again.
>
> ("To Jane.")

"With A Guitar, To Jane" is worth dwelling on as a sample of playfulness in a tricky area of selfhood. Despite an "airy" quality appropriate to its speaker, Ariel, the poem is worked out with a beguiling and somewhat bizarre intricacy. It resembles a set of Chinese boxes, with each new box announcing a new identity. At the outset, Shelley turns himself into two "singing" personae, one—Ariel—through allegory, and one—the guitar—through metonym:

> Ariel to Miranda;—Take
> This slave of Music for the sake
> Of him who is the slave of thee;
> And teach it all the harmony
> In which thou can'st, and only thou,
> Make the delighted spirit glow,
> 'Till joy denies itself again
> And too intense is turned to pain.
>   (1–8)

This double instance of "a going out of our own nature," to borrow Shelley's definition of love, is part of a complex courtliness, and is not to be taken literally. But its imagery is developed in too much detail, with too little qualification, to be *merely* courtly:

> When you die, the silent Moon
> In her interlunar swoon
> Is not sadder in her cell
> Than deserted Ariel.
>
>   (23–26)

>   [The guitar] knew
> That seldom-heard mysterious sound,
> Which, driven on its diurnal round
> As it floats through boundless day
> Our world enkindles on its way.
>
>   (74–78)

However fragile the fantasy, the two tree-born singers have taken up, multiplied, and elevated Shelley's identity, and for good measure have put his poem, a complimentary, occasional verse, into transit as a little myth or idyll.

But I spoke of Chinese boxes. Neither Ariel nor the guitar is a fixed form; each contains identities other than its own. Ariel, now Miranda's guardian spirit, is said to be "Imprisoned, for some fault of his, / In a body like a grave" (38–39), a patently self-reflexive allusion to Shelley. The result is a trick with mirrors: Ariel, as we know, is an interim self half-whimsically assumed by Shelley—and yet Shelley is presented here as an interim self, one of many, reluctantly assumed by Ariel. The myth-making poet is thus unmade by his own myth, though only, of course, so long as he consents to go on making it. As for the guitar, it is the transfigured form of the tree mentioned earlier, the one that "Died in sleep and felt no pain / To live in happier form again." When played properly, the guitar transmutes into song the "harmonies"—the "sweet oracles of woods and dells" and of "many-voicéd fountains"—that it knew as a tree. In the right hands, it speaks not as an instrument but as a tree spirit released, like Ariel, from the "knotty entrails" of nature (*Tempest*, I, ii, 295). Questioned "skillfully," it answers "in language gentle," talking "according to the wit / Of its companions"; but to those who "cannot question well / The spirit that inhabits it" (80–81), the guitar is just a guitar.

Amid all these fluctuations of identity, Shelley himself is dispersed and evaporated. He becomes, so to speak, a pure principle of the interim, the emptiness contained in the last Chinese box. To be in this "humbler, happier lot" expresses his literally selfless devotion to Miranda, who significantly becomes "Jane" again in the last line. It is Jane alone who returns to an integral, unchanging self. Shelley's wit, his fantastic gallantry, is to claim that a world of sheer deliquescence, drawn from the "goings out" of his own ego, attends lovingly on her centered being.

"With A Guitar" is in some ways a serious poem of renunciation and devotion, but it hides its seriousness, modifies its latent pain, under the high gloss of its fancifulness. Shelley did, though, confront the harsh prospect of a destructive transit at least once, in *The Triumph of Life*. The severest anguish in this self-chastising poem is a parody of the ecstatic "rising" transit that prevails in Shelley's work. Its distinctive feature is a self that falls to the ground from sheer depletion of spirit, a self so changed that, without being anything positive, it exists only to signify that it has lost its identity. Rousseau, another Shelleyan alter ego, is the exemplary figure of the poem, and the repetition of his collapse—in effect a transfiguration gone wrong, driven perversely backwards toward non-humanity and even non-being—is the primary unit of form. As might be expected, this negative transcendence of Rousseau's is associated with a negative music—really a kind of anti-music, a sonorous collage of "many sounds woven into one / Oblivious melody, confusing sense / Amid the gliding waves & shadows dun" (340–42). This is the "measure" heard in the air around the "shape all light" whose allure—

resembling Asia's in every way except that *the shape does not listen*—brings
Rousseau to his doom:

> "And still her feet, no less than the sweet time
> To which they moved, seemed as they moved, to blot
> The thoughts of him who gazed on them; & soon
>
> All that was, seemed as if it had been not."
> (382–85)

It is shocking to see a transit in Shelley cancel out being, and worse, all of
being, yet so it happens; and in this moment Shelley approaches the abyss of
musical silence that opens in Chopin's F-Minor Prelude. It is, of course,
tempting to think that *The Triumph of Life* signals a decisive reversal in his
career, but the temptation is sentimental; the very different lyrics to Jane
Williams are, after all, exactly contemporary. But one can well say that Shelley begins here to see transfiguration in dialectical terms, something that
makes *The Triumph*—though convention may make this sound odd—a
very Chopinesque poem.

VI

Chopin and Shelley did not originate the transit of identity, but they were
perhaps the first to explore it systematically. Certainly, it is in their work
that ontological insecurity as a principle of form finds its widest range and
sounds the limits of its values and possibilities. In some ways, the history of
transitivity after these two—figures unique in their blending of formal rigor
with unremitting intensity—is a history of decline. Gradually, both in music and poetry, transit comes to appear as something to be resisted, at least to
some minds, but those seminal ones. Transit is frozen out by the strict dual-
isms that one finds in poets like Yeats and Stevens, foreclosed by the strict
orderings of twelve-tone composition in much of Schoenberg's and Webern's later work. In poems like "A Dialogue of Self and Soul," in music like
Webern's Piano Variations, the sheer impermeability of the critical elements
to a fluctuation of identity is virtually the triumph of the vision. Perhaps
this resistance is a response to the destructive impulse that always seems to
shadow identity when it becomes fluid. Certainly, as the nineteenth century
progressed, such destructiveness seemed to get out of hand. Rimbaud's self-
accusatory fantasies in *A Season in Hell* are strong testimony:

I became a fabulous opera. . . . I thought that every being deserved several *other* lives. That gentleman doesn't know what he's doing: he's an angel. That
family is a litter of dogs. With some men, I talked out loud with a moment of
their other lives.—That's how I got to love a pig. . . .

My health was threatened. Terror approached. I would fall into sleeps of several days and go on with my bad dreams after waking up. I was ripe for
death . . . my weakness led me to the world's edge and to Cimmeria, land of
shadows and whirlwinds.

Even more anguished, because less buffoonish, are the incessant failures and
changes of selfhood in Eliot's *The Waste Land*, a poem in which the speaker
is ultimately indistinguishable from the phantasmagoria that envelops him.
And it is surely no accident that the climactic moment of Berg's *Wozzeck*—
the orchestral postlude that follows Wozzeck's death—is a shocking plunge
from the atonal norms of the opera into a tragic D minor.

To put it very simply: the transit of identity is precariously close to the
collapse of identity—is, as Rimbaud says, a perilous path, *une route de dan-
gers*. Evidently, to take on the task of formalizing the very principle that
erases one's form is to make a Faustian bargain. Mephistopheles may at first
take the form of a mere poodle—but he won't keep it for long.

5

Song

Sphere-born harmonious sisters, Voice and Verse,
Wed your divine sounds, and mixt power employ,
Dead things with inbreathd sense able to pierce.
(MILTON, "At a Solemn Music")

no carnage, but this single change:
Upon the steep floor flung from dawn to dawn
The silken skilled transmemberment of song.
(HART CRANE, "Voyages III")

In its traditional definition, song is a form of synthesis. It is the art that reconciles music and poetry, intonation and speech, as means of expression; and Milton, among many others, takes its "mixt power" as a reflection of the original synthesizing power of divine creation. Why, then, does Hart Crane in "Voyages" call song a "transmemberment"? The word is a portmanteau combining "transformation" and "dismemberment"; in a poem about the links between poetry, love, and loss, it appropriately evokes the figure of Orpheus, the archetypal poet/singer who transforms both the world and the underworld until the Bacchantes dismember him. But the image of a transmemberment also points to something primary—and disharmonious—in the nature of song itself.

By "song" here, I mean primarily the classical art song: an independent composition for any number of voices in which, according to Edward T. Cone, "a poem . . . is set to a precisely composed vocal line united with a fully developed instrumental accompaniment."[1] Perhaps the most widespread view of song in this sense is one that regards the musical setting of a

---

[1] Edward T. Cone, *The Composer's Voice* (Berkeley: University of California Press, 1974), p. 5.

poem as a supplementary expression of poetic meanings. The song, from this standpoint, is mimetic of the text, or a kind of translation of it. Goethe, for one, seems to have taken this position, as we know from his praise of "compositions [that] I feel to be, so to speak, identical with my poems."[2] Cone once suggested a less extreme version of the same view when he wrote that "Ultimately there can be only one justification for the serious composition of a song; it must be an attempt to increase our understanding of the poem"—a position he would apparently no longer maintain.[3]

Song may encourage this way of thinking because it so often employs pre-existing texts that enjoy a high cultural status. Moreover, many songs do rely on translation effects, particularly to establish an initial point of contact between the text and the music; examples range from the hurdy-gurdy imitation that starkly accompanies "Der Leiermann," from Schubert's *Die Winterreise*, to Schoenberg's teasing use of E-major triads in *Pierrot lunaire* to evoke an "old fragrance from *Märchen*-times." Nevertheless, it seems odd to think of composers as merely writing footnotes to poems, even if we acknowledge the possibilities of reciprocal influence and ironic contrasts between the poem and the composition. A more plausible view is that poetry for the composer is only part of the "raw material" for composition. The phrase is Cone's, and both he and Suzanne Langer have helped to shape a view of song as the appropriation rather than the imitation of a text. In *Feeling and Form*, Langer explains the notorious fact that feeble texts often make for great songs by arguing that a poem, once enveloped by music, loses its individual identity; it simply becomes part of the song.[4] A more fully developed theory is offered by Cone in *The Composer's Voice*. Song, he argues, is an interplay of several dramatic personae—those of the singer, the accompaniment, and the composer. But *not* of the poet:

> A song is not primarily the melodic recitation or the musical interpretation or the criticism of a poem. Although it may be any or all of these things it is first of all a new creation of which the poem is only one component. The familiar pun that accuses composers of using texts as pretexts goes too far, but it contains an element of truth nevertheless. The composer is not primarily engaged in "setting" a poem. As I have pointed out elsewhere, a composer cannot set a poem directly, for in this sense there is no such thing as "the poem"; what he uses is one reading of the poem—that is to say, a specific performance, for even

[2] Quoted by Cone, *Composer's Voice*, p. 20.

[3] Edward T. Cone, "Words Into Music: The Composer's Approach to the Text," in *Sound and Poetry*, edited by Northrop Frye (New York: Columbia University Press, 1957), p. 15.

[4] Susanne Langer, *Feeling and Form* (New York: Scribner's, 1953), pp. 149–68.

a silent reading is a kind of performance. He must consider all aspects of the poem that are not realizable in this performance as irrelevant. And to say that he "sets" even this reading is less accurate than to say that he appropriates it; he makes it his own by turning it into music. What we hear in a song, then, is not the poet's persona but the composer's.[5]

The arguments of Langer and Cone are plainly more faithful to our musical experience than the notion of translation, but they do not yet capture the quality that Crane touched on with the word "transmemberment." The problem, which seems to rest on a commitment to the ideal of organic form, is that Langer and Cone represent the appropriation of the poem as a smooth, unambivalent, almost alchemical process. Some songs do, of course, give that impression, particularly when the instrumental texture is so elaborate that the voice is reduced to the status of one tone-color among many; Mahler's "Der Abschied," from *Das Lied von der Erde*, is one such song. Far more often, though, the poetry and the music will pull the voice in different directions, and the more so to the extent that the listener takes the text seriously. A poem is never really assimilated into a composition; it is *incorporated*, and it retains its own life, its own "body," within the body of the music. Moreover, the appropriation of the text by the music is not a *fait accompli* that is given to the listener with the sound of the first note. It must be enacted, must be evolved, during the course of the music itself. And to quote another poet, Wallace Stevens, "There is a conflict, there is a resistance / Involved." A song, we might say, does not *use* a reading; it *is* a reading, in the critical as well as the performative sense of the term: an activity of interpretation that works through a text without being bound by authorial intentions. On this view, the relationship between poetry and music in song is implicitly agonic; the song is a "new creation" only because it is also a de–creation. The music appropriates the poem by contending with it, phonetically, dramatically, and semantically; and the contest is what most drives and shapes the song. As Cone observes, the composer must consider as irrelevant whatever cannot be realized in his reading. But this act of exclusion is an audible process in the music, and its presence necessarily evokes the specter of a counter-reading that seems to radiate from the poem being appropriated, to be what the poem "wants to say." The song is thus permitted to make its reading only by violating another reading—unless the composer really does want to write a footnote. And that, of course, would be a kind of reading in itself.

Both composers and poets have sometimes recognized that song is, to a large and literal extent, an arbitrary form, the expression of an interpretive

---

[5] Cone, *Composer's Voice*, p. 19.

will to power. Ives, for example, is characteristically forthright and pugna-
cious about the matter:

> [A] song has a *few* rights, the same as other ordinary citizens. If it feels like
> walking along the left-hand side of the street, passing the door of the physiol-
> ogy or sitting on the curb, why not let it? If it feels like kicking over an ash can,
> a poet's castle, or the prosodic law, will you stop it? Must it always be a polite
> triad, a "breve gaudium," a ribbon to match the voice?[6]

From a very different temperament, Rilke's, comes an acknowledgment of
the same violence, the same loss of original poetic authority to a musical co-
ercion:

> I am . . . quite sincerely averse to any accompaniment—musical as well as illus-
> trative—to my works. It is after all my aim to fill with my own creative output
> the whole artistic space that offers itself to an idea in my mind. I hate to believe
> . . . that there could be any room left over for another art, which would itself
> then be interpretative and complementary. . . . *We* are faced with the task of
> each clearly deciding for *one*, his own, form of expression; and to this creative
> activity, enclosed in *one* province, all coming-to-the-rescue on the part of other
> arts becomes weakening and dangerous.[7]

Nietzsche, writing as both a composer and a poet, argues for an even more
radical incongruity than this, an audible disunion of elements that borders
on a repudiation of language:

> When the composer writes music for a lyrical poem . . . he, as a musician, is not
> excited either by the images or by the feelings speaking through this text. . . . A
> necessary relation between poem and music . . . makes no sense, for the two
> worlds of tone and image are too remote from each other to enter more than an
> external relationship. The poem is only a symbol and related to the music like
> the Egyptian hieroglyph of courage to a courageous soldier.[8]

---

[6] Charles Ives, *Essays Before a Sonata, The Majority, and Other Writings*, edited by
Howard Boatwright (New York: Norton, 1970), p. 130.

[7] Rainer Maria Rilke, *Letters, 1910–1926*, translated by Jane Bannard Greene and M. D.
Herter Norton (New York: Norton, 1969), p. 246.

[8] Friedrich Nietzsche, "On Music and Words," translated by Walter Kaufmann, in *Between Romanticism and Modernism: Four Studies in the Music of the Later Nineteenth
Century*, by Carl Dahlhaus, translated by Mary Whittall (Berkeley: University of California Press, 1980), p. 112.

Song, we seem forced to conclude, is not a refined way to throw language into high relief. It is a refined form of erasure.[9]

II

The dissociative, agonic quality of song is inherent in the fusion of words and music—so much so that vocal styles are perhaps best described by the ways in which they attack the text. The exaggerated accentuation of children's and nursery songs, the crooning of American popular song, the amplified detonations of rock, all make the point in ways appropriate to their social function. More broadly, we can refer to the almost universal use of sustained vocalic sounds and melismatic undulation as expressive devices. The style of the classical art song since the Renaissance heightens the tension between words and music in two fundamental ways: first, by adopting an intonational manner that presents the voice as a precisely tuned instrument rather than as a source of utterance; and second, by opening the possibility of a musical response to the poetry that is complex enough to raise questions of interpretation. Other features—the expressive forcing of high and low tessitura, where the sound of the words inevitably fades into the effort of attacking the pitch; the complication of rhythm and the varied movement of the voice toward and away from speech-like patterns; the repetition, alteration, and syntactic breakdown of the text—also contribute to alienating the singing of the words from any plausible speaking of them, any context in which they might function as a speech-act.

The art song, of course, is my concern here, so the following discussion will jump to it unapologetically after some further discussion of the fundamental issue: the disintegrative effect of music as such on words as such. Most of the songs to be considered are Lieder, a choice that reflects the historical fact that the Lied brings the question of interpretive response to its fullest development. My brief excursions outside of this repertoire reflect

---

[9] David Lewin, "*Auf dem Flusse*: Image and Background in a Schubert Song," *19th-Century Music* 6 (1982): 47–59, has recently developed a sophisticated version of the idea that a song "expresses" its text. The music, he argues, chooses from among various plausible readings of the poem as an actor does with a script; reading here takes on the sense of expressive performance, of staging, and Lewin is able to show how such stagings influence such deep compositional structures as are posited by Schenkerian analysis. From the standpoint of this chapter, Lewin's model is not ineffective but is incomplete, since the kind of representation he discusses is usually only an early phase in a large appropriative process. Lewin's own theatrical/performative model betrays the impossibility of restricting the text-music relationship to "plausible" meanings. (A reader-aloud once intoned Wordsworth's line "With rocks, and stones, and trees"—the conclusion of the Lucy poem "A Slumber Did My Spirit Seal"—in a manner more appropriate for the last act of *King Lear*. When challenged, he is supposed to have replied, "But the poor woman is dead!")

the conviction that the same question is also raised elsewhere, though perhaps less consistently.

From a phenomenological standpoint, song is a partial dissociation of speech: a loosening of phonetic and syntactic articulation and a dissolving of language into its physical origin, vocalization. If speech is taken as a norm, song is a regressive form of utterance, and its linguistic regressiveness seems to have a psychosexual dimension. Some lines from Wordsworth's "Michael" are suggestive:

> Never to living ear came sweeter sounds
> Than when I heard thee at our own fire-side
> First uttering, without words, a natural tune;
> While thou, a feeding babe, didst in thy joy
> Sing at thy Mother's breast.
> (345–49)

This association of song with what Erik Erikson calls "basic trust" in inner and outer continuity, the primary bonding of the infant to both others and to his own identity, may help to explain why the primary use of song in social life is to create intimacy, to relax inhibitions, and often to release erotic feeling.[10] Other suggestive links are not far to seek: the therapeutic effect of song on stuttering; the fact that to overhear spontaneous singing is to intrude on the singer's privacy; the more aggressive intrusiveness of forcing someone to sing, which Rilke evokes in the episode of the Danish girl in *The Notebooks of Malte Laurids Brigge*. With all this as a context, the various adaptations of vocal composition to speech rhythm and speech accentuation that dot musical history take on the air of sublimations, an effect that is underlined by the images of purity and service that have historically justified text-centered styles. No matter how muted or naturalized it may become, the primary fact about song is what might be called a topological distortion of utterance under the rhythmic and harmonic stress of music: a pulling, stretching, and twisting that deforms the current of speech without negating its basic linguistic shape.

The art song as a genre is the exploitation of this expressive topology—its shaping both as a primary musical experience and as a reflection of the contest between musical and poetic meanings. Some songs, in fact, are little more than topological etudes that waver purposefully between the overt and the covert remolding of textual enunciation. Vocal melody does not necessarily have to be either arresting or memorable; its power can come directly from a dis-articulation of language that blends with a harmonic rhythm. Schumann's *Dichterliebe*, for instance, is melodically richest in its piano postludes, while its vocal line often depends on the coincidence of under-

---

[10] On "basic trust," see Erik Erikson, *Childhood and Society,* 2d ed. (New York: Norton, 1963), pp. 247–51.

stated topological twists with points of harmonic tension and release.

The result of topological variation is to defamiliarize utterance; to give it a stylized, even a ritual, quality in which the vocal line becomes an image of speech in much the way a mimed movement is the image of an action. The most immediate impact of song is to convert this dissociated speech-image into an occasion of expressive intimacy. By replacing the phonetic/syntactic integrity of the text with the gestural continuity of a melodic line, song reconnects the impulse to speak with its basis in physical sensation and the felt continuity of the ego—the subjective preconditions of communication. The most striking way to make this point is to contrast song with *Sprechstimme*. Schoenberg's declamatory invention is a technique of alienation, and the reason that it evokes genuine queasiness before one gets used to it (and even after) is that it carries out a topological distortion of speech without the consoling, enveloping presence of a continuous pitch-contour. Commenting on his Four Orchestral songs, Op. 22, Schoenberg himself once claimed that song is a rhythmic imitation of the movement between pitches that characterizes the voice in expressive speech.[11] If he was right, then song is in essence a stylization of the sound and feel of the self in its openness.

III

Predictably enough, composers have not agreed on what to make of the topological force of song. In a comment on his Mallarmé cycle, *Pli selon pli*, Pierre Boulez seems to relish the musical abolition of language: "As to the general understanding of the poem in its musical transposition, how far can one cling to this? To what point must this be considered? My idea is not to be restricted to immediate understanding, which is only *one* of the forms (the least rich, perhaps?) of the transmutation of the poem."[12] Boulez, of course, speaks as a dogmatic avant-gardist, but that more intuitive experimentalist, Robert Schumann, seems to have held similar views. Schumann spoke disparagingly of poetry and considered it secondary in song; his own songs alter their texts freely, even carelessly. Several of his remarks suggest that he thought of the Lied as a form of lyric piano piece—a "song without words" but with words—and his habit of doubling the vocal melody of his Lieder on the piano bear this definition out.[13] The voice, not the poem, is what matters.

[11] Arnold Schoenberg, "An Analysis of Arnold Schoenberg's Four Orchestral Songs, Op. 22, by the Composer, as Read by the Late Hans Rosbaud for Radio Frankfurt on February 21, 1932," translated by Claudio Spies; in the booklet accompanying *The Music of Arnold Schoenberg* (Columbia M2S 709), v. 3, p. 28.

[12] Pierre Boulez, notes to the recording of his *Pli Selon Pli* (Columbia M30296).

[13] See Eric Sams, *The Songs of Robert Schumann* (New York: Norton, 1969), pp. 1–3.

At the other extreme, Sir Michael Tippett has expressed compunctions about the damage that music does to poetry. "Nowadays," he remarks, "I am disinclined to 'destroy' the verbal music of any real poetry by instrumental or vocal music and prefer to 'manufacture' a scenario of words myself."[14] The comment refers to Tippett's "Words for Music Perhaps"—not a song cycle on Yeats's Crazy Jane lyrics, but a series of interludes that "protect" the poems by alternating with recitations of them.[15]

As Tippett suggests, it is hard to separate the defamiliarizing of an utterance from the destroying of it. Vocal music always seems to be struggling against a latent impulse to dissolve its language away. More often than not, this is a background effect; the music gives it realization as a tension, an expressive sense of inner pressure, that takes the foreground with vocal pyrotechnics at climactic, usually closing moments. Such topologically drastic inflections generally blot out the text as a direct, essentially willful transcendence of it; they seem caught up by what Nietzsche describes as "a musical excitement that comes from altogether different regions" than does poetic excitement.[16] This is especially true in popular song, where interpretive response is subordinated to a generalized expressiveness, and in opera, where "musical excitement" and dramatic action are in constant tension with each other. In certain vocal pieces, however, the topologically drastic climax appears as a concrete interpretive gesture. These pieces are typically concerned with emotional and metaphysical extremes, blurrings of ego boundaries, and transits of identity; in them, the disintegration of language by melisma, tessitura, or sustained tones becomes a major goal of the musical form.[17] We can call this expressive process "overvocalizing," with the proviso that the term does not suggest something excessive; it simply refers to the purposeful effacement of text by voice. Major examples can be taken from Beethoven, Schubert, and Brahms.

The solo quartet on "Wo dein sanfter Flügel weilt" in the finale of Beethoven's Ninth Symphony calls forth an expressive dissolution of the text that is both transcendental and heroic. The passage, a cadenza transformed from ornament to structure and from the virtuosic to the sublime, is arguably the most critical moment in the "Ode to Joy." Formally, its purpose is to usher in the coda—which is to say the closure of the movement and the

[14] Quoted by Nicholas Kenyon, "Birthday," *The New Yorker* (January 28, 1980): 98.

[15] Though I am not discussing opera here, it may be worth recalling that Wagner, the most word-enamored of composers in theory if not in practice, thought of the triumphant fusion of words and music as a morally uplifting sacrifice on the part of the music.

[16] Nietzsche, "On Music and Words," p. 112.

[17] An impressive modern variant appears in George Crumb's *Ancient Voices of Children* (1970), where the vocal line begins in the linguistic void of an undulating vocalise and gradually wends its way to enunciated song.

symphony—by resolving an extended harmonic digression into a tonic triad
(D♮). Expressively, it seeks a moment of epiphanic finality, a gesture of singular intensity that can stand as a full realization of joy in music. But the joy
is not to be identified with Schiller's Daughter of Elysium and her spreading
wings; that picturesque allegory is about to be overcome by purely musical
images of continuity and all-inclusiveness. Beethoven forms his climactic
gesture by erasing Schiller's language, Schiller's imagery, in the strain of pronouncing them. The headlong drive of the music to its final cadence is thus
made to emerge from a moment in which the poetic text disappears, or more
exactly to burst forth from the awed silence that follows. For this purpose,
the sense that the singers are under stress is essential, so it is no accident
that the passage marks the end of a vocal line that is notorious for its repeated challenges to accuracy, smoothness, and breath-control, an open gamble
with the limits of the voice as an instrument.[18]

The process begins with an extreme melismatic extension of "sanfter"
that passes form voice to voice in ecstatic triplets; the soprano and tenor
dominate, consistently emphasizing their upper registers. A brief pause for
the soprano and alto follows, then one for the tenor: written-out catches of
breath that seem to poise the singers on the verge of some supreme effort.
Meanwhile the bass renews—has already renewed—the triplet figuration on
"sanfter" and rises with it over virtually the entire compass of his voice to a
climactic high E. After repeating this note, the bass sinks quickly below the
staff; but what Beethoven wants to span here is not just the compass of one
voice but the very compass of the human voice, and so, with the mutual sup-
portiveness that is characteristic of this passage, the soprano is called on to
continue the ascent. Slowing expansively, she draws out the sustained first
syllable of "sanfter" into a melismatic *crescendo* and rises to a penetrating
pair of high B's on "Flügel." Beethoven marks the second of these *decrescendo*, as if to suggest a self-consuming intensity at work; and from here the
soprano sinks to a more comfortable F♯. The passage ends in the next measure with a single sustained D-major triad, in which the singers' final outpouring can expand freely, luminously, and with only the barest trace of a
text (Ex. 31). The expressive goal of the whole symphony arrives in the form

---

[18] Commentators like to point to a passage where the chorus sopranos must sustain a
high A for some twelve measures, but my own favorite rough spot is the six measures for
solo tenor on "Freudig wie ein Held empor," which is so taxing with its high A's and B's
that Beethoven permits the soloist to omit it. Anthony Hopkins, in *The Nine Symphonies of Beethoven* (London: Heineman, 1981), p. 277, notes that the A that Beethoven
"remembered from the days when he could hear" was a semitone lower than ours, and he
has "read of a performance given a semitone down in which the alleged difficulties all
but vanished." It is not surprising to find Beethoven's judgment vindicated, but the point
is that the singers are not being challenged merely to produce certain tones but to produce them with a seeming effortlessness and purity of intonation that is difficult—not
impossible—to achieve and sustain.

of the most elemental sound in Beethoven's musical language: four solo voices meshed in a tonic chord.

EXAMPLE 31. Beethoven, Ninth Symphony, finale (voices only).

In six-four position, that chord itself is technically a transitional sonority, but Beethoven conceives of it as a consummation, a consonance on the largest scale. He evolves the D-major harmony so smoothly that the chord seems less to arrive than simply to be there, to have been there, when it needs to be. When the soprano is released from her brilliant high notes, the chord to which she sinks is a B-major triad. The alto responds at once with a compensating increase in brilliance, rising by skip to her high D♮, and thus changing the chord to B minor, the relative minor of D. This prepares for the D-major resolution, which then emerges almost imperceptibly with a B-A step in the bass. All that remains is for the vocal sonority to grow more radiant as the orchestral strings fall silent and the clarinets and solo bassoon, in weak registers, enrich the texture all but inaudibly. Beethoven infuses the entire climactic passage with a similar combination of urgency and serenity. Urgency, because the voices are asked for great suppleness in long phrases and high tessitura, and because the music—starting on the dominant of B major— takes so indirect a route to the tonic. Serenity, because the tempo is relaxed, the final chord an expansive release from vocal strain, and the harmonic movement carried out with the utmost transparency and simplicity.

Because this climax is so carefully shaped, the collapse of the poetry into rhapsodic vocalization suggests a literal movement from the expressible to the ineffable. Schiller's genially conventional iconography of Joy is displaced (not "set") by a sonorous image of harmony as vocal communion, a representation of four solo voices as complementary aspects of a single continuous voice. In particular, Schiller's personification of joy, a figure that Beethoven has so far accepted, is now cancelled out by a reverse figure in the music, one that can be said to de-personify the singers. Completing each other's gestures at the extremes of breath, range, and strength, the voices are transformed by a loss of distinctiveness; they become impersonal, like the ecstasy, the going-out of the self, that their song celebrates. Where Schiller's classical figure humanizes a joy that is supposed to be divine, Beethoven's overvocalizing draws forth a countervailing sense of otherness, an awed acknowledgment of mystery. By dis-articulating the pictorial rhetoric of the text, Beethoven claims for voice its ancient privilege of communicating transcendental immediacy. There is a curious poetic justice in this, given Schiller's own claim in the essay "On Naïve and Sentimental Poetry" that the excellence of "modern" art depends on ideas that cannot be represented in bodily form. A letter of 1817 shows Beethoven elevating music over poetry in just these terms: "in this respect [visual representation] the poet, too, whose sphere in this case is not so restricted as mine, may consider himself to be more favored than my Muse. On the other hand my sphere extends further into other regions and our empire cannot be so easily reached" (to Wilhelm Gerhard, July 15, 1817).

The close of Schubert's song "Ganymed" also evokes a feeling of rapture, but one based on an idealized eroticism that is very remote in spirit from the "Ode to Joy." The text, by Goethe, represents the union of Ganymede with Jupiter as a dissolution of the ego brought about by an ecstatic immersion in nature. The source of this ecstasy is Ganymede's own imagination, which projects his aroused sexuality into the progress of a spring morning:

> Dass ich dich [Frühling] fassen möcht
> In diesen Arm!
>
> Ach, an deinem Busen
> Lieg ich, schmachte,
> Und deine Blumen, dein Gras
> Drängen sich an mein Herz.
> Du kühlst den brennenden
> Durst meines Busens,
> Lieblicher Morgenwind!

Could I but grasp you [Springtime]
In my arms!

Ah, on your bosom
I lie and languish,
And your flowers, your grass
Press themselves to my heart.
You cool the burning
Thirst of my bosom,
Beloved morning wind!

Schubert's song underplays the shaping, striving aspect of Ganymede's consciousness. Drifting through unrelated keys and constantly varying its melody, the music stresses the bedazzled movement of the poem rather than the powerfully generative sequence of images that leads with intuitive logic from rising mist to descending clouds, from the personified breast of Spring to the mythified lap (*Schoss*) of the god.[19] This creates a "yielding" sensuousness in the music that undermines the fusion of active and passive eros suggested by the climactic cry "embracing embraced!" (*Umfangend umfangen!*). When Ganymede's ego melts away at the close of the song, his rapture appears as an exalted passivity, a supreme letting-go. Schubert embodies this release in the almost unbearably prolonged melismatic distortion of the poem's last line, "all-liebender Vater" (Ex. 32). The self dissolves along with the words that it fails to command.

EXAMPLE 32. Schubert, "Ganymed" (voice only).

Both Beethoven in the Ninth Symphony and Schubert in "Ganymed" focus on extremes of psychological union and separation. So, too, does Brahms in his *Alto Rhapsody*, another work that overvocalizes its primary moments of transition and resolution. Goethe's text, excerpted by Brahms from *Harz-*

---

[19] For a detailed gestural analysis of "Ganymed," see my "The Schubert Lied: Romantic Form and Romantic Consciousness," in *Schubert: Critical and Analytic Essays*, edited by Walter Frisch (Lincoln, Nebraska: University of Nebraska Press, *forthcoming*).

reise im Winter, is an evocation of both human and natural wastelands (*Wüste*):

> Aber abseits, wer ists?
> Ins Gebüsch verliert sich sein Pfad,
> Hinter ihm schlagen
> Die Sträuche zusammen,
> Das Gras steht wieder auf,
> Die Öde verschlingt ihn.
>
> But apart there, who is it?
> In the brush he loses his way,
> Behind him strike
> The branches together,
> The grass rises again,
> The emptiness swallows him up.

The music begins with a C-minor *Adagio* in which the movement of the voice is inhibited repeatedly until it dissolves into the "pathlessness" of complete immobility. The vocal line is broken into detached phrases that obscure the sense of Goethe's sentences; these forlorn arcs of melody move entropically, all of them ending with a melodic descent that retards the pace of the alto, which is already enervatingly slow. This pattern reaches a numbing climax with the distended vocalizing of "Öde" at m. 42, where its impact is articulated with a remarkable harmonization: a bare F♯ octave in the deep bass tritonally posed against the alto's C. Brahms's voice-leading does not at first resolve this bleak dissonance (Ex. 33). Like the trills in the introduction to Beethoven's Third "Rasumovsky" Quartet, the queasy descent of a minor ninth that completes the enunciation of "Öde" is harmonically impotent; it

EXAMPLE 33. Brahms, *Alto Rhapsody.*

can only circle back to the very F♯-C dissonance that produced it. (And for similar reasons: the F♯-C tritone, as I have argued elsewhere, can be heard as the primary harmonic goal of the *Adagio*.[20]) The deferred resolution that follows, a prolonged half-cadence tinged with non-harmonic dissonance, is weak at best—perhaps feeble is more like it—and registers only a confirmed immobility, matched by emotional paralysis, in the two-measure overvocalizing of "verschlingt" (mm. 44–45).

The real resolution of the intractable F♯-C interval is not, in fact, the dominant G in m. 44, but something on a larger scale. The primary structural downbeat of the *Alto Rhapsody* as a whole is the revivifying turn of the music from the C minor of its opening to the C major of its close. The transitional movement is carried out by a slow-moving series of dominant-tonic progressions, each of which is cued by a prominent melodic resolution from F♯ to G. As its last expressive gesture in C minor, the alto line overvocalizes Goethe's phrase "aus der Fülle der Liebe trank" through a tortuous series of dissonances; the large-scale melodic movement is from C to G, with a closing resolution through F♯ (Ex. 34). Though it is still posed against a C, the F♯ at this point forms part of a strongly directional chord, V⁷/V, which at once

EXAMPLE 34.   Brahms, *Alto Rhapsody*.

resolves to the dominant followed by the tonic major (mm. 107–8). The orchestra repeats this pattern of resolution three times, with varied harmonic contexts for the F♯-C interval; the eventual result is a perfect cadence that brings C major home to the music over quickening pizzicato triplets in the cellos (mm. 115–16). This long-range harmonic reply of one overvocalized gesture to another is the expressive pivot of the composition. "Liebe" exhausts the alienating power of "Öde," even though Goethe's text still links

---

[20] For a discussion and further analysis, see my "The Mirror of Tonality," *19th-Century Music* 4 (1981): 196–98.

love only to "hatred of mankind" (*Menschenhass*). And the music that follows belies Goethe's text still further—or else suggests its unacknowledged impulses: for where the poem turns to a prayer for consolation that is rhetorically hedged with uncertainty and the consciousness of waste, the radiantly diatonic music is already a consolation—not a prayer for a "heart-quickening tone" but the realization of one.

Overall, the C-minor half of the *Alto Rhapsody* creates an ironic relationship between the music, which seems frozen in despair, and the poem, which describes an implacable wandering. The implication is that the anguished journey *"abseits"*—apart, away from the path—is more than the outer projection of the wanderer's sense of alienation as the poem describes it: "He feeds on his own worth in secret, / in barren self-seeking." The wandering suggested by Brahms is not a projection but a compensation, though a barren one: a replacement of numbness with pain, of self-seeking with object-seeking, of stagnation with wandering. It is consistent with this that Brahms makes no attempt to reproduce the poem's rhetorical stresses; so "hinter" receives more emphasis than "schlagen." The purpose of the music is to interrogate Goethe's poem, not to recite it.

IV

British and American Romantic poets, who provide a rich phenomenological record of how song is heard—what John Hollander calls "great anatomized acts of listening[21]—follow the composers in singling out the climactic moment when the music of song all but erases its speech. In a central Romantic genre, the poet hears a song that assumes epiphanic power precisely because it is unintelligible, and often at the very point where it passes the threshold of intelligibility. The singer in these poems is usually either a bird (Keats's "Ode to a Nightingale," Shelley's "To a Skylark," Whitman's "Out of the Cradle Endlessly Rocking"), or a girl (Wordsworth's "The Solitary Reaper," Stevens's "The Idea of Order at Key West"); either way, the listener/poet acts out a large-scale rhythm of verbal effort and exalted release from it, both movements shaped by the music. The poet's imagination is initially aroused by the impulse to insert his own words in the linguistic gap opened by the song. Once in place, these words gradually dissolve like the song's own, leaving the poet mute and transfixed, usually in a posture of intenser listening.

In "The Solitary Reaper," to take a seminal instance, Wordsworth turns his inability to understand the "melancholy strain" that fascinates him into

[21] John Hollander, "Wordsworth and the Music of Sound," in *New Perspectives on Coleridge and Wordsworth*, edited by Geoffrey Hartman (New York: Columbia University Press, 1972), p. 59.

a speculative rapture, an epiphanic act of hearing.[22] As he listens, he improvises a poetic text to replace that of the reaper's song. This text, in turn, represents her singing as a free movement of imagination that recalls Coleridge's description of a magical, synthesizing power in which discordant qualities are reconciled. The near and the far, past and present, heroic and humble, all blend together as the possible subjects of the song:

> Will no one tell me what she sings?—
> Perhaps the plaintive numbers flow
> For old, unhappy, far-off things,
> And battles long ago:
> Or is it some more humble lay,
> Familiar matter of today?
> Some natural sorrow, loss, or pain,
> That has been, and may be again?
>
> (st. 3)

Animated by this imaginative overflow, the song breaks the linguistic frame in which Wordsworth has placed it and enters a virtual eternity that is purely musical. More exactly, there is a double eternity: one in the immediacy of the poet's rapt listening, in which "the Maiden sang / As if her song could have no ending," and one in his recollection of the indecipherable music, which is the origin of his poem: "The music in my heart I bore / Long after it was heard no more." This eternalizing process finds its focal point in the singing voice itself—the voice in the act of vocalizing, the agent that decreates speech into pure music. (The suggestion could be added that this focus on the voice has a sublimating effect that keeps Wordsworth's rapture from becoming captivation. A similar poem, "To a Highland Girl," has overtones of Romantic repetition that "The Solitary Reaper" escapes). Here, as in its other features, "The Solitary Reaper" is exemplary; its "thrilling voice" is echoed in the "full-throated ease" of Keats's nightingale, the "thousand warbling echoes" that Whitman spins from "the mockingbird's throat, the musical shuttle,"[23] and the voice that Stevens hears creating a world at Key West:

---

[22] See also Geoffrey Hartman, *Wordsworth's Poetry, 1787–1817* (New Haven: Yale University Press, 1964), pp. 3–18.

[23] Whitman's version of the vocal pattern is especially intricate. "Out of the Cradle" begins with a fully intelligible song—the mockingbird's—which becomes epiphanically "speechless" when it migrates into the poet's selfhood, appearing there as the "melody" of his own "thousand songs" *before* he has words for them.

It was her voice that made
The sky acutest at its vanishing.
She measured to the hour its solitude.
She was the single artificer of the world
In which she sang.

(33–37)

One thing that is missing from Wordsworth's poem, however, is a recognition of the emotional and erotic violence implicit in moments of overvocalizing. For a recognition of this turbulent core of song, one might turn to Berg's *Lulu* Suite, where the physically staggering *Totenschrei* of Lulu is torn from its dramatic context to explode into the undefended ear. A more explicit instance can be found in a reckless and demanding passage from Whitman's *Song of Myself.* Though the ostensible subject here is opera, Whitman is interested in voice, not musical drama. What he depicts is the flood of transcendental intuitions—the "exquisite meanings" in the "volumes of sound"[24]—that overwhelms him when language is effaced by singing:

I hear the violoncello ('tis the young man's heart's complaint,)
I hear the key'd cornet, it glides quickly in through my ears,
It shakes mad-sweet pangs through my belly and breast.

I hear the chorus, it is a grand opera,
Ah this indeed is music—this suits me.

A tenor large and fresh as the creation fills me,
The orbic flex of his mouth is pouring and filling me full.

I hear the train'd soprano (what work with hers is this?)
The orchestra whirls me wider than Uranus flies,
It wrenches such ardors from me I did not know I possessed them,
It sails me, I dab with bare feet, they are lick'd by the indolent waves,
I am cut by bitter and angry hail, I lose my breath,
Steep'd amid honey'd morphone, my windpipe throttled in fakes of death,
At length let up again to feel the puzzle of puzzles,
And that we call Being.[25]

(596–610)

These lines trace the step-by-step dissociation of the poet's identity as his response to the music intensifies. The most striking feature of this process is

[24] Walt Whitman, "That Music Always Round Me," line 7.

[25] John T. Irwin, in "Self-Evidence and Self-Reference: Nietzsche and Tragedy, Whitman and Opera," *New Literary History* 11 (1979): 177–92, reads this passage as formulating an ideal of poetic self-referentiality. But Whitman, characteristically, focuses on the music as epiphanic rather than as self-referential—as both a vision that comes forth and as a personified otherness that arouses and envelops him.

the continuous sexualization of musical response, and more particularly the
juxtaposition of images that displace erotic feeling from instrumental to vocal objects and back again—for instance by identifying the cello with the
young man's heart's complaint, then turning to the openly phallic cornet.
(Whitman himself gives the clue to this cathectic freedom a few lines earlier:
"I hear the sound I love, the sound of the human voice, / I hear all sounds
running together, combined, fused, or following.") Though the music seems
to lure, even to seduce the ear by eliciting an aroused and arrogant vitality—
"This indeed is music—this suits me"—its primary effect is to thrust the
listener into an erotically charged passivity, most tellingly so when it "fills"
him with the tenor "large and fresh as the creation." Disorientation and
self-estrangement follow in the form of unsuspected "ardors" and a phantasmagoria of place. Finally, in rapid succession, the music wounds, lulls,
and kills the ego.

Taken as a whole, the process depicted here is a translation of the experience of song into a sensuously detailed imitation ("fake") of death, a movement of transcendence that is at once orgasmic and maiming. The exultant
perversity of being thus "steep'd in honey'd morphine" is redoubled by the
suggestion of oral sexuality in the "orbic flex" of the tenor's mouth. At the
same time, the conversion of erotic delirium into a kind of visionary free
fall appears in the paradox that the tenor's mouth re-creatively fills with
song the ego whose boundaries it devours. For our purposes, the most significant aspect of this sweetly destructive transit of identity is its link to
overvocalizing. Whitman's ravishment by the music is so complete that he
himself disarticulates the soprano's text by losing track of what she is singing: "I hear the train'd soprano (what work with hers is this?)." (The original
1855 version of the poem reads here: "she convulses me like the climax of
my love-grip"; the revision reads like a metonymic movement from cause to
effect.) This dissolution of the word is then magnified by the death that the
poet suffers amidst a final series of erotic displacements. As meted out by
pure voice, by music as lover, death is experienced as a throttling, the crush-
ing of the windpipe—that is, of the organ of speech, the source of all the
"talk" that does not "prove" the poet's ego:

> Come now, I will not be tantalized, you conceive too much of articulation,
> Do you not know O speech how the buds beneath you are folded?
> . . . .
> Writing and talk do not prove me.
>   (569–70, 579)

Whitman's interim self is an ecstatic mute, "steep'd" in an erotic music of
the spheres.

V

Less all-consuming ways of disarticulating poetry by music depend largely on the stature of the poetry at issue. Some poems, notably the feeble ones that still make for good songs, exhaust themselves in the process of identifying the music with an imaginary circumstance. Their purely reifying function, in fact, is the reason why they do not need to be much good. A banal bit of versifying can supply the basic rubrics and images of a fiction as well as a work of genius; the poem does not have to operate as poetry, but only as language. Most often, a song based on such a marginal text will treat it directly as a verbal failure. The fictional framework will be shown up as flimsy; the song will brush it aside, belie it, with an obviously more resonant fiction of its own. Schumann set the tone for this technique of outdoing the text with the uncharacteristically acerbic remark that the poem must be crushed and squeezed of its juices like an orange.

Beethoven's Ninth Symphony is probably the most dramatic example of outdoing in all of music because it willfully contends with a significant text. Beethoven was aware of this: "The composer," he remarked in 1809, "must be able to rise far above the poet. Who can do that in the case of Schiller?"[26] Nietzsche was perhaps the first to argue that the finale of the Ninth was the answer to that question:

> That Schiller's poem "To Joy" is totally incongruous with this dithyrambic world redemption jubilation and that it is inundated by this sea of flames as if it were pale moonlight—who would take away from me this most certain feeling? Indeed, who would be able to dispute my claim that the only reason why this feeling does not find overwhelming expression when we listen to this music is because the music blinds us totally to images and words and *we simply do not hear anything of Schiller's poem?*[27]

A less "dithyrambic" but openly disruptive instance of outdoing appears in Schubert's "An mein Herz"—at least if the performers are not afraid to realize the tempo suggested by the accompaniment.[28] In this song, the composer sets a breathtakingly banal poem by Ernst Schulze in which the speaker resigns himself to the loss of his beloved by producing a string of clichés. The poem is written in a tone of reasoned calm and develops at a slow, reflective pace. Ruminative in the worst sense, it arrives at a muted close

---

[26] Ludwig van Beethoven, 1809; quoted in *Beethoven, The Man and the Artist, as Revealed in His Own Words.* Compiled and annotated by Friedrich Kerst; translated by Henry Edward Krehbiel (1905; repr. New York: Dover Books, 1964), p. 22.

[27] Nietzsche, "On Music and Words," pp. 112–13.

[28] The recording on *Schubert: Songs; Schoenberg: The Book of the Hanging Gardens,* Nonesuch H-71320, by Jan de Gaetani and Gilbert Kalish, may be taken as a model.

through a series of conditional arguments, each of which is blown up into a
full stanza:

> Und gab auch dein junges Leben
> dir nichts als Wahn und Pein:
> hat's ihr nur Freude gegeben,
> so mag's verloren sein!
>
> Und wenn sie auch nie dein Lieben,
> und nie dein' Leiden verstand,
> so bist du doch treu geblieben,
> und Gott hat's droben erkannt.
>
> And if your life in youth
> Brought only illusion and pain,
> If only it gave her joy
> Let all such loss remain!
>
> And should she never acknowledge
> Your suffering and your love,
> You still kept true in loving
> And God knows it above.[29]

Schubert's response to these features is to ignore them. The piano part of his
song overrides the resignation of the poem with a continuous chain of agitated ostinato chords. *Forte* or *piano*, minor or major, the nervous throbbing
of this accompaniment suggests the psychic impasse of Romantic repetition,
and it leads the song (as it must) to an arbitrary, short-winded close: not a
surrender of the heart's agitation, but an external rejection of it. Meanwhile,
the voice sings the poem too fast for comfort, with minimal pauses between
the stanzas and awkward repetitions within them. Schulze's ruminations
break down at this pace into a distraught patter; if the words were enunciated much faster, they would be garbled. It is as if the voice were frantically
pretending to control the heart by keeping pace with it—only, of course, to
echo its turmoil and to turn the pieties of the verse into nonsense. The song
thus moves in a zone of feeling—of rampant subjectivity, manic, defensive,
duplicitous—that is not simply left out of Schulze's test but is simply incon-
ceivable in terms of the text's tepid, idealizing rhetoric.

More subtle, almost subliminal forms of outdoing are also available to the
composer. In the first aria of his Cantata No. 199, Bach is faced with an absurd series of oxymorons: "Stumme Seufzer, stille Klagen, / Ihr mogt' meine
Schmerzen sagen / Weil der Mund geschlossen ist" ("Silent sighs, mute la-
ments, / You might express my griefs / Since my mouth is shut"). Bach's re-

---

[29] Schulze's text is drawn from the Breitkopf and Härtel Critical Edition of Schubert's
Complete Works, edited by Eusebius Mandyczewski (1884–97; repr. New York: Dover
Books, 1965), v. 16.

sponse is to repeat the verses over and over with increasingly elaborate melismas on key words. This kneading of the text reaches its climax with a breathless melisma on "geschlossen" that persists over the whole second part of the shapely oboe theme that leads the accompaniment. The sighs and false perplexities of the words are erased by the music and dissolved into a lyrical, almost purely melodic, gesture. In the first part of his "Lamento d'Arianna," Monteverdi begins the setting of Ottavio Rinuccini's conventionally overheated love lament, "Lasciate mi morire," with a chromatic approach to what turns out to be the subdominant minor. Appoggiatura-laden voices then rise, fall, and overlap over seven slow measures before establishing the tonic with a perfect cadence on "morire." The implicit identification of death with harmonic destination—home, resolution, rest—gives the music a psychological tension, a complex inwardness, that is beyond the reach of the text and converts a cliché into an insight. And in an almost antithetical esthetic framework, Ravel's "La Flûte enchantée" refuses to follow the movement of its text from the "sweet shadow" of desire to the "mysterious kiss" of a lover's flute. The song is conceived as a circular movement back to the initial scene of desire, with its slow tempo and identifying flute melody. After a brief *allegro*, the tempo is gradually braked until the opening re-emerges. Fragmented and varied forms of the flute melody intertwine with the voice in the middle section, but the melody only appears as an integral gesture in isolation from the voice, and the close that it brings to the song, while squarely on the tonic triad, is noncadential. Ravel thus presents as a frail, perpetually unsatisfied fantasy what the poet, "Tristan Klingsor," somewhat fatuously presents as romantic magic. (Perhaps he shared his namesake's view of gardens.) Klingsor, of course, was of the opinion that Ravel had been a servant of the text.

Poetry more substantial than Schulze's, Rinuccini's, or Klingsor's poses a greater difficulty for the music that tries to surpass it. A composer who sets a work by Goethe or Shakespeare, Blake or Rilke, will not find it so easy to suggest an imaginative space that the text is unable to occupy. This problem is compounded by the listener's relationship to the text. An insignificant poem may be known only or mainly through its setting, so that a listener may look at it rather indifferently. An important text will be known in its own right, and many listeners will have internalized it through various acts of interpretation. Significant texts tend to expand their suggestiveness by assimilating the network of interpretations that develops around them; a piece of vocal music based on a well-known poem necessarily risks a comparison that may make it seem expressively inferior. A composer will not simply be able to break such a poem down. In order to violate the "language barrier" against its expressive autonomy, the music will have to grapple with the accumulated force of meaning lodged in the poem: to recognize and to overcome the listener's probable prior reading. Interpretation is the contested area; possession of the text—in this context a kind of incantation, a word-object that is numinous regardless of what it means—is the reward. "Appropriation" is not a casual term, as anyone who has ever read Heine's line "Im wunderschönen Monat Mai" by mentally hearing Schumann's music has demonstrated; and Rilke's anxiety about "esthetic space," Beethoven's worry over besting Schiller, shows that poets and composers take the issue seriously. A song that masters a significant text, then, does so by suggesting a new interpretation—specifically a skeptical interpretation, one that rewrites the text in some essential way. In other words—slightly exaggerated but only slightly—the music becomes a deconstruction of the poem.

This process of rewriting can take place by means of techniques that I will call expressive revision, imitation, and structural dissonance. The first two are widely recognized, though more often observed than studied. An expressive revision occurs when the music and the text of a vocal composition are incongruous according to a fairly straightforward set of conventions. With song, this usually means a music continuously at odds with the poetry, though the more operatic practice of creating commentary with leitmotifs does occur, particularly in song cycles. (*Die schöne Müllerin* and *Dichterliebe* both contain examples.) The effect of an expressive revision is to suggest that the text is trying, naïvely or defensively, to suppress something, to inhibit the possibility of a reading that the song insists on pursuing. A latent discontinuity in the poetry is thus made explicit in the projected form of an open tension between the poetry and the music. The exact nature of that tension depends on what kind of suppression is implied—a refusal, forgetting, disavowal, or some other mode of concealment.

This technique has the attractive knack of sounding simple while it charges the voice with ambivalence, splitting the vocal persona between blindness and insight. The fifth song of Schumann's *Dichterliebe*, for example, is based on this text by Heine:

> Ich will meine Seele tauchen
> in den Kelch der Lilie hinein;
> die Lilie soll klingend hauchen
> ein Lied von den Liebsten mein.
>
> Das Lied soll schauern und beben
> wie der Kuss von ihrem Mund,
> den sie mir einst gegeben
> in wunderbar süsser Stund'.
>
> I'll plunge down with my soul,
> In the lily's cup it will dart;
> The lily shall ring and suspire
> With a song of my sweetheart.

> The song shall thrill and tremble
> As her mouth did with that kiss,
> The one that once she gave me
> In an hour of marvellous bliss.

Heine's focus here is on a moment of arrest, a sexual awakening so poignant that the memory of it precludes any fulfillment other than an idealized repetition. By eroticizing his sensuous response to the lilycup, the speaker creates a synesthetic quivering in which sensation takes on the power of fantasy. The flower and its "singing" fragrance combine to form an afterimage of the speaker's beloved, or more exactly of her felt presence, from which he once again receives the agitated kiss that exposes her love. The kiss is a kind of archetypal gift. It acts as an epiphany of desire as a mutual, not a solitary, feeling, and at the same time it grants the speaker a new identity based on that mutuality—something confirmed by the return of this kiss to him as a song, the token of his power as a poet. It is not the implicit impulse behind the "schauern und beben" that provides his fulfillment, but the "flowering" of relatedness that the kiss embodies. And the fulfillment is inexhaustible, because when the desire awakened by the kiss re-emerges it immediately returns upon its origin in the "wunderbar süsser Stund'." The poem is a little idyll that claims to be innocently content with Imaginary relationships; and this it tacitly justifies with its studied naïveté.

Instead of accepting this excess of erotic security, Schumann distances it with a rueful B-minor music and confronts its constantly heightening emotions with a feeling of constriction. The music is notably cramped in register, with the piano part confined to two octaves and the voice, remarkably, bound within the compass of a minor sixth. The vocal line is also cramped in contour; moving almost entirely by step, it consists of nothing but repetitions of and oscillations around the tones of the tonic and the mediant.[30] The harmony contributes by keeping within a narrow compass—basically tonic/dominant movement briefly tilted toward the mediant—without genuine modulation. Until the piano postlude, chromatic dissonance is kept to a minimum and the subdominant is pointedly avoided; the postlude then harps on both with altered chords and subdominant triads, heightening the air of pathos without actually widening the scope of the harmony.

This expressive revision by the music responds to a certain feeling of rigidity, something ritualized or charm-like, in the speaker's repetition of the images that link him to his privileged moment. The pleasure that he seeks is, after all, not primary but substitutive; its precondition is an absence, whether of his beloved herself or the freshness of their initiatory hour together. His synesthetic fantasy is a compensation: it attempts to replace the singular

---

[30] Schumann uses a similar melodic pattern elsewhere in the cycle as a sorrowing leitmotif; the second, fourth, and thirteenth songs furnish instances.

focus and intensity of desire for the beloved with a multiplicity of sensuous pleasures that imitate erotic feeling and diffuse it along a chain of metonyms. More disturbingly, the specifically genital implications of the first image, that of plunging into the lilycup, suggests an unappeased sexual longing that the speaker tries to displace onto a memory—and which the memory cannot help betraying by its emphasis on quickening and trembling. The feeling-tone of the music intrudes these features on the poem as an uneasy current of unacknowledged yearning. The song evokes a regret for the diminished—constricted—power of substitutes for primary pleasure, while not quite renouncing their easily idealized allure.

The second deconstructive text-music relationship, imitation, makes special use of a common technique: the creation of sonorous images that mimic the kinetic quality of a feeling or a natural process. In song, these images are always based on the text, and it may seem odd at first to consider them subversive. It is just here, in fact, that the music openly seems to accept its expressive dependency on a fiction. But even with imitation an interpretive contest is possible. The musical image is based on the referential aspect of the poetic image; it does not necessarily need to take over the connotative or the structural aspects. What *is* taken over is the figurative function of the poetic image. The imitative music acts like a trope—an explicit site of connotative flexibility, of suggestion and signifying play. The musical image is only marginally dependent; it is perfectly free to support a reading of the poem that denies or emends the one "intended" by its poetic counterpart.

For an example we can turn to Schubert's "Erlkönig." Goethe's poem presents a frantic night ride on which a father loses his son to what the son says is a supernatural force. Schubert's song responds with figuration that imitates both the hoofbeats of the father's horse and the heart-pounding emotions of both father and son. Ostinato triplets swing back and forth between insistent octaves and harmonically restless chains of chords in a pulse that saturates the accompaniment. The match in atmosphere—haunted, driven, cruel—is perfect. But in one respect, at least, Schubert's ostinatos rewrite what they express; they constitute a substitution of tragedy for irony.

Goethe's text consistently separates the father and the son from each other. The two speak at cross-purposes throughout, as if their voices were interfering echoes. The son can do nothing but ask questions until the Erlking seizes him; and all his questions are pleas for a sharing of perception, for an intersubjective unity with his father: "Mein Vater, mein Vater, und hörest du nicht / Was Erlenkönig mir leise verspricht?" ("My father, my father, and can't you hear / What the Erlking is whispering in my ear?") Three times, as his desperation mounts, the son addresses his father doubly; it is as if the man who is clasping him could confirm the bond of true fatherhood only by acknowledging (and so banishing?) the Erlking as a threatening false father. But this is just what the father is unable to do. His replies to his son's questions are reassurances in intention, but refusals of communion in effect:

"Sei ruhig, bleibe ruhig, mein Kind, / In dürren blättern säuselt der Wind" ("My son, set your mind at peace, at peace; / the wind is just whistling in withered leaves"). The exclusion is systematic; the father can neither see (stanzas 2, 6), hear (st. 4), nor feel (st. 7) what his son does. As the son is drawn more and more into fantasy or vision, the father insists more and more on what he thinks of as real, impotent to question it on his son's behalf. When the boy dies, the image of his body in the father's arms only repeats as narrative the separation already presented as voice.

This separation is something that the song will not let stand. Schubert's ostinato triplets, unrelievedly harsh and mostly in the minor, sound as a unifying pulse through both the son's questions and the father's replies, in opposition to playful triplets in the major for the Erlking's lures. This creates a dramatic duality, with the natural, embodied by a parent and child, engaged in a tragic struggle against the fantastic. Such, of course, is the way the father sees things, so we might say that a latent impulse in the song is to lament the failure of paternal power. That is certainly the role of Schubert's narrator, whose introduction of the father in confident major keys leads to an anguished, harmonically troubled close. The song may even suggest that the loss of identification with the father is a death-blow to the self. The poem, skeptical and indeed mistrustful of fatherhood, presents the son by contrast as a middle term between the natural and the fantastic, and suggests that what destroys him is the psychic stress of living between the two realms, which leaves him unable, as Geoffrey Hartman has remarked, of maintaining his separateness from either.[31] The boy can neither stop encountering the seductive Erlking nor stop dreading him.

A second example of deconstructive imitation appears in the sixth song of *Dichterliebe*, "Im Rhein, im heiligen Strome." Heine's poem begins with a massive reflection of Cologne and its great cathedral in the waters of the Rhine. The speaker then recalls how a picture of the Virgin in the interior of the actual cathedral once illuminated the "wilderness" of his life by presenting him with the features of his beloved. Schumann's setting of the first stanza uses deep bass octaves under a resonant dotted rhythm to create an E-minor tone-image of cathedralesque weight and vastness. When the speaker turns his mind's eye to the picture in the second stanza, the music seems to follow his movement from sublimity to intimacy by withdrawing the octaves and working the dotted rhythm into a lyrical texture. But the change is deceptive—an unstable, ambivalent acceptance of the speaker's point of view that the rest of the song will reverse. As the music continues, it slowly reconstructs the solemn texture of the opening, and in the process reduces the speaker's memories to gossamer; the visual imagery of the picture is dissolved away before the more "substantial" sonorous image of the cathedral.

---

[31] Geoffrey Hartman, "Wordsworth and Goethe in Literary History," in his *The Fate of Reading* (Chicago: The University of Chicago Press, 1975), pp. 179–202.

Schumann sets the second and third stanzas to music of constantly increasing harmonic uncertainty, with emphasis throughout on the uneasy sonority of the subdominant minor; the vocal line also is steeped in poignant inflections—first minor, then chromatic as well. For the third and most intimate stanza, Schumann brings back the "cathedral" octaves in soft cross-accents, as if the sublime imagery of place were echoing subversively through the speaker's sentimental reverie. A sort of breaking point is reached when the highly charged image of the beloved's lips—Schumann repeats the phrase "die Lippen"—is set antithetically to a diminished dominant triad over the tolling of one of the octaves. A few measures later, the vocal line fades away into uncertainty, deprived of internal closure by a dominant ending. The octaves of the opening then return in the piano postlude on an emphatic perfect cadence that resolves the long-range harmonic tension that has been accumulating; and they resonate into the foreground with a powerful syncopated descent as the music closes. In the text, the rather soggy transfer of feeling from sacred to profane love paradoxically dwarfs the gothic splendor of the Rhine riverscape. Schumann refuses the paradox. His tone-painting turns the speaker's fantasy into an ephemeral, almost trivial side-effect of standing in a privileged place, "the great and holy Cologne." The cathedral and its image in the river transcend and dispel all merely personal vision, much as the cathedral music does in the closing movements of the "Rhenish" Symphony.[32]

A third way for the music of a song to deny interpretive authority to its text is to undercut the text's structural rhythm. The music and the poetry do not have to be convergent for this to happen; all that is required is for the music to deny its expressive support in a crucial way or at a crucial moment. What this often entails is a disparity in one of the obvious formal features that music and poetry have in common: closure, sectionalization, repetition, the differentiation and affiliation of material, and so on. The special advantage of this structural dissonance is that it can give full play to the mimetic dimension of song while still allowing the music to "re-read" a poem radically. Another piece by Schubert, "Gretchen am Spinnrade," provides a striking example. In treating Gretchen's broken lament for Faust, Schubert wrote music that is universally admired for its simple yet devastating sadness; most likely—composing the song at seventeen on a single October day—he had nothing else in mind. Yet his song has something in mind that Goethe didn't.

As a poem, "Gretchen am Spinnrade" uses the relationship between its refrain and its nonrepeated stanzas to expose a surging cathectic rhythm

---

[32] Heine seems to have been half aware that a reading like Schumann's was possible. In 1839, the year before Schumann wrote the song, Heine issued a third edition of his *Buch der Lieder* in which "heiligen" ("holy") in the first line of the poem is changed to "schönen" ("lovely"). The change trivializes the line, but it effectively defends the poem against a reader more interested in the sacred than in the saccharine.

within a lament that seems static, consumed by its own hopeless monotony. Though fairly long, the poem requires full quotation; as a convenience, I have marked its division into three groups of stanzas:

Meine Ruh ist hin,	(I)	My peace is gone,	(I)
Mein Herz ist schwer;		My heart is sore,	
Ich finde sie nimmer		Never will I find it,	
Und nimmermehr.		Nevermore.	

Wo ich ihn nicht hab,	Wherever I lack him,
Ist mir das Gab,	That place is my grave;
Die ganze Welt	My whole world
Ist mir vergällt.	Turns into gall.

Mein armer Kopf	My poor head
Ist mir verrückt,	Is madly turned,
Mein armer Sinn	My poor mind
Ist mir zerstückt.	Is shattered.

Meine Ruh ist hin,	(II)	My peace is gone,	(II)
Mein Herz ist schwer;		My heart is sore,	
Ich finde sie nimmer,		Never will I find it,	
Und nimmermehr.		Nevermore.	

Nach ihm nur schau ich	Only for him
Zum Fenster hinaus,	Do I gaze from the window,
Nach ihm nur geh ich	Only for him
Aus dem Haus.	Do I go from the house.

Sein hoher Gang,	His proud step,
Sein edle Gestalt,	His noble form,
Seines Mundes Lächeln,	The smile of his mouth,
Seiner Augen Gewalt,	The power of his eyes,

Und seiner Rede	And his talk's
Zauberfluss,	Magic stream,
Sein Händedruck,	The touch of his hand,
Und ach, sein Kuss!	And ah! his kiss!

Meine Ruh ist hin;	(III)	My peace is gone,	(III)
Mein Herz is schwer;		My heart is sore,	
Ich finde sie nimmer		Never will I find it,	
Und nimmermehr.		Nevermore.	

Mein Busen drängt	My bosom urges
Sich nach ihm hin.	Me after him,
Ach, dürft ich fassen	Ah could I but clasp him
Und halten ihn	And hold him close

Und küssen ihn,	And kiss him
So wie ich wollt,	As my heart would choose,
An seinen Küssen	In his kisses
Vergehen sollt!	To swoon, to die away!

Each group of stanzas here begins with the refrain, Gretchen's cry of anguish, then continues by spelling out the particulars of her situation. The refrain combines the specific sensation of an absence within the self ("Meine Ruh' ist hin") with a free-floating sense of emotional agitation. The continuations refer to both of these elements, first making an implicit equation between Gretchen's absent peace and the absent Faust, then portraying the impact of that double absence on Gretchen's feelings. But this sequence is worked out with telling differences as the poem unfolds.

As the continuations succeed each other, they register the changing nature of Gretchen's agitation. At first, her emotions are invested in self-conscious representations of inner emptiness—a world gone sour, a mind shattered, Faust's absence as a grave. In the second continuation, this gives way to a series of impassioned, alluring images of Faust that slowly accumulate an erotic charge; the third continuation is a more intense, more erotically explicit play of images that seems to absorb Gretchen completely. By the close of the poem, the agitation of grief has become indistinguishable from sexual desire, the imagery of mourning indistinguishable from sexual fantasy. The emergence of this ambivalence suggests an unacknowledged struggle in Gretchen between pain and desire, or more exactly between two kinds of pain: one redoubled by self-consciousness, and one mitigated by desire (an antithesis: other-consciousness). In the end, it is desire that controls the foreground. The missing Faust is restored in imaginary, and Imaginary, form, so much so that he nearly takes over the poem; and Gretchen's fantasy about him becomes a partial compensation for the absence that calls it forth. The detailed, arousing imagery that envelops the figure of Faust contradicts the closing insistence of the refrain that what is lost—really the part of Gretchen's ego that is identified with Faust—can never be found again. Gretchen reintegrates her "shattered mind" by spontaneously internalizing the object of her love.

As the persistence of the refrain reminds us, Gretchen's passage from self-alienation to desire is a movement of reinterpretation, not one of difference. The desire acts as a sublimation of the violent misery and ritualized searching—the trips to the window and into the street—by which her "poor head" is turned/maddened ("verrückt"); sexuality appears as a sublimating, not the sublimated, force where identity is concerned. Goethe articulates this process by giving each continuation an influence on the recurrence of the refrain. The first continuation, barren of fantasy, fixed in the "grave" of Faust's absence, lasts for two stanzas, suggesting a norm that is also observed by the final stanza-group. The second continuation, in which the threshold of fantasy is imperceptibly crossed, lasts for three stanzas, as if Gretchen were able to defer the outbreak of lament by spinning out the images in which her desire is beginning to find itself. The effect of a deferral is very specific; it is the extra, third stanza that makes the erotic element in the poem explicit for the first time. The climactic cry of this stanza, "Und ach, sein Kuss!" is the culmination of a series of images that re-creates Faust's body from scattered reminiscences of his gait, figure, smile, and so on. The movement of integration also reverses the imagery of fragmentation attached to Gretchen's mind and body in the first continuation. But the final continuation does even better than this. Not only is it a violent and open expression of sexual fantasy, but it also defers the refrain indefinitely, so that the poem ends with an image of passion, indeed of the "fading (*Vergehen*) of the subject" into the other that comes with sexual fulfillment, rather than with the abstract "nevermore" of barren despair.

Schubert's treatment of "Gretchen am Spinnrade" is based on a structural dissonance that turns Goethe's pattern inside out. Goethe's lament—the refrain—becomes Schubert's mitigation, while Goethe's mitigation—the pattern of continuation—becomes the basis of Schubert's lament. The curve of anguish traced by Schubert ascends with the curve of sexual desire, and is relieved only by the sense of isolation from the beloved that appears in the refrain. This structural rhythm leads Schubert to make a famous alteration, the repetition of the first couplet of the refrain at the close of the song. For musical as well as dramatic reasons, Schubert wants the song to end with a release of tension; like Goethe, he directs Gretchen's pain toward a sublimation. But Goethe's sublimation is a spasm of desire, while Schubert's is a lapse into resignation. Where Goethe completes a continuous transformation of Gretchen's disturbed peace, Schubert posits an exhausted ebbing of passion. This change, one might add, is not necessarily to Schubert's advantage, though the fierce emphasis of the song on the pain in sexual longing partially compensates for the loss of Goethe's evocation of the mobility of intense emotion.

The structural rhythm of Schubert's song matches that of the poem, with three large-scale *crescendo*s to parallel the three groups of stanzas, but the matched rhythms move in opposite directions. Where Goethe starts with a cry of pain and dilutes it with the flow of images, Schubert starts with a sorrowful whisper and intensifies it almost to a scream. Each section of the music begins *pianissimo*, with the refrain sung over a D-minor "spinning" figure in the accompaniment. The *crescendo*s mount through the continuations—to *forte* the first time, *fortissimo* thereafter—while the spinning figure exposes the self-torturing core of Gretchen's grief by imperceptibly shifting the imitative focus from her wheel to her wheeling emotions. The vocal line for the Faust imagery of the second continuation does seem to seek the balm of desire, but there is a poignant inflection at the thought of emotional intimacy—"Seines Mundes Lächeln, / Seiner Augen Gewalt" set

to restless harmony—and this prepares the way for an aggrieved conclusion
at the remembrance of physical intimacy—"Sein Händedruck / Und ach,
sein Kuss!" ("Sein Händedruck" is sung as a d²–f² oscillation, the melodic
pattern that will later dominate the despairing D-minor vocal line of the last
stanza.) For Schubert's Gretchen, imagery fails—and worse: it steadily
heightens the consciousness of separation. Desire is present, certainly, but it
is unable to internalize the images of Faust, impotent to convert the imagery
into fantasy.

This pattern produces two crises in the musical design. The first of these
comes at the close of the second *crescendo*, the setting of "Und ach, sein
Kuss!" At this point the spinning figure, which has been continuously sustained since the beginning, is abruptly replaced by clamorous *sforzando*
chords while the voice mounts to an overvocalized cry of pain on "Kuss,"
the erotic turning-point of the poem. Gretchen's anguish is marked in the
vocal line by an anti-cadential movement from D (the tonic tone) to G on
"sein Kuss"; the G of "Kuss" is the dissonant tone of the dominant-seventh
chord that bursts forth in the accompaniment, and it turns the word into an
almost inarticulate protest against frustration and rejection. The overflow
of sexual feeling momentarily brings the song to a halt, producing a strong
structural dissonance by breaking continuity; in the poem, the quasi-incan-
tatory rhythm that leads smoothly from stanza to stanza is essential in articulating the always transitional character of Gretchen's feelings. The impression of a sonorous void is heightened as the dominant-seventh chord
under "Kuss" fails to resolve, transforming itself instead into a drawn-out
diminished seventh (Ex. 35). The suspension of harmonic motion registers
the paralysis of Gretchen's ego.

EXAMPLE 35. Schubert, "Gretchen am Spinnrade."

Several measures of the spinning figure now follow *pianissimo*, echoing
Gretchen's anguish by elaborating the diminished-seventh chord that con-

summates her cry. Twice the figure breaks off after a painful dissonance, a bare minor ninth, as if the emotional and harmonic impasse reached in the second *crescendo* could admit of no recovery. Then the figure smooths itself out and the refrain returns, exchanging Faust's all-too-seductive image for the vacant shelter of Gretchen's heavy heart. The return is momentarily placating, the more so because its figuration now provides the deferred resolution of the climactic dominant-seventh chord. But the music rises inexorably into the third and most turbulent *crescendo*, this one marked by a thickened texture for the spinning figure and by prolonged *fortissimo* writing. For a climax, the voice turns to three plangent outbursts on "Vergehen sollt'," the last two capped by melodic leaps at "Vergehen" that reach a sustained high A over a *forzando*-laden accompaniment. (The 'open" sonority of these moments supports their stark intensity; each high A forms part of a bare fifth that represents the dominant-seventh chord.) At the same time, the text is successively condensed. First we hear the last two stanzas in full, then only the last stanza—as revised by Schubert to incorporate a rhetorically intensified first line, "O könnt' ich ihm küssen" ("O if I could kiss him"). Finally, the death-driven closing couplet stands alone. The effect of this gesture is to expel, even to exorcise, all of the elements of pleasure and intimacy—the embracing, holding, uninhibited kissing—from Gretchen's sexuality, until all that is left is a hopeless wish for obliviousness. Where the "Vergehen" of Goethe's Gretchen unifies an evolving sexual fantasy with the image of a swoon, the increasingly shrill "Vergehen" of Schubert's Gretchen exposes a thwarted and fixated consciousness trying to exhaust itself. Schubert's condensations and repetitions constitute Gretchen's attempt to blot out—more literally to displace—the seductive images that torture her awareness of separation beyond enduring.

With this new impasse, the song reaches its second crisis, one that appears mainly as an unappeased need for psychic defense and esthetic distance. Nothing is available to limit the fragmentation and depletion of the self except the refrain, with its protective sense of imageless solitude. Yet to bring the refrain back at this point would close the song with a moment of calm, something without warrant in the relentlessly downward curve of feeling throughout. As we know, Schubert brings the refrain back anyway, perhaps partly from a sense that the inevitable return of the music to the tonic would subvert any implication of total collapse. His quiet ending contradicts the statement of the refrain, "Meine Ruh' ist hin," much as the rise of passion in the poem contradicts the numb passivity of "Ich finde sie nimmer." But where Goethe's ending is a closure, the outcome of a process that shapes the whole poem, Schubert's is suspended, rootless. Its arbitrary quality, coupled with its undeniable effectiveness, suggests that Schubert far more than Goethe read "Gretchen am Spinnrade" as a study in Romantic repetition, with the characteristic pattern of captivation, absent others, erotic despair, and unprepared conclusions.

A more subtle yet more disruptive instance of structural dissonance, withheld to the point of closure and then sprung like a trap, appears in "Erlkönig." Goethe's poem is a ballad with a frame. It both begins and ends with a stanza assigned to an anonymous narrative voice; the middle section is taken up by the dramatic voices of the father, son, and Erlking, which clash and intertwine without interruption by the narrator.[33] The effect of this frame structure is to lure the reader into an empathetic response and then to cast a chill over it. The narrator's scene-setting—an abrupt question and answer, then a breathlessly repetitive description in the present tense—begins the poem with a plunge into immediacy. The agitated play of voices that follows heightens this both through suspense over the boy's fate and through a dramatic intimacy produced by leaving out all narrative transitions. But after the son's climactic cry, "Erlkönig hat mir ein Leids getan," all feeling of immediacy evaporates. The return of the narrative voice for the final stanza is presented as a circular symmetry that distances the death of the child through Romantic irony. (Several of the most famous German ballads—for instance "Herr Von Falkenstein" and "Schondilie"—begin with narrative and end in dialogue.) The narrator's first words here are recapitulatory, teasing; they do little more than withhold information from our aroused curiosity, and the almost cinematic "cut" to them after the boy's cry is an open manipulation of the reader. Goethe makes the foregrounding of form especially intrusive and self-conscious by echoing the images of the first stanza with those of the last. He even echoes the initial rhyme of "Wind" and "Kind":

> Wer reitet so spät durch Nacht und Wind?
> Es ist der Vater mit seinem Kind;
> Er hat den Knaben wohl in dem Arm,
> Er fasst ihn sicher, er hält ihn warm.
> [st. 1]

> Dem Vater grausets, er reitet geschwind,
> Er hält in Armen das ächzende Kind,
> Erreicht den Hof mit Müh' und Not;
> In seinem Armen das Kind war tot.
> [st. 8]

> Who rides so late through the windy night?
> It is a father, his son held tight.
> He holds the boy closely in his arms,
> He holds him safely, he holds him warm.
> [st. 1]

---

[33] My account of the voices in the poem differs in several details from Cone's in *The Composer's Voice*, pp. 24–25.

> The father spurs quickly, beset with fright,
> His moaning son in his arms wound tight;
> He reaches the farm all panting and wild.
> His arms were wound tightly around his dead child.
> [st. 8]

The distancing process is completed in the last line, which moves from evocative narration to flat statement, and from the present tense to the past.

Goethe's formalizing move alters the very genre of his poem. "Erlkönig" is not what it seems to be at first, a grim and affecting ballad, but an interrogation of the ballad form, a nest of enigmas. Was the child really lost to supernatural forces or did he die of his own imagination—and in any case what does the ambiguity imply about imaginative processes and their origins? Why do the father's rational "reassurances" focus more and more on withered forms as the Erlking's fatal lures grow more erotic? Why does the circular form of this art-ballad violate the blunt narrative linearity of most folk-ballads? And why does the narrator submerge himself under the play of voices throughout, to return only with news of death—news announced with a neutrality so toneless that it is brutal?[34]

Schubert's song does not resolve any of these questions; instead it breaks the frame that raises them. At just the point where the poem heightens the feeling of distance, the song heightens empathetic participation by means of a sharp structural dissonance between narrative and harmonic movement. The moment of collision comes during the most critical episode in the music, the return of the tonic. It is precipitated by the accompaniment, which, feverish throughout, at last reels out of control and carries the voice along with it.

The accompaniment in "Erlkönig" is frankly obsessive. The music opens in a vehement G minor, with G octaves introducing the ostinato triplet pulse over a theme in the bass built from a rising scale (G to E♭) and a falling tonic triad. The heart of what follows is a projection of this basic texture over a wide range of tonalities; with two interruptions for the Erlking's light whispers, the process is continuous throughout the song. As dramatic tension rises, the harmony grows increasingly volatile, more as if it were rejecting than diversifying the tonic, but there is no escape from the narrow rigidity of expressive gesture. This clash, which contributes much of the overwrought feeling of the song, seems to respond to the dilemma of the father, who is in desperate flight from a figure who always looms *ahead* of him. Once again Schubert's strongly father-centered reading of the poem comes to the fore.

The harmonic design of the song as a whole is extreme, a study in pungent voice-leading, jarring contrast, and unexpected shifts of direction. Schubert

---

[34] See Hartman, "Wordsworth and Goethe," p. 192.

repeatedly punctuates the question-and-answer pattern of the text with harmonic changes, especially with collisions between close relatives of the tonic
and remote key areas. There is virtually no middle ground to connect these
harmonies; mediating movement around the circle of fifths is sparse or absent. Approached and left abruptly, and often with much chromatic agitation, the remote tonalities are intrusions, trespasses, in keeping with the father's experience of the Erlking. Throughout the song, in fact, the harmony
seeks to create images of intrusion with insistent stabbing dissonances that
break out and break off with equal abruptness. As the father's control over
the dramatic situation deteriorates in the final moments, the intrusions become longer and more elaborate, as if to anticipate the Erlking's inevitable
triumph. Ironically, the only passages in the interior of the song that have
any harmonic stability are the ones devoted to the Erlking's lures. The lurch-
ing, dizzying quality of this music, its patchwork of stark juxtapositions, is a
vivid translation of Goethe's constant shifting of voices and desires. Yet by
making so much volatility basic to the musical structure, the translation itself becomes the rationale for Schubert's violation of Goethe's design.

   That violation begins soon after the boy's cry of pain sends the music
back to the obsessive G minor of its opening. The move sounds at first like
an imitation, a structural consonance aimed at Goethe's stiff-jawed frame
structure, but the impression is a snare. After eight measures of recapitulation (the only ones in the song), the tonic lapses into the subdominant. A
turn to the dominant might be expected to follow, but instead a menacing
bass rises by semitones onto a root-position Ab-major triad (Ex. 36). Schubert insists strongly on this Neapolitan sonority; he cadences to it at once
through a dominant substitute (vii°⁷/Ab over an Ab pedal). The voice then
embarks on a hushed Ab-major recitative to announce the death of the boy.
Unlike Goethe, Schubert wants the narrator's "In seinem Armen das Kind
war tot" to sound heartbroken, and he asks the voice to falter movingly before declaiming the last two words. The most telling thing about this expressive pause is the note that precedes it on "Kind" (Ex. 36)—a subversive, initially unaccompanied G. I call the G subversive because G is the tonic note
of the song, and the voice responds to its pull here by treating it as a destination of sorts. But this particular G is a far cry from the tonic: it is nothing
more than the Neapolitan leading-tone. When he halts the recitative, Schubert interrupts a smooth melodic cadence in Ab; dangling uncomfortably,
the exposed G only heightens the harmonic tension *against* the tonic. The
tension is wound still tighter as the piano adds a diminished-seventh chord,
vii°⁷/Ab; a fermata extends the mystification. It is up to the once-more-un-
accompanied voice to settle matters, which it does by dropping a tritone to
articulate the deferred "war tot" as C#-D. The D points to the dominant of
G, but its proximity to Ab gives it a dissonant aura that is at once shocking,
frightening, and poignant. The song then comes to an abrupt end with a rit-
ualistic cadence formula, V⁷-I, that carries little conviction. The tonic has

EXAMPLE 36. Schubert, "Erlkönig."

been dissociated, largely depleted of its closural power, in order to enact a tragic recognition. Like the father, the listener is confronted with the blank arbitrariness of final things.

Schubert, then, ends in a remote, uncanny atmosphere that threatens to deconstruct not only the text but also his own harmonic and (thanks to the recitative) stylistic language. Where Goethe moves in a tight circle to break the mood of his poem and focus on enigma rather than emotion, Schubert rejects an incipient circling movement to produce the most emotionally taxing measures in his song. The formal discontinuity of the music is not self-conscious, but naïve in Schiller's sense of the term; what we hear is a dramatic repudiation of Romantic irony. Schubert does not accept the poem as an ambiguous text that raises questions about the daemonic aspects of the imagination; he rewrites it as the terrified recognition of something elemental and malevolent, as if to compensate for the poet's seeming reluctance to confront what the narrator has overheard. Schubert's Erlking is an objectified, alienated form of everything that inevitably fails in human love—the "ruin" that Shelley once called "Love's shadow." When the Erlking's whisper turns from a lure to a lustful demand, his music loses its frolicsome, dancelike character and becomes an ominous version of the triplet ostinato associated with the father, son, and narrator. The harmony disintegrates to evoke the full otherness of the Erlking (Ex. 37), while the figuration identifies that otherness with the characters who disavow it. The Erlking seizes

EXAMPLE 37. Schubert, "Erlkönig."

them all on behalf of a love that is indifferent to its object: "Ich liebe dich, mich reizt deine schöne Gestalt; / Und bist du nicht willig, so brauch' ich Gewalt!" ("I love you, your youthful form is so fine; / Come! or I'll force you and make you mine!") At "Gewalt," Schubert calls for an *fff* outburst that binds the son's voice and the Erlking's into a single measure—for at this point both the daemon lover and his beloved exclaim at the contact between them (Ex. 37). And from here on, the triplet ostinato is not the sound of fear and flight, but of possession.

A possible term for the esthetic of Schubert's "Erlkönig" might suggest a reversal rather than simply a rejection of Romantic irony; we might speak of a Romantic pathos that solicits an overidentification with the illusions of art. Like the child in the song, the artist is vulnerable to the objectified forms of his angers and desires. To accept that vulnerability without defensiveness is to redefine the imperatives of form. Intensity of vision may demand a form that is self-consuming as a function of its very strictness; and so it happens in "Erlkönig," which ends by overextending the controlled harmonic volatility that animates it throughout. The danger of passivity in this attitude is obvious, and in places like the finale of his C-minor Piano Sonata, Opus posthumous, Schubert is not always immune from failures of esthetic will. But it is still not unjust to say of Goethe's great poem what Schubert's song does, that its form is too self-assured, its authorial control too rigid, almost obsessional. Keats's "La Belle dame sans merci," also a ballad that asks what is and isn't there in what the imagination sees, begins with an extrinsic narrator who promises a frame. The promise, as in Schubert, is not kept. Instead, Keats's woebegone knight closes the poem by echoing the questions put to him by the narrator. By having it so, Keats poses all of Goethe's enigmas without pretending that he or his poem have mastered them.

VI

Within the large-scale rhythm of a song cycle, certain structural dissonances can take on the status of tacit leitmotives; the motivic or harmonic unity of the cycle may thus be matched by a consistency of deconstructive play. Schoenberg's first fully atonal work, *Das Buch der hängenden Gärten* (*The Book of the Hanging Gardens*), to texts by Stefan George—a cycle whose extraordinary sensuous beauty has still not received the recognition that it deserves—offers a tantalizing instance of this.

Schoenberg's selection of poems from George's larger cycle constitutes a tragic quest romance. The speaker finds himself in a phantasmagorical garden-world identified with the hanging gardens of Babylon; there he courts, wins, and loses a mysterious woman/priestess. The love-affair rouses extreme but passive hungers in him that repeatedly emerge into open masochism. The garden-world itself, supposedly a paradise, is as ambivalent as the love that it sanctions. It is lush, ponderously sensuous, smothering, ruined, full of alluring surfaces and castrating edges—a mingling of golden reeds and crooked ridges, shimmering fishponds and fans with knifelike points. Schoenberg translates the sensuous and erotic ambivalence of the gardens with a musical one. His songs are steeped in a chromaticism that has cut its ties to tonal centers, poising itself on the edge of a harmonic void. But the music also seeks analogues to tonal form with a restless inventiveness. Motivic repetition and transposition, parallels to tonal voice-leading, and circular movements of harmony all work to naturalize the strange "osmosis of tones" that gives the songs their distinctive texture.[35]

The focus of structural dissonance in the cycle is a tension between gestures of this order, which echo the procedures of tonal resolution in the absence of their harmonic basis, and actual tonal reminiscences. With surprising consistency for so varied a work, *Das Buch* makes an association between heightened moments of erotic passivity and the vestigial appearance of tonal harmonies, usually through a quasi-cadential movement. The eighth song is perhaps the most open and plangent example of this tonal nostalgia. Schoenberg begins by stating the augmented triad F–A–C♯ in both

---

[35] "Osmosis": Hans Heinz Stuckenschmidt, *Arnold Schoenberg* (Zürich: Atlantis Verlag, 1951), p. 35.

voice and piano, and goes on to saturate the music with the notes of this
chord by spelling them out in the bass at the head of insistent angular figurations. A point of supersaturation is reached at "fieberheissen"—fever-
heat—in m. 17, where the full augmented chord returns dramatically to ac-
company its own arpeggiation (Ex. 38; note the reinforced C♯, an echo of
earlier emphases, as well as the G♭–F step in the voice). The same measure
also introduces an emphatic C♯–C♮ step that precipitates an extended resolution of the augmented triad into a triad of F minor, with the leading tone
superimposed (Ex. 38). The song closes by attacking this F-minor chord five
times in the bass, under strongly accented resolutions of the flat to the

EXAMPLE 38. Schoenberg, *Das Buch der hängenden Gärten*, No. 8.

raised leading-tone in the middle voice and contradictory sonorities in the
upper ones (Ex. 39). Desperate erotic longing blends into a tonal aspiration
that is partially satisfied, partially denied, as the text supplicates: "Let some
coolness spring to the fevered brow / I tottering lean upon."

EXAMPLE 39. Schoenberg, *Das Buch der hängenden Gärten*, No. 8.

The third song provides an instance richer in internal conflict, but before we turn to it a brief digression will be necessary in order to consider some special problems posed by the analysis of atonal music. A freely atonal work cannot be referred to what George Perle calls "a preestablished harmonic unit" external to it; motivic and harmonic material have no context, no definition, outside the work itself.[36] One consequence of this is that the language of traditional musical analysis becomes, strictly speaking, meaningless when confronted with a work like *Das Buch*, because there is no way to decide whether, say, a four-semitone interval is a major third (a consonance) or a diminished fourth (a dissonance). The presence of residual tonal features only complicates matters, because the basic structural procedures of atonal pieces are almost always independent of them. Often enough, these features emerge only when the listener focuses attention on attack patterns, ignoring intervening or tied material as "non-harmonic" if it is registrally distinct enough to be heard as a background.

I can only respond to these difficulties here, not pretend to resolve them. The discussions that follow assume that pitch-complexes with familiar sonorities are usually heard as such, so that it is reasonable to speak, for instance, of conjunct major thirds as augmented triads. (No less an authority than Roger Sessions insists that so-called "tonal associations" are virtually impossible to avoid in atonal music.[37]) My labeling of chords and intervals follows Schoenberg's notation, on the understanding that notational choices often suggest ways of hearing. As to the presence or absence of residual tonal features, the basic question is always what a listener for whom tonal relationships have the status of a natural language—which is still virtually any listener—is likely to make of the sonorous fabric that the composer presents. If tonal allusions appear, the question of their expressive role in their atonal context immediately follows. These issues are especially relevant to the early music of Schoenberg, which is in the process of emerging from and altering the sound-world of traditional tonality.

The tonal motifs in *Das Buch* tend to focus on the related tonalities of G and D, a disposition introduced into the cycle by the second and third songs, which initiate the speaker's erotic quest and establish its passive character.[38] The text of the third song begins with a plea for the priestess of the gardens

---

[36] George Perle, *Serial Composition and Atonality*, 4th ed. (Berkeley: University of California Press, 1977), p. 1.

[37] Roger Sessions, "Problems and Issues Facing the Composer Today," in *Problems of Modern Music*, edited by Paul Henry Lang (New York: Norton, 1962), pp. 21–33.

[38] The second song begins with a primary seventh chord of D minor and recapitulates it a few measures before the close. In Classical tonality, this sonority usually resolves to the subdominant—here G—and in fact a melodic movement from D to G is carried out by the voice after each i[7] chord, with an accentual pattern that suggests this resolution. It was Webern who first pointed out the G-major allusions of the song.

to elect the quester "to [the ranks of] those who serve" her, and ends with a plea for pity and patience "for one who stumbles in so strange a path." (It is impossible not to hear the composer's voice in that plea.) The response of the music to the quester's tremulous humility is a rhythmically urgent texture crisscrossed by clashing sonorities.

The first three measures of the song are built over an oscillating bass that seems to swing down the circle of fifths from D to G to C and return through G to D. A D-minor feeling emerges as the accompaniment forms accents on the third beat of each measure, where a D-minor triad is attacked over a C–G pedal. At the same time, the accentual pattern of the vocal line produces a firm large-scale tonal articulation—again of the D-minor triad (Ex. 40).

EXAMPLE 40. Schoenberg, *Das Buch der hängenden Gärten*, No. 3.

After measure 3, the D-minor atmosphere—despite all the emphasis, it is not a real key—disintegrates into a rich atonal texture. The voice pulls apart from the piano in free elaborations and transpositions of a small intervallic cell; the accompaniment is dominated by transpositions of the opening material and by a heavy chordal passage that is repeated at fixed pitches. At its climax, however, the song pulls back toward D as the voice and bass, in similar disjunct motion, attack the bare fifth D-A (Ex. 41). A recapitulation of the D-G-C bass progression follows, and leads to a fragmentary return of the original D-minor allusions. The voice intones "fremden stege" ("strange path") in tortured melisma; then the D-minor triads heard earlier reappear in their third-beat position, this time without a pedal tone to veil their sonority (Ex. 42). The brief coda is teasingly ambiguous. Over a "non-harmonic" bass, the final measure repeats the whole-tone descent in thirds, Eb-G to

EXAMPLE 41. Schoenberg, *Das Buch der hängenden Gärten*, No. 3.

EXAMPLE 42. Schoenberg, *Das Buch der hängenden Gärten*, No. 3 (piano postlude).

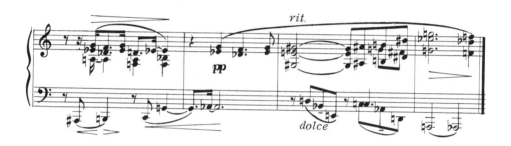

Db-F, that begins the right-hand piano part. But the progression at this point also constitutes a "fictitious resolution" to D minor.[39] The closing chord, if its flat tones were allowed to resolve by half-step in response to the F octave interlocked with them, would produce a D-minor triad (Ex. 42).

The basis of Schoenberg's antithetical association between the primary rhythm of musical fulfillment and a recurrent moment of personal depletion is the fact that tonal cadences and resolutions are regressive elements in the atonal sound-world of the cycle. The cadential moments are much like the perfect cadence in Monteverdi's "Lamento d'Arianna" in their suggestion of withdrawal and enervation, only here the suggestion has, so to speak, been psychoanalyzed. Schoenberg's design reduces the tonal cadence to its etymo-

[39] Jim Samson, in *Music in Transition: A Study of Tonal Expansion and Atonality, 1900–1920* (New York: Norton, 1977), pp. 160–61, gives a diagrammatic analysis of this song that also notes a fictitious resolution—but, in my view, an implausible one that does not adequately reflect Schoenberg's voice-leading.

logical root; it is a fall, a false step on the "strange path" that leads to genital love. The quester's erotic will is frail and secondary; his real object is the peace of separation, as the twelfth poem can be read to affirm:

> When in holy rest in deep-slung hammocks
> Across our sleep our hands nestle
> Devotion damps the burning in our limbs.

The projected form of the quester's passive, self-denying eroticism is the destruction of the garden, which is inevitably realized as he subtly resists and degrades the woman's yielding to him. The last song, submerging the quester in "clouded-over, stifling night," marks his final fall by sinking into an atmosphere of D minor; a fictitious resolution to the D-minor triad is the closing gesture of the cycle.

Schoenberg's harsh reading of George's texts is consistent with the relentlessly tragic view of sexuality that shapes his other expressionist vocal works, *Erwartung*, *Die glückliche Hand*, and *Pierrot lunaire*. What we hear, as Carl Schorske puts it, is a conversion of the Wagnerian *Liebestod* to a *Liebestöten*.[40] The link made by *Tristan* between the flow of desire and the prolongation of tonal uncertainty finds its mirror-image in *Das Buch*, where tonal presence marks the failure of desire. Like Schubert's Gretchen, Schoenberg's quester is in flight from desire, but his flight is a destruction, not a sublimation; the song-cycle acts out an unconscious rejection of the ego, the "I" in whom genital sexuality is articulated.

The centers of cadential collapse in *Das Buch* are the fifth and tenth songs, which the music takes as a pair against the will of the poetry. The text of the fifth song begins by asking on what path the beloved is going to walk, and ends with the speaker's masochistic wish to make his face her footstool. As the wish is intoned, the bass embarks on a series of three movements from D to G in octaves, suggesting a V–I cadence (Ex. 43). The repeated octaves intrude a tonal contour on the song with an authority that matches their sonorous weight; Schoenberg's later music would avoid octaves for that very reason. With each approach to G, the upper voices pull closer to a tonal sonority; in the last measure, this process yields a chord that can be heard as a G-major triad colored by a non-resolving appoggiatura (E♭) to the dominant (D). The withheld resolution, however, has in a sense already taken place, because the vocal line has repeatedly used an E♭–D descent to form melodic cadences. The vocal D has acted as a subliminal dominant throughout the song. The humiliating wish-structure of the speaker is thus set forth

---

[40] Carl Schorske, *Fin-de-Siècle Vienna: Politics and Culture* (New York: Alfred A. Knopf, 1980), p. 354; Schorske's whole discussion, pp. 344–64, is illuminating. See also my "Schorske's Ring Cycle, Schoenberg's *Liebestod*," *19th-Century Music* 5 (1981): 76–81.

EXAMPLE 43. Schoenberg, *Das Buch der hängenden Gärten*, No. 5.

in an atmosphere haunted by the tonal memory that intimates the death of desire.

The exotic text of the tenth song would clearly like to affirm the speaker's erotic will, but Schoenberg will not let it. The poem unfolds in an overripe atmosphere of wetness, roundness, and softness, all put to the service of a passive, unconsummated sexual expectancy. The garden scene is presented as a thinly veiled evocation of the beloved's genitals, but its would-be idyllic character clouds over almost immediately with an anxiety that hovers around castration; the "lovely [flower] bed" ("schöne beet") is rimmed by "purple-black thorns / through which thrust flowercups with flecked [stained, splotchy] spurs." The closing lines blur the genital focus—openly displace it, really—and retreat into an idealizing fantasy: "her moist mouth [is] / like sweet fruit from heaven's fields." Schoenberg captures the enervating quality of the speaker's passive eros with a remarkably candid atmosphere of D major/minor. The first three measures are entirely taken up by the smooth stepwise resolution of non-triadic dissonances into plain triads of D major and minor. The passage, for piano alone, is later repeated with a vocal overlay that embroiders and extends the triadic resolutions. The second half of the song is devoted primarily to expanding a conflict implicit in the first measure between thirds and fourths as resources of sonority and structure. The conflict ends with a reminiscence of the first measure, as Schoenberg smoothly resolves a fourth-chord into a D-major triad (Ex. 44). The closing passage responds to the failure of erotic nerve at the end of the poem by echoing the degraded close of the fifth song. The D-major triad that acts as a chord of resolution is supported by a D octave in the bass, which falls cadentially to a G octave. Over this G, the upper voices rise to a fictitious G-major resolution (Ex. 44). Tonal satisfaction is thus made to coincide with an edgy evasion of sexuality, a kind of corrupt modesty. The tension between erotic imagery and action that emerges is not unlike the one

EXAMPLE 44. Schoenberg, *Das Buch der hängenden Gärten*, No. 10.

suggested by Schumann in "Ich will meine Seele tauchen," except that Schoenberg has stripped away the reassuring gloss of idealization. It is no accident that the next song isolates the voice to ask whether the sexual union that eventually took place was really the bliss that the lovers had imagined. Where consummation ought to spring, Schoenberg inserts an abyss.

VII

Schoenberg's vocal style in *Das Buch* generalizes the impression of continuous intensity and erotic disturbance by vacillating between chromatic oscillation and the kind of disjunctive contour that some later composers would turn into a mannerism. The musical gestures of the voice are almost too fluid, too autonomous, to be reconciled with utterance—enough so that Schoenberg felt called on to defend his technique, with some help from Schubert. "Even Schubert," he wrote, "does not set off words singly in any marked fashion according to the weight of their meaning. Rather, by means of a comprehensive melody, he may pass over a salient textual feature, even when it is most important in regard to poetic content and poetic substance. It should not be surprising, then, that a genuine melody will arise relatively seldom from a procedure which strongly emphasizes the text."[41] Schoenberg identified his own "comprehensive melody" with the continuous variation that he tried to make the basis of musical structure. To appropriate the language and meaning of a text much further than his Expressionist style does, one would have to warp them beyond recognition.

Some later styles, of course, have done just that. The avant-garde composers who came to maturity after the Second World War have at times been openly, even extravagantly, antitextual. In Luciano Berio's *Sequenza III*, for instance, written in 1966, the singer is asked to maul the text with breath

[41] Schoenberg, "Analysis," p. 27.

tones, spoken pitches, sounds of minimal duration, laughter, mouth clicks, coughing, closed-mouth vocalization, and vocalization with hands muting the mouth. Milton Babbitt's 1974 "Phonemena" dispenses with a text altogether in favor of abstract strings of phonemes. Such avant-garde vocalism represents an attempt to get beyond the expressive tradition that begins with the text-centered styles of the Renaissance and their imperative "to express and paint in tones the outer world of nature and the inner reality of man."[42] But the result all too often suggests a desperate virtuosity that only makes explicit—and so slackens—the tension at the basis of the earlier styles. Expressive song has harbored anti-textual elements throughout its history. What animates the vocal style in both Monteverdi's "Lamento d'Arianna" and, say, Peter Maxwell Davies's *Dark Angels* (1974) is the demand that the anti-textuality of the music must be part of a response to the poetry rather than merely an exploitation of it. That the response "opens," rewrites, even defaces the text is only to be expected; the music adopts the poetry as an origin, and then treats it the way all origins are treated, by departing from it. Most composers in the expressive tradition would agree with Schoenberg, in practice if not in theory, that song brings poetry to life not by resembling it, but precisely by being different.

No matter, then, how silken it is, song is always a transmemberment of speech. At a primary phenomenological level, the unfolding of a song is a volatile interplay between two attempts to be heard—that of the music and that of the poem. In the absence of external cues—a text, a program, a stylization or allusion—music acquires what Cone calls "human content" by evoking a movement of intuition, a play of possibilities like Wordsworth's improvisation in "The Solitary Reaper," but one that can represent the tacit connotations of the music only so long as it is not verbalized. This is not an embryonic text, nor can it be represented by a text, as the language of program notes shows all too well. The play of possibilities is, rather, a free flow of visual, tactile, and pre-verbal interpretants with primary-process overtones; it is more lawless and paratactic than not, a tacit speculation without a center. When words are added to music, the result is not a shift away from this characteristic mode of musical expressiveness, but a tension. It is true, as Cone points out, that words do not limit the music in the naïve sense of violating its ineffability,[43] but here again "There is a conflict, there is a resistance / Involved." The music of a song is a composition before it is a setting, and it never ceases to radiate a tacit richness of implication, to insist on the paradoxical blend of particularity and indefiniteness that belongs to mu-

---

[42] Edward E. Lowinsky, "Music in the Culture of the Renaissance," in *Renaissance Essays*, edited by Paul O. Kristeller and Philip P. Wiener (New York: Harper and Row, 1968), p. 380.

[43] Cone, *Composer's Voice*, p. 167.

sic alone. The more fully developed the instrumental lines, the more true this is likely to be, though it can hold good for an unaccompanied vocal line. Meanwhile, the poetry of the song sanctions, in fact compels, a mimetic response that identifies what the music is expressing with a dramatic and affective situation. Explicit fiction-making threatens to displace tacit speculation as the primary vehicle of response and interpretation. We might put this by saying that the rhetorical mode of music is an extreme metonymy, and that the language of song constantly tries to reinstate the imagery that the music of the song displaces and elides.

To go a step further, we might even conjecture that the language of song always reinstates the *wrong* images, much the way that a dream does—and for much the same reasons of compromise and disguise, defense and veiled disclosure. Let me close with a question, then: Is song so intensely, and so *erotically*, expressive because it comes exquisitely close to intoning all those things that we forbid ourselves to say?

6

"A Completely New Set
of Objects"

The katy-dids at Ephrata return
But this time at another place.
It is the same sound, the same season,
But it is not Ephrata.

(WALLACE STEVENS, "Memorandum")

Charles Ives's instrumental pieces are probably the most word-hungry non–vocal compositions by any major composer. More than Liszt, more than Berlioz, Ives is extreme, even reckless, in subjecting his work to the programmatic demands characteristic of the nineteenth century. Almost any example of European program music will have an intelligible form independent of its program; the same cannot be said for "Decoration Day," "The Fourth of July," or "Hallowe'en." Ives's extreme allusiveness, however, is not a mere eccentricity, but a response to a cultural imperative that has haunted American art since its first maturity: the need to reconcile a transcendental vision, a sense of the absolute, with a texture and a form that are distinctively American. To alter a phrase of Wallace Stevens, Ives regards his music as the cry of its occasion. And the occasion—the discovery of an American absolute—must not only call forth the cry but also be perfectly audible in it.

Stevens is the poet closest to Ives in his response to the same demand, though the position of the two men is not historically the same. Ives is the first American composer of stature to insist on a music that reflects its region; his place as a musician is analogous to Whitman's as a poet. Stevens, in sharing Ives's insistence, is only one of Whitman's heirs. Yet it is Stevens—not Williams, or Frost, or Hart Crane—who sees most clearly what the demand for an American absolute, "a local abstraction," means; and he sees what Ives could not help seeing, and what Whitman did not need to see. For poets like Williams and Crane, the question of local abstractions is one of means. Their aim is to domesticate an alien tradition; what they ask is how to Americanize the imagination, how to justify Whitman's boast that, once asked to "migrate from Greece and Ionia," the Muse would pack her bags and come to install herself "among the kitchenware." For Stevens, as for Ives, the issue is not defined so simply, and it is not a question of how but of whether. Stevens and Ives confront the need to treat place transcendentally as a metaphysical burden, not a rhetorical challenge. They deal with it as a dilemma, in full recognition of the difficulty, even the near impossibility, of finding solutions.

The burden itself can be defined as the task of creating what Stevens calls "a completely new set of objects": works of art in which the local and the absolute, the contingent and the transcendent, fuse into a single form. Both Stevens and Ives feel emphatically that this cannot be accomplished simply by giving poetry or music a local character. The problem cannot be solved for poetry as Williams tried to solve it, with an infusion of idiomatic speech and imagery taken from the gritty streets of home. Nor can it be solved for music as Ives is often misunderstood to have solved it, by incorporating folk and popular elements into sophisticated compositions; Daniel Gregory Mason could do that. As Ives put it with a case in point: "Someone is quoted as saying that 'ragtime is the true American music.' Anyone will admit that it is one of the many true, natural, and, nowadays, conventional means of expression . . . . But it does not 'represent the American nation' any more than some fine old senators represent it."[1]

For Stevens and Ives, the problem of making a completely new set of objects is defined by the fact that the local and the absolute are fundamentally incompatible with each other. These terms form part of a rigorous dialectic, drawn by Ives from the Concord Transcendentalists, and familiar in Stevens as the quarrel between reality and the imagination.[2] For both men, art is the expression of a transcendental force, a faculty of mind or spirit which is the source of all value and the interpreter of all desire. Stevens, of course, calls that faculty the imagination, and it is worth noting the persistence of the definite article; there is only one imagination, though its embodiments are

---

[1] Charles Ives, *Essays Before A Sonata*, edited by Howard Boatwright (New York: Norton, 1970), p. 94. (*EBS* in text.)

[2] In this chapter, I will make use of Stevens's *The Necesssary Angel* and Ives's *Essays Before A Sonata* to open interpretive possibilities. To do so raises the much-debated question of how or whether to integrate an artist's conscious intentions into an attempt to understand that artist's work. My position is that Ives and Stevens are being taken as critics, not as creators whose comments have the authority to guarantee an original or primary meaning. Not all artists are good critics, especially of their own work. Mahler tinkered with programs and then withdrew them; Eliot came to find the notes to *The Wasteland* an embarrassment; Stravinsky was inconsistent about tempos when conducting his own music. Robert Browning was once asked what his obscure early poem "Sordello" meant, and replied to the effect that when he wrote the poem only he and God knew what it meant and now only God knew. For me, Ives and Stevens are good self-interpreters, and their comments are important here not because of who made them but because of what they suggest. The same considerations will apply later to Elliott Carter.

infinitely various. For both Stevens and Ives, the imagination is transcendent of all local facts, all the contingent realities of historical place and time—everything that makes up the landscape of individual life, and in so doing inevitably defines the limits of individual life. Both men also maintain, however, that the imagination can only act, only speak, through the local things to which it does not belong. "It is one of the peculiarities of the imagination," writes Stevens, "that it is always at the end of an era. What happens is that it is always attaching itself to a new reality and adhering to it. It is not that there is a new imagination but that there is a new reality."[3]

The process of this "attachment" is neither smooth nor simple. The imagination and reality are not passive opposites; they resist and belittle each other, and they cannot be made to go hand in hand without a strain. In order to attach itself to a reality, the imagination must at the very least create a momentary disordering or distortion; a violent disruption is equally possible and perhaps more tempting.[4] To use the imagination, according to Stevens, is to generate "those violences which are the maturity of [our] desire" (*NA* 63–64). Prior to *Notes Toward A Supreme Fiction* (1942), such violences in Stevens's work usually take the form of thrusts or displacements; that is, the imagination makes room for itself in reality by shoving reality out of the way. In "The Idea of Order at Key West," the song of "the maker," the girl on the beach, displaces "the dark voice of the sea":

> It may be that in all her phrases stirred
> The grinding water and the gasping wind;
> But it was she and not the sea we heard.
> (12–14)

The same thing happens more rudely in "The Man With the Blue Guitar," where the world is reduced to the ball on the nose of a clown by the guitar player's "fat thumb":

> He held the world upon his nose
> And this-a-way he gave a fling.
> His robes and symbols, ai-yi-yi—
> And that-a-way he twirled the thing.
> (XXV)

Between *Notes* and "Description Without Place" (1945), the thrust at reality tends to become a cut, a tearing—the parting of one thing from another by abstraction, which, according to Stevens, is the imagination's essential activ-

---

[3] Wallace Stevens, *The Necessary Angel: Essays on Reality and the Imagination* (New York: Vintage Books, 1951), p. 22. (*NA* in text.)

[4] On the violence of Stevens's imagination, see J. Hillis Miller, *Poets of Reality* (New York: Atheneum, 1974), pp. 251–54.

ity. In "Description," for example, the workings of the imagination appear in the gap between the way a place looks—its description—and the place itself. The description comes to us as "a sight indifferent to the eye," "a little different from reality." Yet the result of this abstraction, "an artificial thing that exists," is not entirely satisfactory. Even though it shapes a place on which the dove of creation alights, the description without place is incomplete: "a knowledge incognito," a "column in the desert," "an expectation, a desire" (V).

In the work of Stevens's last decade (1946–55)—the portion of his poetry that most converges with Ives—the thrust or cut of earlier imaginative acts is replaced by a fusion in which the imagination coincides with the reality that it transcends. Stevens compares the imagination in this aspect with light (NA 60): like light, it adds nothing to reality except its own presence. The poetic form taken by this strange addition—an "addition" of sheer transparency—is the pivotal use of minimal descriptions: local place-names. Named in the presence of the imagination, the local becomes an abstraction, an imagined thing; while the imagination "localizes" itself in the act of naming. In "Reality Is an Activity of the Most August Imagination," for example, Stevens places himself on a drive between Cornwall and Hartford on a given Friday night. The placement is emphatic: the night, we read, was "not a night blown at a glassworks in Vienna / or Venice"; it is pure Connecticut, pure Americana. Stevens's drive becomes an act of the imagination as the movement of the car creates "the visible transformations of summer night"; and the presence of the imagination constitutes Cornwall and Hartford as the borders of an absolute space. The poem calls that space "night's moonlight lake," an area defined by what it is not—"neither water nor air"—and where it is not, just as a moonlight lake is neither moonlight nor a lake. Night's moonlight lake is a composite form—a space, a duration, a perception—in which the local and the absolute overlap: a visionary locality that blends into one thing both the night's "visible transformations" and its fixed identity as the darkness between Cornwall and Hartford.

Ives fully shares Stevens's sense that the maturity of desire involves the "violence" of transformation. For Ives, there is a radical duality to be found between "substance" and "manner," terms that he applies freely to action, to the self, and to art.[5] Ives's "substance" corresponds roughly with Stevens's "imagination," though Ives literally thinks of it as absolute in the sense of being noumenal, unlike the skeptical Stevens, for whom the absoluteness of the imagination is itself finally an imagined thing. "Manner," in turn, aligns itself with Stevens's "reality": the local, the contingent, the historical. For Ives, the aim of art is to consume manner by substance. "We are going to be arbitrary enough to claim," he writes,

[5] Ives, EBS, pp. 75–77

with no definite qualification, that substance can be expressed in music, and that it is the only valuable thing about it; and, moreover, that in two separate pieces of music in which the notes are almost identical, one can be of substance with little manner, and the other can be of manner with little substance.

(EBS 77)

Obviously, the way to write inauthentic music is to let manner predominate over substance; and for Ives, this means in particular to be hemmed in by the musical equivalent of locale, whether it belongs to the Boston Symphony—a *bête noire*—or to ragtime. His remarks on the subject ought to dispel forever the notion that he is a straightforward nationalist or local colorist; in fact, Ives insists that if local color is a part of manner, then "either the color part is bound eventually to drive out the local part, or the local drive out all color" (EBS 78). Indigenous material belongs in music only as an echo, a precious trace, of substance, a musical memory linked to a transfiguration of locality that forms part of the composer's "spiritual consciousness." (What this often means for Ives is an idealized boyhood on a Wordsworthian model.[6]) It does not matter how such material sounds as long as it carries the music into "the showers of the absolute" (EBS 92). A self-conscious folk-tune is no more than a song about "the cherry on the cocktail."

Ives's most characteristic way of subsuming American material into the substance of an absolute is a form of allusion that is often misunderstood as quotation. Stevens offers a close parallel in his use of American place-names. To take Stevens first, it is generally true that when he wants to symbolize the imagination in radical opposition to reality, he uses exotic imagery in order to do it. This is most characteristic of his early poetry, where the imagination appears in the shapes of savage and tropical lushness, as in "Floral Decorations For Bananas," where leaves "plucked from Carib trees" go "Darting out of their purple craws / Their musky and tingling tongues." When, however, Stevens wants to represent reality yielding to the pressure of the imagination, he commonly represents it by the locale of his native regions, Pennsylvania and Connecticut. For Stevens, when an ordinary evening becomes the scene of an "inescapable romance," it is an ordinary evening in New Haven. An important poem in this mode, though a little-noticed one, is the lyric that gives this chapter its title:

> From a Schuylkill in mid-earth there came emerging
> Flotillas, willed and wanted, bearing in them
>
> Shadows of friends, of those he knew, each bringing
> From the water in which he believed and out of desire

---

[6] See Stuart Feder, "Decoration Day: A Boyhood Memory of Charles Ives," *Musical Quarterly* 66 (1980): 234–61.

Things made by mid-terrestrial, mid-human
Makers without knowing, or intending, uses.

These figures verdant with time's buried treasure
Came paddling their canoes, a thousand thousand,

Carrying such shapes, of such alleviation,
That the beholder knew their subtle purpose,

Knew well the shapes were the exactest shaping
Of a vast people old in meditation . . .

Under Tinicum or small Cohansey,
The fathers of the makers may lie and weather.

In this poem, the imagination is the force that brings "alleviation" to human desire by shaping new objects through meditation; reality is the local, pure and simple; and the two become one. This fusion has its source in a quality that can simply be called "thirdness"—the quality that arises when the means of perceiving an object is the impossibility of saying that the object is one thing or another.[7] Thirdness is the basis for one of Stevens's rhetorical fingerprints, the extended description that vaporizes its object with an intricate "as if" sequence or play of appositives. Elsewhere, the quality is more direct. In "Reality Is An Activity," thirdness compels the poet's recognition that night's moonlight lake is neither water nor air. In "A Completely New Set of Objects," it compels the reader to recognize that the poem's images are neither literal nor figurative. Stevens's river, for instance, is neither literally the Schuylkill and figuratively a visionary form, nor the reverse; and the figures in the flotillas are neither literally images of the beholder's friends and figuratively spirits of place, nor the reverse. Both the river and the figures are third things, parts of a new set of objects. Thirdness like this is the mark of fusion in Stevens; it is the way that things are perceived when the imagination has integrated itself with a local reality, the form in which a vision of mid-earth—of earth as imagination *and* reality—is a trip to Pennsylvania.

Where thirdness marks the fusion of a locality and an absolute, Stevens turns the locality into a privileged spot, a permanent threshold of fusion, by pronouncing its name as a kind of numinous formula. Set within the imaginative rhythm of the poem, the name behaves as a trope—a metonym for the transfiguration of the local scene. The essential feature of place-names in this essentially Ivesian role is that their presence is incantatory rather

---

[7] I am not alluding here to C. S. Peirce's concept of thirdness—the realm of intention, meaning, the "contingent rules" that shape experience—though Peirce's phenomenology is not incompatible with Stevens's. On Peirce's thirdness, see Richard J. Bernstein, *Praxis and Action* (Philadelphia: University of Pennsylvania Press, 1971), pp. 177–87.

than referential. "Tinicum" and "small Cohansey," for instance, are names deliberately chosen for their obscurity, their lack of rich associations; and even the Schuylkill, admirable river though it is, does not have the resonance of the Mississippi or the Rio Grande. Unlike a poem such as Whitman's "Crossing Brooklyn Ferry," where the rhapsodic naming of locality forms an intimate bond between the poet and those who live after him in the places that he names, "A Completely New Set of Objects" addresses its names to unalterable strangers, readers for whom the names are essentially empty. This "emptiness" in the name is strongly in accord with the principle that reality becomes imaginative only by means of abstraction. In order to embody its fusion with an absolute, a locality is forced to make a kind of dialectical bargain: the price that a named place pays to transcend itself is its disappearance into a place-name. In turn, the name becomes less the designation of a particular locality than a signifier for locality as such, the core of definiteness over which thirdness hovers. It is in this abstract version of the local that reality and the imagination meet.

In some poems, Stevens rarefies this pattern of local abstraction still further by trading away the actual name. A place may be transformed without an imaginative christening; the mere possibility of finding a word, a name, a syllable, that belongs to it might be enough:

> [She wanted] the two of them in speech,
>
> In a secrecy of words
> Opened out within a secrecy of place,
>
> Not having to do with love.
> A land would hold her in its arms that day
>
> Or something much like a land.
>   ("Two Letters," II)

> Little existed for him but the few things
> For which a fresh name always existed, as if
> He wanted to make them, to keep them from perishing.
>   ("Local Objects")

In "Old Man Asleep," the unspoken name is half-realized as the literal cry— or vocable—of its occasion; the "whole peculiar plot" (place/story) of the self is fused with "the earth" in "the drowsy motion of the river R." In poems like these, we might say, it is the emptiness of the name, not the name itself, that is most "pronounced."

What Stevens does with place-names, real and potential, Ives also does with the hymns, folk songs, rags, and barroom tunes that turn up continually in his music. These local melodies are almost never simply quoted by Ives;

they are nearly always distorted, either in their own right, or by their placement in a polytonal or polyrhythmic texture that leaves them sounding at once naïve and defamiliarized. Perhaps the most startling instance of this occurs in "The Revival," the last movement of Ives's Second Violin Sonata. After a series of variations on "Shall We Gather at the River," the music explodes into a long coda in which the hymnody of the violin is swamped by a crashing hubbub of tone-clusters and dissonant chords on the piano—all over a dominant pedal (Ex. 45). The manifestation of "substance" is virtually literal, as sheer volume of sound in a jagged rhythm becomes the expression of harmonically intelligible sonority. By contrast, Berg's quotation of a

EXAMPLE 45. Ives, Violin Sonata No. 2, finale.

Bach chorale melody in the finale of his Violin Concerto is curiously free of tension, despite its intrusion of tonality into a twelve-tone texture. Not only does Berg derive the quotation from the tone-row on which the concerto is based, but the words to the chorale, "Es ist genug, Herr, wenn es Dir gefällt" ("It is enough, Lord, if it be Thy will"), are at one with the expressive purpose of the music, which is to respond to the death of a friend's daughter.

Ives almost always excludes continuities like these when he echoes a hymn tune or a traditional melody. His music is modeled on personal rather than musical memory, and a sudden, irrelevant outburst of "Dixie" against independent chromatic lines—a major event in the opening movement of his Second String Quartet—is more his style. Another treatment of "Shall We Gather at the River," in the last movement of the Fourth Violin Sonata, makes a closure out of his characteristic warping of aural perspective. The hymn does not appear without distortion, sometimes grotesque distortion, until the final measures. When it does emerge at last in pristine form, the music has to stop—and it does, pointedly cutting off the closing phrase of the hymn. Here, as in Stevens, the local makes a dialectical bargain with the absolute: in order to be heard, it reduces to an allusion to itself. Or, to generalize in a way that will cover both the local tune and the place-name: the local, in order to lend an identity to the absolute, is forced to surrender its own identity. The "local object"—the tune or the place—is not represented mimetically, but instead is translated, abstracted, into a function of the imagination—the act of naming or alluding. To vary Stevens's formula, the imagination in these cases may add only itself to the local scene, but it also takes away whatever is not itself.

Both Ives and Stevens return often to this method of forming local abstractions, but neither is entirely satisfied with the divided consciousness that it refines, half-conceals, but cannot overcome. As Stevens exclaims, it is "As if, as if, as if the disparate halves / Of things were waiting in a betrothal known / To none, awaiting espousal to the sound / Of a right joining" ("Study of Images II"). In his Second Piano Sonata of 1911–15, "Concord, Massachusetts, 1840–1860," Ives attempts to find that reconciling sound by forming "impressionistic pictures" (*ESB* xxv) of a moment in history that fleetingly seemed to possess a more-than-historical unity—to be "nontemporaneous" (*ESB* 52). "Perhaps," writes Ives, "music is the art of speaking extravagantly" (*EBS* 52), and in the "Concord" Sonata he extravagantly takes the Transcendentalism of Concord to represent an exemplary unification of place and spirit. The sonata derives its formal coherence from nineteenth-century models of motivic transformation, but it also demands an active and complex extra-musical definition. The sonorous presence of the music must be heard in the process of emanating from an extrinsic source—a transfigured place-consciousness; and to bring this paradox to life, Ives immerses the listener in a densely textured, often massively physical current of sound. That current is meant to wind slowly and erratically back into its semi-divine origin, arriving as the work ends at a musical image of a place—Walden Pond—irradiated by " 'Transcendent Thoughts' " and " 'Visions' " (*EBS* 101). The music memorializes the fusion of the local and the absolute by re-enacting it as a structural rhythm.

The programmatic apparatus for the "Concord" Sonata makes that of Berlioz's *Symphonie fantastique* look like a model of economy. The four movements—"Emerson," "Hawthorne," "The Alcotts," and "Thoreau"— are intended to "present (one person's) impression of the spirit of transcendentalism that is associated in the minds of many with Concord, Mass." (*EBS* xxv). The score of the sonata was originally meant to be interleaved with a group of essays on the subjects of the various movements, together with a prologue and an epilogue outlining Ives's musical esthetic. The essays were published separately at first, under the title *Essays Before A Sonata*, but when Ives had the chance to publish a second edition of the sonata in 1947, he returned to his original plan and interleaved the movements with excerpts from the essays. "The spirit of transcendentalism" is obviously meant to guide performance as much as the musical notation and musical structure. Ives even directs the performer to establish new tempo relationships on a personal and programmatic basis each time the sonata is performed—as he did himself. "There are many passages," he says in a note to the score, "not to be too evenly played and in which the tempo is not precise or static. It varies usually with the mood of the day, as well as that of Emerson, the other Concord bards, and the player."[8]

Ives's combination of musical and extra-musical values is most crucial where it is most obvious, in the choice of motivic cells. The sonata is organized around a pair of these: the declamatory opening figure of "Emerson," which forms the basis of the free-flowing dissonant polyphony that runs throughout the work, and the motto from Beethoven's Fifth Symphony.[9] The significance of Beethoven's contribution is established at the close of the "Emerson" essay:

> There is an "oracle" at the beginning of the *Fifth Symphony*; in those four notes lies one of Beethoven's greatest messages. We would place its translation above the relentlessness of fate knocking at the door, above the greater human message of destiny, and strive to bring it towards the spiritual message of Emerson's revelations, even to the "common heart" of Concord—the soul of humanity knocking at the door of the divine mysteries, radiant in the faith that it *will* be opened—and the human become the divine! (*EBS* 36)

The Beethoven motive is Ives's embodiment of "substance" in the sonata. As the most widely known phrase in musical history, it metonymizes the total human effort to make a music that speaks "a language so transcendent that its heights and depths will be common to all mankind" (*EBS* 8). Set against this primal musical shape is the incessant shape-changing of the Concord material, which represents the Transcendentalists' Concord as the seedbed of indigenous American "divinities" and "place-legends" (*EBS* 101), a privileged form of the spirit of place in its striving for illumination by "flashes of transcendent beauty" (*EBS* 30).

The sonata prepares for its fusions of "the disparate halves of things" by continually working varied and fragmented forms of the Beethoven motive into the teeming Concord polyphony. There are inversions, retrogrades, retrograde inversions, rhythmic restatements with varied interval-content, separate developments of the upbeat and the downbeat—the one focused on the level ♪♪♩ rhythm, the other on the characteristic interval of a falling

---

[8] Charles Ives, prefatory note to his Second Pianoforte Sonata, "Concord, Mass., 1840–1860," 2d ed. (New York: Associated Music, 1947).

[9] The "Concord" Sonata contains certain features and nodal points of significance on which there seems to be general agreement. The broad outline of my account here agrees with both those of Henry Cowell, *Charles Ives and His Music* (New York: Oxford University Press), pp. 190–207; and Wilfrid Mellers, *Music in a New Found Land* (New York: Hillstone, 1975), pp. 48–56, though with considerable difference in emphasis and some in detail.

third—and melodic elaborations of the upbeat followed by deferred statements of the downbeat. Before long, the formal properties of the Beethoven
motive are so thoroughly disseminated into the polyphonic texture that
when the motive returns in its primary form, as it does repeatedly, it evokes
a pair of antithetical meanings. Partly defamiliarized, partly all-too-familiar,
the motive is at once an integral part of the music around it and yet something irrevocably extrinsic, an oracular intrusion. At such moments, assimilation and allusion overlap to produce a completely new object, a local abstraction that comes and goes like an epiphany:

> The leaves were falling like notes from a piano.
>
> The abstract was suddenly there and gone again.
> The negroes were playing football in the park.
> The abstract that he saw like the locust-leaves, plainly:
>
> The premiss from which all things were conclusions.
> [STEVENS, "Contrary Theses (II)"]

Ives saturates the music with this process, so much so that the to-and-fro
movement of fusion and dispersal is the only formal contour that the sonata
has. The piece as a whole forms a fantasy, in both a musical and a psychological sense, of hovering on a threshold, of expanding Stevens's "As if, as if,
as if"; it seems to fill out a gigantic generative interval in which an inchoate
pattern of integration is continually clarified and re-obscured. Yet for all its
dualistic flux, the music does embrace a controlling subtext: a generative
rhythm that "has not yet passed the border line between subconsciousness
and consciousness" (EBS 7). Through a series of highly charged transitions,
the sonata makes its way from a dialectical to an organic interplay of discourses.

In the first movement, "Emerson," the initial juxtaposition of materials
sets the local and the absolute in radical opposition. The music begins as the
germinal Concord figure—a chain of descending seconds and thirds—
sounds forcefully in the bass under an ascending version of itself; this leads
without transition into free polyphonic and polyrhythmic elaboration. Before long, overlapping statements of the Beethoven motive appear in the
outer voices of a four-part texture, but the counterpoint is so closely spaced
and its inner voices are so active that only a vaguely allusive cross-rhythm
reaches the ear before heavy chords embark on a variation of the opening
chain of intervals. Not to be stifled so easily, the Beethoven motive plunges
abruptly to the lowest registers of the bass and cuts across the rhapsodic, unfocused flow of the Concord music with startling rhythmic violence (Ex.
46a). Unmistakable this time, the "oracle" presents its first epiphany as a
visceral jolt.

As "Emerson" proceeds, this extravagant antithesis slowly yields to a ten-

tative integration. Returning at unpredictable intervals, the Beethoven motive undoes its original rhythmic character a bit at a time. There is no hurry
about this, and no very marked beginning to the process, which is not meant
to be followed in action but recognized and wondered at in retrospect. For a
while, the motive continues to clash with the Concord material in the most
drastic of terms. The opposed motivic statements do not coincide anywhere;
they are metrically free, they form polyrhythms with each other, and they

EXAMPLE 46.   Ives, "Concord" Sonata, rhythmic pattern of "Emerson."

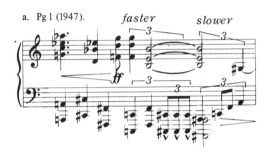

d. pg. 18

e. pg. 19

* to be heard as a kind of an overtone

avoid rhythmic unisons (overlapping downbeats). Then, imperceptibly, a *rapprochement* develops as now one, now another of these sources of discontinuity is removed. By the close of the movement, a full reversal has taken place; the basic materials of the music dovetail smoothly. On its last appearances, the Beethoven motive assimilates itself to a rhythmic texture that is almost Classical. Submitting to a foursquare beat set by the Concord material, the motive domesticates its polyrhythms into syncopations and consistently resolves its syncopated attacks into rhythmic unisons. Example 46 gives an abbreviated outline of the overall pattern of transformation.

Ives's turn from disjunction to integration in rhythmic texture has a harmonic counterpart that is based on the tonal definition of the Beethoven motive. The harmonic process develops independently of the rhythmic one, but begins and ends in consort with it. When the Beethoven motive first breaks into the foreground, the tonal memory associated with it comes into conflict with the intuitive, pre-tonal, linear harmony that marks the opening of "Emerson." Yet the tonal memory itself is discordant—thrown out of tune as far as possible; the motive is bargained away dialectically like one of Ives's hymns or rags. At the height of a massive *crescendo*, Ives transposes Beethoven's opening upbeat by a tritone and alters the descent of the downbeat from a major to a minor third (Ex. 46a). No one needs perfect pitch to hear so frank a distortion of those particular four notes or to connect the transposition antithetically to the sound of Beethoven's original music. The connection—experienced mainly as a feeling of discomfort—proves to be prophetic. In its later appearances, the motive exhausts the total chromatic with some help from its variants, but its ultimate point of reference remains the form of its original statement in the Fifth Symphony, G–E♭. About a third of the way through the movement, and again just before the close, a double statement of the G–E♭ motive is hammered out *fortissimo* as part of a variously ornamented dominant progression in D major (Ex. 47). The shift from allusion to quotation corresponds to the resolution of a large-scale dissonance. With this esthetically risky gesture, Ives at once endows the sonata

EXAMPLE 47.   Ives, "Concord" Sonata, "Emerson."

with a tonic, the emergent D major, and encapsulates the harmonic design of "Emerson," which represents that tonic by its dominant alone. At the same time, by assimilating the motive in its pristine form to a progression that substitutes for a decisive cadence to the tonic (ii⁹–V⁷ for V⁷–I), Ives gives the sonata's overarching fusion of materials a specifically cadential value on the largest scale, something that will be fully realized in the cadence that finally emerges at the end of the last movement. A similar feeling of enormously extended resolution even plays at this point about the historical, "intertextual" relationship of the music to Beethoven's Fifth. The Classical tonality that shapes the symphony is transformed, *relocated,* within the quasi-improvisatory dissonant polyphony that drives the sonata.

The concluding measures of "Emerson" confirm both the harmonic integration and the rhythmic one, yet they also suggest that something is still missing, still inaccessible. The coda is preceded by an eerie passage in which an obbligato viola whispers *pianissimo* for two measures, as if to announce the sought-for fusion by "transcending" the instrumental sonority of the sonata. The viola part consists of slowly descending semitone figuration, accented so as to articulate a pair of medium-range descents, C–B–B♭ and A♭-

G-F♯. The melodic contour alludes to the characteristic motion of the Concord figure but "tightens" its interval structure, while the pairing of the semitonal groups a descending third apart echoes the characteristic interval of the Beethoven motive. After this, the whole harmonic career of the motive is encapsulated as varied forms of Ives's opening tritone transposition softly return above the Concord figure; these lead directly to a statement of the original G–E♭ motive that falls just shy of an A-major resolution. A lyrical arpeggio then swirls upward over four octaves, its seemingly unfocused dissonances eventually settling into a full dominant-thirteenth chord of D major with the eleventh altered from D to D♯. The resolution of the D♯ dissonance substitutes for a cadential resolution of the chord as the Beethoven motive tolls faintly over the sustained notes of the arpeggio in the minor-third form F–D, the pitch of its sequential continuation in mm. 3–4 of the Fifth Symphony (Ex. 48). The large-scale process of the movement finds its

EXAMPLE 48. Ives, "Concord" Sonata, "Emerson" (notation simplified). Note the articulation of the dominant-seventh chord as the arpeggio concludes.

consummation in this quiet gesture. Bathed in tranquility, the absolute takes the local as its transient origin: it materializes, only a little changed, to resolve the contingent harmonies of place.

After this, the Beethoven motive sounds once again in its primary G–E♭ form over a quasi-cadential bass (Ex. 46). Falling from A to D♯, A to F♯, the bass points toward a harmonic resolution in D major. The D♯ is enharmonically equivalent to the E♭ of the Beethoven motive, and it seems as if the local and the absolute could achieve a final reconciliation through another resolution of D♯ to D♮. Yet in the final measure the bass slips strangely from A to F♮ and sticks there. If we want to know why, we have to recall again the motivic continuation at the beginning of Beethoven's Fifth. The measures following the arpeggio are saturated by allusions to Beethoven's G–E♭, F–D sequence, all of which break off before moving from F to D. The final bass descent is simply the last of these. Its F is a preparation for a D that never arrives, at once the announcement of a resolution and the deferral of one. D as a motivic note is represented only by the listener's half-conscious memory of the Beethoven symphony. D as a tonality is represented only by the almost subliminal chiming of its leading tone in the third C♯–E, a sonority that pervades the closing measures—"to be heard," says Ives, "as a kind of an overtone." Beethoven's motive and Ives's tonality thus join together in a ghostly polyphony of discourses, but the music displaces tonal resolution by tonal dissolution.

The two middle movements align the local and the absolute elements more loosely, allowing a period of release from the tension of seeking a perfect unity. The second movement, "Hawthorne," is said by Ives to be "phantasmal." It is meant to be dreamlike: to enter a collective or impersonal unconscious in which the local and the absolute mingle freely but distractedly, passing, so to speak, in the night. Both are contained; neither is resolved into the other. The movement, writes Ives, has to do perhaps with "something personal, which tries to be 'national' suddenly at twilight, and universal suddenly at midnight" (EBS 42). Ives's commentary places the music where terror can no longer be distinguished from delight, where "the ghost of a man who never lived" may be at one with a hymn tune that haunts a churchyard or with children's excitement on a frosty Berkshire morning; and the self, in that place, is open to the showers of the absolute in the negative sense that everything there is arbitrary.

The pandemonic reign of this arbitrariness begins with a dissonant pinwheel, as flurries of upper notes revolve ever faster and louder over a nonharmonic ostinato bass; the whirling energy then fans out into a cacophonic free-for-all. Before too long, a hollow and mysterious ne plus ultra emerges as a hushed series of black-note tone clusters sounds in the high treble—not struck but gently set vibrating by depressing a strip of board on the keys. Since Ives says that "[t]he use of the sustaining pedal is almost constantly required" in "Hawthorne," these dim sonorities should combine to form a quivering blur, laden with overtones from the lower voices, which becomes a twelve-tone cloud as the pp black-note clusters pivot around an ff white-note one. At the limit of its uniqueness, the local thus appears as an undifferentiated Ur-sound, a "verticalized" form of the chromatically saturated polyphony of "Emerson." Spinning madly on, the movement conjures up fleeting scraps of half-remembered tunes that blend with each other and dissolve. The Beethoven motive comes and goes, sometimes careening into ragtime and then bouncing away, without integration. During one memorable episode, it slithers in and around a melody that is trying very hard to be "Columbia, The Gem of the Ocean." Eventually, the music finds an end, though not an obviously impossible closure, by disintegrating once more into nonharmonic noise.

Like "Hawthorne," the third movement—"The Alcotts"—is hyperbolical: it makes self-conscious nostalgia of the unity and serenity to follow in the finale ("Thoreau"), as "Hawthorne" makes delirium of the multiplicity and dialectical conflict that precedes it in "Emerson." The unsheltered, un-localized space of chaotic memory and fantasy gives way here to the shel-tered parlor at "Orchard House" where, writes Ives, stands "the spinet that Thoreau gave and where Beth played the Scotch airs and played at the *Fifth Symphony*" (*EBS* 47). The "played-at" Fifth Symphony opens the movement calmly over off-key hymn harmonies; as Wilfrid Mellers observes, its bi-tonal sweetness in this guise both mimics the sound of an out-of-tune piano and evokes a feeling of domestic stability.[10] But the Beethoven motive can only be travestied by its domestication, and it accordingly tends to disinte-grate as the music proceeds. Enervated by the parlor harmonies, its rhythm most often pursues a kind of fuzzy half-life, more "manner" than "sub-stance." Nonetheless, Ives does find a "spiritual sturdiness" in the Alcott's coziness, "a kind of common triad of the New England homestead" (*EBS* 47). Near the close of the movement, this spirituality asserts itself with a modalized C-major statement of the Beethoven motive in majestic parallel triads. Still nostalgically hymnlike in feeling, yet reunited with substance by sheer naïve panache, the theme suddenly seems to transfigure the domestic simplicities that have denatured it. This reversal of values is genuinely re-velatory, but it necessarily fades back into the homespun sounds of the par-lor. C major falls out of tune again as the melodic line descends softly over a group of B♭ triads and resolves onto a lingering B♭. Then another fade, this time back to the C-major triad, ends the movement, as if the domestic B♭ sonority had been dissipated by the force of a vision that it could not hope to sustain.

With the final movement, Ives turns from recalling the piano that Tho-reau gave, to depicting Thoreau himself as a transcendental musician: a composer of Æolian music (*EBS* 53), a transmitter of the monodic "har-mony" of Nature. It is through the image of Thoreau's music, intertwined with his own and with Beethoven's, that Ives will evoke "the sound / Of a right joining" that marries place to substance.

In "Thoreau," the Beethoven motive is not sounded until the close, but the persistence of a kind of pre-echo of it turns this deferral into a form of germination. After an interval of indefiniteness, built of soft arpeggios and swirling figures, the music begins to unfold over a tranquilly ascending os-tinato bass. Tolling recurrently through the movement to hint at some vi-sionary "elevation," this three-note figure begins with a rising third that gradually establishes itself as a mirror-image of the distinctive falling third of the Beethoven motive, a role foreshadowed by the inversions and retro-

---

[10] Mellers, *Music in a New Found Land*, p. 53.

grade inversions of the motive in the first movement (Ex. 49).[11] A second ostinato, emerging between statements of the first, sustains the texture of allusion. A motivic descent of a third, itself stated in thirds, continues to emphasize that interval over a tolling bass (marked "evenly and perverse-

EXAMPLE 49. Ives, "Concord" Sonata, "Thoreau."

ly"), in which the triple upbeat of the Beethoven motive seems to extend itself indefinitely (Ex. 50). The music is meant to evoke a Thoreauvian revery, and as it takes its slow course "through an autumn day of Indian summer" (*EBS* 67), the upper voices seem to rise continually above and out of the latent presence of the Beethoven motive—fragmented and dissociated—in the bass. To complement the first movement, where the music of the abso-

EXAMPLE 50. Ives, "Concord" Sonata, "Thoreau."

(*evenly and perversely*)

[11] Mellers (*Music in a New Found Land,* p. 55) calls the ostinato an inversion of the Beethoven motive, but it is only that in a rather abstract way (explained by Cowell). What one hears is a trace, half after–image, half premonition, which comes from the foregrounding of the rising interval.

lute gradually reoriginates itself from within the ever-changing multiplicity of local sounds, the music of place here finds its own origin in the fixed, embryonic forms of the absolute.

"Thoreau" now rises to a final synthesis by transferring its polyphonic play of origination to a new area, the fluctuating contour of a uniquely realized single voice. Almost imperceptibly at first, a tranquil melody is played by an obbligato flute. Ives's essay identifies this music with the sound of Thoreau's flute as it rises over Walden Pond at the end of the day's meditation: "It is darker—the poet's flute is heard out over the pond and Walden ... faintly echoes—is it a transcendental tune of Concord?" (*EBS* 69). The answer to that is "Yes," of course, as "Concord" assumes a double meaning. In the sound of Thoreau's magic flute, the chains of seconds and thirds that form the music of place are seamlessly woven together with the Beethoven motive. The movement of origination becomes mutual and continuous, as the local and absolute themes give way to each other in turn, each a momentary prelude, then postlude, to the other. In its gently sustained act of fusion, this "transcendental tune" provides a consummatory undoing of the fierce collision of materials with which the sonata opens. When the flute falls silent, the fusion is lost; but it has been, to borrow another phrase from Stevens, for a moment final.

Both the finality and the precariousness of this resolution are implicit in the subtle harmonic design of the movement. Ives repeatedly shapes the dissonant polyphony of "Thoreau" to suggest D major as a tonal center and G major/minor as its subdominant. The ostinato, A–C–G, reinforces and sustains the orientation, both by its melodic emphasis on G and by its sonority as an incipient dominant seventh of D. The harmonic role of the flute melody is to coax the tonic, subdominant, and dominant-seventh areas into an exemplary "transcendental" unity. The melody itself is in G minor[12]— more, it is a transparent elaboration of the G-minor triad—and it repeatedly rises to sound the Beethoven motive on the third, D–B♭. The continuity of local and absolute elements is suggested by the recurrent gesture illustrated in Example 51, where a dotted figure based on the D-B♭ third emerges as the tail of the Concord melody and is immediately transformed into the Beethoven motive. At first, the accompaniment during this episode is a lyrical example of freely dissonant voice-leading marked by a slight polyrhythmic displacement from the contour of the melody. Then—after a *crescendo* that half drowns out the flute, as if we had only imagined it—the rising ostinato emerges, this time in the new form shown in Example 52, and the "right joining" perfects itself. By synchronizing its accentual pattern with that of the melody, the softly rocking figure adds tranquility where none was felt to be lacking. Its harmony deepens this feeling that a core of stability has been touched, for the ostinato now outlines a dominant-ninth chord

---

[12] Not, as Mellers says (*Music in a New Found Land*, p. 55), "in or near B♭."

EXAMPLE 51. Ives, "Concord" Sonata, "Thoreau" (flute only).

EXAMPLE 52. Ives, "Concord" Sonata, "Thoreau."

of D major, and with each recurrence it explicitly raises its C♮ to C♯ in order to confirm the dominant-seventh function that it has intimated throughout the movement. The G minor of the melody is thus disclosed as an elaboration of the dissonant tone of the dominant-seventh chord. In sum, the flute passage enacts a full integration in every expressive dimension—gestural, structural, rhythmic, melodic, and harmonic.

The stage is now set for a closing resolution. "Thoreau" is the only one of the four movements to end with a definite key-feeling, not a deferred or ambiguous harmony; only after nearly fifty minutes of music will the sonata allow any sense of closure. The concluding D-major sonority emerges from the quick, irridescent shimmer of a dominant arpeggio, identical to the one that opens the movement (Ex. 53); the cadential resolution to the tonic from this huge four-octave chord represents a specific fulfillment of the unfinished D-major cadence that closes "Emerson." As the ostinato sounds in the bass for the last time, a lingering C♯ in the treble resolves into a series of D–A fifths that spell out the rhythm of the Beethoven motive; a dying murmur in the middle voices follows with a last touch of subdominant coloration, which is absorbed into the prevailing sonority. The last note to sound is a

EXAMPLE 53.   Ives, "Concord" Sonata, "Thoreau" (notation simplified).

prolonged C♯, the leading tone of D, which forms a seventh above the bass. This sonority can only confirm the presence of the tonic, and yet it also gives the ending a faintly phantasmal quality, like the atmosphere of rising mists described by Thoreau in the poem that Ives quotes in his commentary:

> Dew-cloth, dream-drapery,
> Drifting meadow of the air . . . .
> (quoted in *EBS* 67)

The concluding C♯ might be meant to echo and clarify the overtone-like C♯s at the close of "Emerson," which also carry a feeling of mysterious quietude. Or, since the D-major phrase at the end of "Thoreau" is a form of the Beethoven motive, the C♯ to which it leads may recall and demystify the brooding C♯ octaves in "Emerson" that introduce the Beethoven motive into the sonata. Ives's essay suggests something of the sort; "Thoreau," he writes, gazes over the water after his flute melody ends and "catches a glimpse of the 'shadow-thought' he saw in the morning's mist" (*EBS* 69). But we cannot be sure. The sonata ends in peace, not certainty; or, as Keats might have said, "It ends in Speculation."

II

Stevens's equivalent to the fusion found in Ives's transcendental tune comes not in massive ventures like the "Concord" Sonata but in poems notable for their chastened quality, a severe humility before the absolute. Yet these poems do reconcile place and spirit much as the sonata does, by bringing them into a relationship of origination. As usual, Stevens's method for this relies on the principle that the imagination works by abstraction—in this case by a pair of abstractions, one a presentation, the other a withdrawal. Stevens begins with the abstraction of imaginative naming, the act by which a local name becomes a metonym for the transfiguration of place by an absolute. He then turns to a second abstraction that disregards the place-name and identifies the absolute directly. This rhythm—we might call it naming and un-naming—at once establishes the local scene as the source of a visitation, an oracular or omphalic threshold, and finds in the absolute the ultimate ground for whatever visionary presence the local has called forth.

Stevens frequently associates naming and un-naming with rivers and river names, as if to suggest an image for the underlying rhythm by which a name will enter the poetry only to flow away as "an apostrophe that [is] not spoken." In "Thinking of a Relation between the Images of Metaphors," a local "variation" on the absolute leads to a direct intuition of the "unstated theme" as the place-name ebbs away together with the generic names appropriate to the place. The poem begins with the many-sided perception of a locality and ends with a re-perception of the same scene in the "one eye" and "one ear" of epiphany. At first, "The wood-doves are singing along the Perkiomen. / The bass lie deep, still afraid of the Indians." By the close, the many doves have become one dove, and the bass, the Perkiomen, and the Indians—who gave the river its name—have been condensed into the image of "the fisherman," an anonymous figure who stands as "the single man / In whose breast, the dove, alighting, would grow still." The religious overtones of the alighting dove are not casual; Stevens, like Ives, is trying to sacralize consciousness by committing it to "place-legends." In "This Solitude of Cataracts," the speaker desires to transcendentalize the seeming stillness of a river that is "Fixed like a lake on which the wild ducks fluttered, / Ruffling its common reflections, thought-like Monadnocks." His goal is the perfect fixity found in the unnamed form of what he sees: "a permanent realization, without any wild ducks / Or mountains that were not mountains," a location at "the azury center of time." And in "Extraordinary References," "The cool sun of the Tulpehocken refers / To its barbed, barbarous rising and has peace." The Tulpehocken fuses the violent history of place—the ancestral territory of Stevens's family, to be exact—with the peace of the imagination that inherits the place-legends. This fusion of barbarous origins and cool distance is transferred from place to person as the poem proceeds:

> *My Jacomyntje! This first spring after the war,*
> *In which your father died, still breathes for him*
> *And breathes again for us a fragile breath.*

Fragility is paramount here, as "a second-hand Vertumnus / Creates an equilibrium"; but even a second-hand Vertumnus is a spirit, a *genius loci* in "the inherited garden," and the equilibrium is real. The poem closes by un-naming Jacomyntje, turning her into a personification of the vulnerable local self adorned with its imaginative protections: "The child's three ribbons are in her plaited hair."

Perhaps the poem that most richly embodies the rhythm of naming and un-naming is "The River of Rivers in Connecticut":

> There is a great river this side of Stygia,
> Before one comes to the first black cataracts
> And trees that lack the intelligence of trees.
>
> In that river, far this side of Stygia,
> The mere flowing of the water is a gayety,
> Flashing and flashing in the sun. On its banks,
>
> No shadow walks. The river is fateful,
> Like the last one. But there is no ferryman.
> He could not bend against its propelling force.
>
> It is not to be seen beneath the appearances
> That tell of it. The steeple at Farmington
> Stands glistening and Haddam shines and sways.
>
> It is the third commonness with light and air,
> A curriculum, a vigor, a local abstraction . . .
> Call it, once more, a river, an unnamed flowing,
>
> Space-filled, reflecting the seasons, the folk-lore
> Of each of the senses; call it, again and again,
> The river that flows nowhere, like a sea.

Stevens's river of rivers is a form of the absolute that is constantly moving on the threshold of a locality. It is both a metaphor and a presence, an imaginative current or "curriculum" and a flowing body of water in Connecticut, something "not to be seen beneath the appearances that tell of it" and a dazzling vision that flashes and flashes in the sun. Most of all, and poignantly in such a late poem, it is a resplendent "vigor" that identifies the transfiguration of place with the transient vigor of life itself. The banks of the river of rivers are free of all shadows—of gaps in the light and dwellers in the underworld. Stevens's Stygia, with its trees that lack the intelligence of trees, suggests what he elsewhere calls the "inert savoir" of the world without imagination. Place without spirit—really a parody of place, a no-place stuck onto the map of the state—constitutes the gloom of the dead. The river of rivers, translating each of the senses into folk-lore, is the "gayety" of the living. It proffers fusion not as an episode in one's "spiritual consciousness" but as the grateful experience of being.

Midway through the poem, Farmington and Haddam are named as momentary sites of the river's presence, so that the two localities fuse with the absolute that flows through them. Yet the places here are not permitted to disappear into their names. Their appearances persist: like the river, they glisten and shine, and the analogy constitutes a heightened blending of the local and the absolute that verges on identification. The river is not seen beneath the appearances that tell of it, but in them or even *as* them.

A responsive un-naming follows: an effort to diffuse the glistening of transcendence over all local sights—or sites. The result is a complementarity. In the presence of its names, the local has appeared as a visible facet of the absolute. With the names withdrawn, the transfigured landscape returns to its visionary origin and appears only as a possibility, a potential shape within the unnamed flowing. But the two perspectives are continuous, intermingled, like the flashing water and the glistening steeple. What each discloses is a river, and it is a river that we are told to call it "again and again." The incantation itself mingles—and mingles us—with the "flashing and flashing" that it celebrates; the vigor that sustains us "far this side of Stygia" is this rhythm of continuities. Naming and un-naming are to be fused in a unique epithet that resolves "the third commonness with light and air" into a tangible singularity, a place without borders: the river that flows nowhere, like a sea.

The rhythms of naming and un-naming in Stevens and of mutual origination in Ives can be taken as mirror images of each other. In the flute episode of "Thoreau," what appears is a spiralling movement in which the local and the absolute have become partners or doubles, so that each arises constantly out of the other. What appears in Stevens's various river poems is a sort of reverse becoming, a flowing movement back into origin as the local is stripped away to reveal its ground in the absolute. Ives seems to see place and spirit as interchangeable grounds for each other, and the fusions that he creates for them are usually seamless. Sound-images in which local and absolute elements are so blended that neither seems to have any stylistic or metaphysical priority over the other recur throughout his works. In the finale of his Fourth Symphony, for example, the gradual superimposition of some half-a-dozen hymn tunes over the cantus-firmus-like melody of "Bethany" ("Nearer, My God, To Thee") produces a unique, densely layered sonority— a substance that is hymnlike but not a hymn. When the music turns toward closure, it is through a vocalise on "Bethany," so that the "cantus firmus"— and by implication the hymn sung in the Prelude, "Watchman, What of the Night"—is disarticulated into overvocalized song. Less majestically transcendental, but equally characteristic, is the closural move in "Washington's Birthday," a fragment of "Goodnight, Ladies" that floats away in the soft, primary string and wind colors of a solo flute and solo muted violin.

Stevens, whose Concord is the home of "Mr. Homburg" as well as of Emerson (who, of course, *is* Mr. Homburg), is more cautious, more detached than Ives about such images; as Helen Vendler once observed, he ends in uncertainty more than any other major poet.[13] The fusions that Ives represents as moments of experience, of realization, of communion, appear in Stevens as tenuous glimpses, possibilities, moments in which "The point of vision and desire are the same" ("An Ordinary Evening in New Haven," III). Stevens's poems of fusion always seem to contain a reservation, however muffled; the presence of death in "The River of Rivers," a version of *et in Arcadia ego*, is no accident. Local objects can always become obstacles to the imagination or travesties of it; absolutes can become "anonymids / Gulping for shape" ("A Lot of People Bathing in a Stream"):

> Gay is, gay was, the gay forsythia
>
> And yellow, yellow, thins the Northern blue.
> Without a name and nothing to be desired,
> If only imagined but imagined well.
>> (*Notes Toward A Supreme Fiction*,
>> "It Must Be Abstract," VI)
>
> The blue sun in his red cockade
> Walked the United States today . . . .
>> ("The News and the Weather")
>
> This structure of ideas, these ghostly sequences
> Of the mind, result only in disaster.
>> ("The Bed of Old John Zeller")

A clue to the sources of Stevens's "restlessly unhappy happiness" might lodge in the fact that his poetry of place is almost always steeped in solitude and often tinged with a sense of loss and abandonment, particularly by parental figures. Ives's music of place, in contrast, almost always refers to a communal or intimate occasion. The Whitmanesque ease with which he approaches fusion seems to be rooted in a secure unity with others that validates his "spiritual consciousness," and the plural, "layered" texture of his music may in part be a reflection of this primary sense of affiliation. The only hitch is that the unity is more past than present; it belongs to an American Eden that is already largely lost by the time that Ives has begun to compose. For Stevens, place is always a latent substitute for persons, native regions for parents. ("Extraordinary References" concedes the point; "The Auroras of Autumn" is almost confessional about it.) One of the notebook entries collected as the "Adagia" admits: "Life is an affair of people not of places. But for me life is an affair of places and that is the trouble."[14] The

---

[13] Helen Vendler, "The Qualified Assertions of Wallace Stevens," in *The Act of the Mind: Essays on the Poetry of Wallace Stevens*, edited by Roy Harvey Pearce and J. Hillis Miller (Baltimore: Johns Hopkins University Press, 1965), pp. 163–78.

[14] Wallace Stevens, *Opus Posthumous*, edited by Samuel French Morse (New York: Alfred A. Knopf, 1957), p. 158.

trouble is that Stevens's moments of fusion occur to a transcendental ego for whom no place is a true origin.

This ambivalence is exposed in "Our Stars Come From Ireland," a double poem that has been unjustly neglected, probably because the poet was at pains to be modest about it in a letter. In the first part, "Tom McGreevey, in America, Thinks of Himself as a Boy," Stevens tries to present the troublesome transcendental ego as an absolute that is born of place—though it is significant that he does so with a dramatic persona, a rarity in his work. The key to the poem is a remark that Stevens made in sending it to Thomas McGreevey himself: "When I look back, I do not really remember myself but the places in which I lived and things there with which I was familiar."[15] McGreevey's thoughts in the poem are of the way that his boyhood imagination turned "him that I loved" into a place-spirit, thereby "making" the place:

> Out of him that I loved,
> Mal Bay I made,
> I made Mal Bay
> And him in that water.

Place is thus an embodied denial of separation from the loved figure, for whom a subsequent couplet strongly suggests a paternal identity:

> Out of him I made Mal Bay
> And not a bald and tasselled saint.

Another late poem, "Celle qui fût Héaulmiette," follows a similar tack:

> Into that native shield she slid,
> Mistress of an idea, child
> Of a mother with vague severed arms
> And of a father bearded in his fire.

As an adult, Tom announces, "I live in Pennsylvania," and then goes on to "make" his new region with an act of imaginative naming. But it is probably Stevens's own childhood voice that sounds here, intruding on the poem to break its narrative fiction; McGreevey lived in Ireland:

> The stars are washing up from Ireland
> And through and over the puddles of Swatara
> And Schuylkill. The sound of him
> Comes from a great distance and is heard.

---

[15] Wallace Stevens, *The Collected Letters*, edited by Holly Stevens (New York: Alfred A. Knopf, 1966), p. 608.

As the stars wash up "through and over" Swatara and Schuylkill, they come from Pennsylvania as well as from Ireland, and as they do the paternal source of self becomes an animate presence in the new locality. The stars, visible at different times from both County Kerry and Pennsylvania, presences moving "through and over" the rivers as both distant lights and near reflections, are figures of pure continuity like the river of rivers in Connecticut, and they, too, compose a "third commonness" that identifies itself with glittering places. It is by naming Swatara and Schuylkill in the presence of this starry thirdness that Tom McGreevey connects his boyhood and adult identities as parts of a larger imaginative self. As the echo of the paternal voice confirms, he makes Pennsylvania a new birthplace "of him / And out of myself," and he succeeds in belonging there, only half in solitude.

The second poem, "The Westwardness of Everything," both re-enacts the first and deconstructs it. Tom McGreevey's fusion of place with the continuity of selfhood reappears abstractly as an absorption of both place and selfhood into a principle of pure origination. All the places that Tom has "made" are un-named and dissolved into the universal presences of sky and water. The western places, Pennsylvania, Swatara, and Schuylkill, become "westwardness"; the eastern ones, Mal Bay, Tarbert, and Kerry, become an "east" that paradoxically appears within the westwardness. No persons enter the poem at all, let alone loved ones; "he" and "I" become simply "the mind." As for the stars, they are seen here only on the edge of vanishing into the dawn—and not a natural dawn but a transcendental one that would constitute "a final change" in which "The ocean breathed out morning in one breath." This etherialized, pneumic morning would be a permanent form of beginning from which nothing would begin, an origin that produced only itself. Coming from Ireland, the stars will also have come away from place itself and faded into an absolute time, a shift that has its cost in a recognition, if not a feeling, of bereavement; the stars, says Stevens, are "Like beautiful and abandoned refugees." Their abandonment is reflected, too, in the rhetorical movement of the poem, which names the "nights full of the green stars from Ireland" only at the beginning, then piles up descriptive and appositive phrases until the object of reference becomes tenuous, almost forgotten by both the poem and the reader. But it is not clear at the close whether the second poem is a consummation of the first or a chilly retreat from it, a completion or an evasion.

III

The scene of fusion, the archetypal Walden Pond where the local and the absolute join in Stevens and Ives, is marked by a pervasive feeling of remoteness. It appears under the spell of a fluid, fantasy-tinged perception that both poet and composer tend to symbolize with bodies of water—a Schuylkill in mid-earth, the Housatonic at Stockbridge. There is a sense of blurred edges, of life in suspension, as if this "shadowy ground," in Wordsworth's phrase, were neither a place nor a state of mind but something in between; Whitman presents the Paumanok of "Out of the Cradle Endlessly Rocking" and "As I Ebb'd with the Ocean of Life" as the same sort of intermediate space. These features perhaps explain why the use of place-names as imaginative abstractions is largely missing from the work of Stevens's American contemporaries. Neither William Carlos Williams nor Hart Crane, in particular—poets whose commanding desire is to marry the local and the absolute—is willing to accept the austerity, to make the dialectical bargains, of the fusion in Stevens.

Williams is such a strenuous nominalist that his place-names have no abstract dimension: they are sounds rather than words, parts of the local scene rather than encapsulations of it. A locality in Williams's poetry is not really a place but a process, a flow of energies saturated in the details of experience. What makes the local into an absolute—and Williams quotes Dewey to the effect that the local is the only absolute—is the irresistible feeling of physical movement that it elicits in a poem.[16] The "dance" of an imaginative "idiom," the unmetrical, asyntactical pirouette of the poetic line, constitutes "a method springing so freshly from the local conditions that determine it" that it becomes epiphanic:

> The red brick monastery in
> the suburbs over against the dust–
> hung acreage of the unfinished
> and all but subterranean
>
> munitions plant; those high
> brick walls . . . .
> ("The Semblables")

It is striking that at the climax of *Paterson*, the epic he devoted to this very issue, Williams does introduce a scene of fusion—names, remoteness, water, even a symbolic stair—to portray a locality that is only absolute because it is lost forever:

> Just off Gun Mill yard, on the gully
> was a long rustic winding stair leading
> to a cliff on the opposite side of the river.
> At the top was Fyfield's tavern—watching
> the birds flutter and bathe in the little
> pools in the rocks formed by the falling
> mist—from the Falls.
> (Book IV)

---

[16] For a discussion see Miller, *Poets of Reality*, pp. 192–304.

The early-American arcadia that northern New Jersey once was lingers metonymically here in the tenseless flutter of birds and in the play of mist over the Passaic Falls.

With Hart Crane, the act of naming remains crucial, but only when it is radically displaced. *The Bridge*, Crane's major attempt at fusion, takes a local object as its central symbol, but refuses to name it; the poetry determines the Brooklyn Bridge as a site of the absolute by withholding its proper name and substituting a series of metaphorical, metonymic, or mythic equivalents. In the Proem, the bridge is addressed as "thee" and "thou," and apostrophized with periphrases—"O harp and altar, of the fury fused!"—but it remains a majestic "anonymid" except in the title, "To Brooklyn Bridge." In the closing poem, "Atlantis," mythic naming takes over; Tyre and Troy are named, but not New York, and the bridge is apotheosized, thrust into timeless otherness, by the transference of names from the "Cathay" of the imagination:

> O Answerer of all—Anemone—
> Now while thy petals spend suns around us, hold
> (O Thou whose radiance doth inherit me)
> Atlantis,—hold thy floating singer late!

When Crane does use local place-names in *The Bridge*, they tend to evoke a degraded landscape that threatens to remain beyond the redeeming embrace of myth:

> Outside a wharf truck nearly ran him down
> —he lunged up Bowery way while the dawn
> was putting the Statue of Liberty out—that
> torch of hers you know—
>
> I started walking home across the Bridge . . . .
> ("Cutty Sark")

Crane's periphrastic method gains an extravagance and intensity, as Williams's indifference to name-magic allows him a vital immersion in place, that is denied to Stevens. Yet neither Crane nor Williams has a secure access to that unique third place where the local and the absolute fuse.

One poet who does have such access is Theodore Roethke, whose "A Rouse for Stevens (To Be Sung in a Young Poets' Saloon)" ends with the couplet,

> Wallace Stevens—are we *for* him?
> Brother, he's our father!

In his later work, especially in "North American Sequence," Roethke adapts Stevens's rhythm of naming and un-naming places and extends it metonymically to generic names, as Stevens himself does in "Thinking of a Relation." The poems in "North American Sequence" follow a broadly regular pattern. The poet comes to a place, or remembers one, usually by water, and describes it in almost too much detail, naming its plants, its wildlife, and often the place itself. The scene troubles him as it promises to fuse both locality and the self with "the other side of light," to become "a place that leads nowhere," resonant with "the murmur of the absolute." The transcendent locality is "made" when Roethke withdraws the plethora of names— perhaps completely, perhaps almost so—and redescribes the scene in terms that refer directly to fusion, so that "the mind moves in more than one place, / In a country half-land, half-water" ("The Far Field"). It is as if the repeated act of naming were a kind of blessing that prepared for the epiphany to follow, a gesture remote in feeling from Stevens's concentrated troping on one or two names, but formally, even religiously, at one with it. In the final poem, "The Rose," the climactic un-naming recalls the scene that Ives evokes for the close of "Thoreau." First the names:

> I think of American sounds in this silence:
> On the banks of the Tombstone, the wind-harps having their say,
> The thrush singing alone, that easy bird,
> The killdeer whistling away from me,
> The mimetic chortling of the catbird
> Down in the corner of the garden, among the raggedy lilacs.

This rhapsodic catalogue (there is much more of it) is an attempt to totalize, to summon up an absolute by summing up local ecstasies. But it is not associated with fulfillment: "Beautiful my desire, and the place of my desire." Fusion comes only when Roethke strips the named birds from the trees and designates the absolute with nakedly paradoxical and abstract language:

> Among the half-dead trees, I came upon the true ease of myself,
> As if another man appeared out of the depths of my being,
> And I stood outside myself,
> Beyond becoming and perishing,
> A something wholly other,
> As if I swayed out on the wildest wave alive,
> And yet was still.

Like Stevens, Roethke finds himself on the ultimate wave that is both being and being-*there* when he peels away a structure of names that he himself has provided to describe the scene of fusion.

As for Ives, his transcendental allusiveness has remained *sui generis*, though it has some points of contact with the disjunctive polyphony of Mahler and middle-period Schoenberg.[17] The music of American nationalism, represented by the "popular" style of Copland and any number of works by Virgil Thomson, is shaped by nostalgia and imitation, not by the will to fusion; its poetic counterpart would be found in Bryant rather than Whitman, in Sandburg rather than Stevens. Ives is probably closer to Stevens in his use of "place-legends" than to any composer, especially when the slightly hermetic, slightly fantastic side of fusion comes to the fore—say in the first movement of the Fourth Violin Sonata, where Ives mixes the hymn tune "Tell Me an Old, Old Story" with a fugue fragment written by his father, or in poems like Stevens's "Metaphor As Degeneration":

> The swarthy river
> That flows round the earth and through the skies,
> Twisting among the universal spaces,
>
> Is not Swatara. It is being.
> That is the flock-flecked river, the water,
> The blown sheen—or is it air?

It is, by the way, typical that Stevens cannot identify the "flock-flecked river" as being until he has denied it the name of Swatara, that obscure little stream just outside of Harrisburg which was his private symbol for native place.

Perhaps the best way to summarize Ives's and Stevens's approach to the problem of fusion is to reconsider two of their central images. Stevens's river of rivers and Ives's flute melody in "Thoreau,"—the epitomes of local abstraction in the two men's work—share certain primary features. Both of them trespass on the boundaries of the work of art: one by the call for an incantatory recognition beyond the close of the poem, the other by its instrumental difference from the music around it. Both, too, trespass on boundaries within the work: Ives's by combining the local and absolute themes into a single melodic line, and Stevens's by flowing nowhere, like a sea. The role of these "trespass images" is to effect a continual reversal of our perception of them. Apprehended as local—the glisten at Farmington, Thoreau's flute—they disclose themselves as absolutes, flowing nowhere, weaving-in the Beethoven motive. Apprehended as absolutes, they reverse the process: becoming Farmington and Haddam, unfolding the local theme.

---

[17] But Ferruccio Busoni, in a pair of important works—the *Fantasia Contrapuntistica* for piano (1910) and the Fifth Sonatina for Piano (1919)—makes structural use of material from Bach that is comparable to Ives's use of Beethoven in the "Concord" Sonata. In addition, both Richard Strauss (in his *Metamorphosen* for 23 strings, 1945) and Sir Michael Tippett (in his Third Symphony and Third Piano Sonata) draw, like Ives, on material from Beethoven.

Their ultimate trespass, it seems, is on the boundaries of the consciousness that tries to contain them. These images, representing the end of striving, are plain and tranquil. A long way from violence, they are in both men's work the final maturity of our desire.

7

Song as Insight—John Ashbery, Elliott Carter, and Orpheus

Saxifrage is my flower
That breaks the rocks.

(W.C. WILLIAMS, "A Sort of Song")

Commenting on his 1978 setting of John Ashbery's poem "Syringa," Elliott Carter suggests that his music is devoted not only to the poem itself but also to "the subliminal background that might be evoked in the mind of a reader."[1] The remark is not meant lightly. Earlier, the ways in which vocal music deconstructs its texts suggested the usefulness of hearing songs as "readings" in an agonic and dramatic sense of the term. What Carter proposes, however, is to put his composition in the subjective position of a hypothetical reader: to "compose" the reading process itself. To organize this substitution—we might say impersonation—Carter grants the text the "classical" privilege of directing the reader's thoughts. He presents his song as an image for the pattern of consciousness that the text might be said to embody.

A song composed along these lines is obviously a form of "translation," but not just any form. Difference, we might agree, is the imperative of song; in sheerly esthetic terms, to ignore it is to court sentimentality or melodrama—Berlioz finding the first, perhaps, in "Le Spectre de la rose" from *Nuits d'eté* and Mahler the second in "Ich hab' ein glühend Messer" from the *Wayfarer* cycle, to take only distinguished examples. But a translation can produce the effect of difference if its object is not to reconstruct the manifest elements of the text, but only the latent ones. As my language here suggests, the closest analogue to this "analytic" form of translation is Freudian dream interpretation, though there may be nothing psychoanalytic about the "latent content" evoked by such a song. The aim, in both cases, is a kind of insight, a recovery of what is unapparent, though not necessarily concealed. In the case of "Syringa," Carter's musical insight reveals a good deal about

---

[1] Elliott Carter, "Syringa" (New York: Associated Music Publishers, 1981), p. iii.

Ashbery's style. It intercepts the poet's concern with "the way time feels as it passes,"[2] his reshuffling and remodeling of the forms of subjectivity, and even his famous difficulty. When the musical and poetic versions of "Syringa" are put together, moreover, they mirror each other in giving the outline of a radical postmodernist esthetic—an esthetic of simultaneity that depends on what Stevens might have called "a tumult of integrations."

II

Since his first String Quartet of 1951, Carter has built his compositions by combining instrumental lines or groupings that are entirely independent of each other. This style is perhaps best heard as an imaginative extension of the basic musical principle of the independence of parts: the demand that melody, bass, and inner voices develop in such a way that they both blend together and retain their individual identities. The projection of such independence onto the broad plane of dramatic gesture and structural meaning has roots in the Venetian polychoral music of the Renaissance and anticipations in both the late quartets of Beethoven and in Mahler's symphonies. But the real progenitor of the style is Ives, in such works as the Second String Quartet, the Fourth Symphony, and *The Unanswered Question*. Carter has never been reluctant to acknowledge the connection: "I have always been fascinated," he once wrote, "by the polyrhythmic aspect of Ives's music, as well as its multiple layering."[3] But Carter has also found himself "perplexed" by "the disturbing lack of musical and stylistic continuity" in Ives, and his own style can be heard as an attempt to give an organic, formally elegant significance to the raw material of Ives's innovations.

Not that Carter is afraid of disjunction; far from it. His layered voices are so independent that they may be sounded simultaneously in different meters, with different thematic or intervallic material, and in tempos that change at different rates. His Third String Quartet (1971), for example, is composed out of two duos, a four-movement sequence for violin and cello in quasi-*rubato* style, and a six-movement sequence for violin and viola in strict time. Seated at opposite ends of the concert stage, the two groups break up their characteristic materials into fragments, shifting back and forth from one to another. The result, says Carter, is "a constant interlacing of moods and materials; for the change within either duo from one movement to another always occurs while the other duo is carrying on the same

[2] John Ashbery, quoted by Richard Kostelanitz in "How To Be A Difficult Poet," *The New York Times Magazine* (May 23, 1976): 18–33.

[3] Elliott Carter, quoted by Vivian Perlis in her *Charles Ives Remembered: An Oral History* (New York: Norton, 1976), p. 145.

movement."[4] Similarly, in the Concerto for Orchestra (1969), all four movements generally sound at once, differentiated by the sonority of the instrumental groupings and by the varied access of each movement to the foreground. The result of arrangements like these is to draw attention away from the linear dimension of the music, its measured propulsion through time, and to emphasize its vertical dimension—not in the pitch-centered terms that define harmony, but as a continuous sphere of activity in which the layers interact, a "tonality" of gesture. Musical time becomes a projected form of "humanly experienced time" (*WEC* 275), "a unity of lived experience" that embraces constant change. One listens hardest to the shifting textures and images produced by the superimposition of voices that sometimes overhear and sometimes ignore each other, but always pursue the structural rhythm that is theirs alone.

III

To see how this multiply layered, polyvocal style comes to impersonate an insightful reader of Ashbery's "Syringa," it is necessary to start where the music does, with an analysis of the poem. Many of Ashbery's poems are elegiac, and they can often be read as attempts to bring together antithetical ways of responding to a loss. Ashbery is capable of a meditative pathos that has the severity of the late Stevens:

> —and winter, the twitter
> Of cold stars at the pane, that describes with broad gestures
> This state of being that is not so big after all.
> ("Summer," *DD* 20)[5]

But his poetry is set in an anti-elegiac time that is constantly leading back "churlishly into life, / Returning, as to the scene of a crime" ("Rural Objects," *DD*, 44). Somehow, both the poignancy of memory and the "free giving and taking" of presence must saturate the poem:

> Who cares about what was there before? There is no going back,
> For standing still means death, and life is moving on,
> Moving on towards death. But sometimes standing still is also life.
> ("The Bungalows," *DD* 70)

---

[4] Elliott Carter, *Writings of Elliott Carter*, compiled and edited by Else Stone and Kurt Stone (Bloomington: Indiana University Press, 1977), p. 320. (*WEC* in text.)

[5] The abbreviations for Ashbery's volumes in the text are as follows: *DD: The Double Dream of Spring* (New York: Dutton, 1970); *SP: Self-Portrait in a Convex Mirror* (New York: Viking, 1975); *HD: Houseboat Days* (New York: Viking, 1977); *AWK: As We Know* (New York: Viking/Penguin, 1979).

"Syringa," a reflection on the myth of Orpheus and Eurydice, is devoted
to this problem. Its solution is to use Orpheus's loss of Eurydice as a deliberately unsubtle metaphor for a personal loss of the speaker's, at the same
time as it declines ever to identify the speaker's loss, or even to allude to it
until the final lines, at which point the personal loss is "no longer / Material
for a poem." The effect of this is slightly dizzying. Someone who meditates
on Orpheus's loss to escape the burden of his own loss is actually just pretending to meditate on Orpheus. The speaker in Ashbery's poem, however,
is *not* pretending that; he is only *pretending* to pretend it. The personal loss
is an open secret; the tale of Orpheus that hides its identity is also an exposure of its presence. As a result, the speaker's refusal to refer to his own loss
does not seem evasive; it seems both ascetic and refreshing, as the elegy casts
off the implicit consolations of personal pathos—praise, memory, understanding—in favor of a loosely focused stream of pastoral and mythic images. At the same time, Orpheus's loss becomes a topic of authentic concern
in the poem, not just a pretext. The poem is, in effect, polyvocal. It has a
meditative voice that engages in a tranquil, often playful consideration of
the problem of loss as presented by Orpheus, and it has an elegiac voice, full
of lament and desire, that uses the Orpheus myth to utter "hidden syllables"
of personal sorrow.

These two voices are always moving in opposite directions. The elegiac
voice, which is to some degree the voice of Orpheus himself, is always retrospective, always "coming back / To the mooring of starting out" ("Soonest
Mended, *DD* 19), the lost past. Against this, the meditative voice poses a refusal to overinvest the self in the "stalled moment" of remembered happiness. Where the elegiac voice resists the passing of time, the meditative
voice seeks to consent to time's every motion, to ask for nothing more than
the "flowing" and "fleeting." Against an Orphean time, it sets a Heraclitean
one. Despite this divergence, however, the two voices of the poem cannot be
separated from each other. One often fades into the other within the movement of a single sentence, and the personal allegory that is always latent renders many passages "undecidable" in tone:

> Of course Eurydice vanished into the shade;
> She would have even if he hadn't turned around.
> No use standing there like a gray stone toga as the whole wheel
> Of recorded history flashes past, struck dumb . . . .
> (*HD* 69)

The conventional way to put this would be to call the speaker ambivalent,
but it is more accurate to say that the two voices give the impression of simultaneity. Ambivalence implies conflict; the poem discloses none. Its feeling-tone is a unity, a singularity; but it is polyvocal. Its two voices compose

only one utterance—just as, say, Carter's Third Quartet is not itself a pair of duos, but music polyvocally *composed* of two duos.

IV

Ashbery's polyvocal texture suggests a "soft" division of the ego, one that appears as a fluidity, not a splitting. The poem neither conceals nor exposes this undulation of mind, allowing it, instead, to blur point of view, to loosen syntactical connections, to elongate the line. Carter's music explicitly re-situates these features in the ego-state that supports them.

"Syringa" is composed for mezzo-soprano, bass, and chamber ensemble. The mezzo takes on the role of the meditative voice of the poem, and it is she who sings Ashbery's text. In music that is simple, graceful, and generally quiet, she articulates each line, each word, with great clarity. Her part, which Bayan Northcott calls "the most conjunct and rhythmically uncomplex melodic line [Carter] has composed since the 1940s," sustains a feeling of unforced contemplativeness that smooths out the often paratactic movement of Ashbery's sentences.[6] Passing through the text without repetition or embellishment, it embodies the superpersonal consent to the passing of time that wants to surrender the image of Eurydice. The mezzo's polyvocal partner is, of course, the bass. His rhythmically independent part realizes the Orphean voice of the poem, filling in the subliminal background that Carter situates in the reading process. The bass intones an agitated, complex, mournful vocal line in ancient Greek, in a melismatic style that suggests an archaic litany. With his impassioned chanting, lingering over the dead in a dead language, he embodies the will to lament, the exaltation of regret, that characterizes Orpheus in the poem and constitutes—for the meditative voice—his "mistake."

Carter differentiates these two voices by giving each one its own repertoire of characteristic intervals and expressive gestures. The bass, as befits his Orphean impatience of limits, has a virtually unlimited supply of melodic and declamatory shapes at his disposal. Those that recur are sharply expressive: oscillations of large intervals in longer note-values; melismatic concentrations of smaller intervals in shorter note-values; the *Tristan*-like inflection of a rising minor sixth (Ex. 54). The bass especially emphasizes larger intervals—"specializes" in them, as Carter might say: major and minor sixths and sevenths, minor ninths, and even wider leaps form his privileged idiom. Adjacent repetition of single pitches is rare—the bass's line moves restlessly, wildly; tritones put their bleak sonority to frequent use.

The mezzo has a more limited repertoire, in keeping with the equable temperament that she represents. The part specializes in smaller intervals:

---

[6] Bayan Northcott, "First Performances: Carter's 'Syringa,' " *Tempo*, No. 128 (March 1979): 32.

EXAMPLE 54. Carter, "Syringa," mm. 201–7 (bass only).

rarely does an interval larger than a sixth appear, and second and thirds are emphasized.[7] Repetition of adjacent pitches is frequent—the mezzo's line moves smoothly, with suppleness and ease; tritones are uncommon, usually reserved for inflections of despair (Ex. 55).

A traditional composition might oppose these two voices through contrastive statements and developments, just as a traditional poem, Tennyson's "The Two Voices," for example, would work them into an antiphonal argument. In either version of "Syringa," the voices are not *opposed* to each

EXAMPLE 55. Carter, "Syringa," mm. 144–49 (mezzo only).

other at all, but *posed against* each other. Neither dialectical nor competitive, they combine without blending to form a singularity, a kind of third voice, which is the integral voice of the work—the voice one hears in how the music sounds, how the poem reads. Carter underscores the radical oneness of this voice by allowing the expressive repertoires of the mezzo and the bass to overlap. Sharing a common origin in a single consciousness, the two voices also share free access to certain intervals: semitones, perfect fourths, and perfect fifths. Occasionally, they also go "out of character" to imitate each other—the bass when his general Orphean volatility dictates, and the

[7] The mezzo's most frequent seventh is a usually rising Db–C, a kind of chromatic counterpart to the falling C–D♯ often heard in the bass.

mezzo when resignation edges over into a moment of hopelessness or when an alien voice, Apollo's, for instance, intrudes on her own.

Carter also brings the two voices together at crucial moments by means of bilingual puns.[8] The most important of these comes at the end of the piece, where the mezzo intones the last word of the poem, "summer," while the bass sings "soma, sema" (body, sign [of the soul]/tomb). This *rapprochement* of the voices is particularly poignant because it occurs as, simultaneously, the meditative voice approaches lament at last and the Orphean voice surrenders lament in exhaustion. Each voice, in other words, takes on the other's role as a way of falling silent, of finding relief from "the evil burthen of the words." In the poem, the same thing happens when the meditative voice acknowledges at last that its own loss constitutes a reanimation of the Orpheus myth, "In whose tale are hidden syllables / Of what happened . . . / In some small town, one indifferent summer." Here, in its one act of personal memory, the meditative voice accepts the identity with Orpheus which it has so far left to its polyvocal partner. Yet at the same time it forecloses all further lament by stopping the poem.

V

So far, the relationship between the voices in both Ashbery's "Syringa" and Carter's has appeared mainly as a form of antirelationship—a pure co-presence; but there is more to it than that. Ashbery's poem gives the impression that its meditative voice is at once both haunted by the figure of Orpheus and far remote from him, a condition that could be described as intimate detachment. I mean this term descriptively, but it also has a psychoanalytic meaning worth a brief digression. Intimate detachment describes the ego-state that prevails when the differentiation between a child and its mother is still recent and the child begins to use language as a way of restoring the lost unity with someone who is now "other." If we associate the heightened self-expression that this state entails with a multiplicity of styles, voices, and phrases—some tender, some aggressive—the suggestion presents itself that some of the power of the polyvocal style—not just in "Syringa" but in general—rests on the combination of desire and expressive fecundity that typifies the ego in its early days.

Throughout Ashbery's "Syringa," the figure of Orpheus fluctuates in its relationship to the meditative voice, sometimes drawing near as a latent alter ego, sometimes hardening into a mythic personage who is merely "thought-provoking":

---

[8] For a discussion of some of these, see Andrew Porter, "Famous Orpheus," *The New Yorker* (January 8, 1979): 56–62.

> The seasons are no longer what they were,
> But it is in the nature of things to be seen only once,
> As they happen along, bumping into other things, getting along
> Somehow. That's where Orpheus made his mistake.
>
> (HD 69)

One odd image even mocks Orpheus as a sentimentality, a cloud with a silver lining, at the same time as it revives him in immediate nature:

> But how late to be regretting all this, even
> Bearing in mind that regrets are always too late, too late!
> To which Orpheus, a bluish cloud with white contours,
> Replies . . .
>
> (HD 71)

In Carter's setting, one gets the similar impression that the bass is trying to "reach" the mezzo, who is most often deaf to his music, a suggestion reinforced by the positioning of the singers at opposite ends of the concert stage. Carter embodies this relationship of unachieved dialogue in his treatment of the instrumental ensemble. The tone-color of the woodwinds is permitted a certain bias toward the mezzo, but with momentary exceptions the accompaniment in "Syringa" aligns itself with the bass. The music is restlessly Orphean, polyphonically dense, and expressively varied. Carter's patterns of attack emphasize rhythmic diversity, while his instrumental voices swirl antithetically around the mezzo's, their tricky, overlapping figurations posed against the mezzo's smooth, sustained line. (A note in the score calls for a flexible interpretation of the mezzo's notated rhythms, so that the part always sounds natural.) Even the timbre of the ensemble is slanted toward the bass. "Syringa" is written for guitar, violin, viola, cello, contrabass, alto flute, English horn, bass clarinet, bass trombone, piano, and percussion. The predominant colors of the piece are accordingly dark, and the mean tessitura is low. This disposition of forces tends to isolate the mezzo in her serenity and detachment against a troubled, sometimes violently agitated background. In part, this is a background that she transcends, hovers over; in part it is the aural landscape that contains her and prompts her song.[9]

---

[9] The mezzo part of "Syringa" can be taken to mark an extreme moment in the development of Carter's polyphony. In most of the instrumental music, the various voices are enmeshed in a sonorous fabric that makes a complete individuation impossible. Extremes of differentiation are reserved for special formal or expressive purposes; the beginning of the Sonata for Cello and Piano (1948), the slow movement of the First String Quartet, and certain climactic moments of the piano piece "Night Fantasies" (1980) offer examples. The sustained differentiation of the mezzo is unique in Carter's work. The soprano line in his other vocal piece, the Elizabeth Bishop song-cycle "A Mirror On Which To Dwell," has pride of place, but is integrated with the accompanimental ensemble, not posed against it.

Carter's instrumental texture also suggests that one source of the intimate detachment in Ashbery's poem is a self-reflexive scruple about the power of poetry. By isolating the mezzo as he does, Carter underscores both the simplicity of her part and its clarity as declamation. The impression that emerges is that what she is doing is closer to recitative—the musical equivalent of speech—than it is to song. The implicit connection between artlessness and serenity is telling. Part of the asceticism of Ashbery's meditative voice stems from a conviction that Orphean song—that is to say, poetry—is myopic in intensity. No matter how severe the loss or how moving the song, "it isn't enough / To just go on singing." The meditative voice does not want to sing because song is the instrument of regret, even of wild grief. It is Orpheus's lament that "rends rocks into fissures" and makes the sky shudder; it is the power of lament that sets the poet against nature in a futile attempt to treasure the stalled moment. The meditative voice therefore tries to write a poem, "Syringa," that is divested of the intrinsic power of poetry to exalt the trauma of grief. This antagonism to the poem, a poem that in some sense demands to come into being because "love stays on the brain," is what prompts the meditative voice to pretend that its loss is too painful to acknowledge. In fact, the self does not need to be protected from the loss at all; rather, the loss has to be protected from the poem. A loss that changes everything, like Orpheus's, is too important and too fragile a thing to be entrusted to the elegiac fury that goes "streak[ing] by, its tail afire, a bad comet," recalling the "wandering mass of shapeless flame," the "pathless comet," that haunts another Orphean mourner, Byron's Manfred. If there must be a song, and it seems there must, then it has to be a song that is content with "the way music passes," that is willing to "participate in the action" of passing time. It must be a song isolated from the "something these people, / These other ones, call life." Such a song casts out remorse, not for the Yeatsian reward of finding that everything we look upon is blessed, but for the simple ability "to utter an intelligent / Comment on the most thought-provoking element" presented by history as it "flashes past." Carter, perhaps, does not follow Ashbery's irony quite that far, but this ascetic song is still what his mezzo—musically isolated, almost reciting—sings.

But why does the mezzo's song coincide with the text of the poem? The answer seems to rest with Carter's situation of the bass voice in a "subliminal" area of consciousness. Ashbery's "Syringa" has two voices but only one speaker, and its speaker is identified with the meditative voice. To that extent, Ashbery "gives" the text of the poem to the more modern of its voices; and Carter, by doing likewise, brings to light both the ghostliness and the primordial force of the speaker's impassioned double. The Orphean voice of the poem is substantial but elusive, a hoarse tone or overtone in the speaker's speech; its place is "the back of the mind, where we live now" ("Saying It to Keep It from Happening," *HD* 30). Sometimes, as Carter says, the Orphean voice comes from the back of the reader's mind. That happens whenever one recalls that the speaker is thinking of Orpheus only because he *is* the Orpheus of "a completely different incident with a similar name," so that everything he says is a covert lament. Elsewhere, the Orphean voice lives in the back of the speaker's own mind, and appears when he lingers over images too poignant or appealing to be confined by the meaning intended for them. When, for example, we hear that to ask for more than the flowing of time is only to become a passive rather than an active part of it, to "become the tossing reeds of that slow, / Powerful stream, the trailing grasses playfully tugged at," we also hear something else, underneath the negation: an Orphean song of unity with nature and of emotional, even erotic, power tenderly used. Carter, of course, intensifies the submerged erotic dimension of the poem by making the intimate detachment of the voices a union/separation of male and female.

Even more telling is the similar polyvocality in the most lyrical and intense passage of the poem, where the Orphean tone is in the open, prolonging itself with finely-wrought details:

> Singing accurately
> So that the notes mount straight up out of the well of
> Dim noon and rival the tiny, sparkling yellow flowers
> Growing around the brink of the quarry, encapsulizes
> The different weights of the things.
> (HD 69–70)

Ashbery's title authorizes us to surmise that the "sparkling yellow flowers" are syringa, which is a form of saxifrage. As its name suggests, saxifrage is a flower that breaks rocks, which it does here at the brink of the quarry. But Orpheus's lament breaks rocks, too—"rends" them into "fissures"; and the connection invests the lament with a sense of fecundity. The flower breaks rocks with its irridescent beauty; it affirms life on a desolate terrain, which is the traditional burden of elegiac song. When song rivals the flowers, the "fissure" of the quarry is transformed into a generative source, "the well of dim noon." The poem presses the point by another play on "syringa," which is derived from "syrinx," the Greek word for panpipe. True, the meditative voice may make this generous acknowledgment of the power of song only in order to get beyond it, to say that "it isn't enough / To just go on singing." But that voice says so, precisely, as it does go on singing, making a poem, "Syringa," which is named for the rock-breaking flower and prompted by loss.

Like its counterpart in Carter's music, the Orphean voice in Ashbery's poem in part assumes its "subliminal" quality by carrying suggestive overtones of earlier "songs." This allusiveness seems to belong to the Orphean voice alone, as a reflection of its impulse to fix on the past—a quality that Carter's bass reflects by its fluent passage through texts by Sappho, Ibycus,

Plato, Aeschylus, "Orpheus," and others. Allusion, except as cliché (" 'The end crowns all' ") tends to resonate with the elegiac strain in "Syringa," which is the price paid by the meditative voice for its ascetic immersion in the flowing present. This happens with the yellow flowers, which recall the traditional flowers of pastoral elegy among their other associations; and it happens, too, with the "bad comet" that suggests Manfred. Manfred is a cautionary instance to the meditative voice, but he is also an Orphean figure who sees his Eurydice after her death, then sees her vanish, and later dies in what he thinks of as triumph, without "mind[ing] so much about his reward being in heaven" ("Syringa," *HD* 70).

This thinning of the meditative texture in favor of elegiac implication—an effect mirrored, as we have seen, by Carter's treatment of instrumental line and color—underlies the seemingly incongruous section of the poem in which some horses reflect on an electrical storm. For the meditative voice, the horses provide another instance of the Orphean "mistake," in this case a belief in the power of music to heal the gaps in nature:

> The horses
> Have each seen a share of the truth, though each thinks,
> "I'm a maverick. Nothing of this is happening to me,
> Though I can understand the language of birds, and
> The itinerary of the lights caught in the storm is fully apparent to me.
> Their jousting ends in music much
> As trees move more easily in the wind after a summer storm,
> As is happening in the lacy shadows of the shore-trees, now, day after day."
>   (*HD* 70–71)

From the meditator's viewpoint, the horses naïvely mythify the haphazard way that things "happen along" in time, defensively idealize the universal pratfall by which things go "bumping into other things," then vanish. What's more, by refusing to acknowledge that the storm is happening to *them*, the horses—innocent egoists—deny the burden of their own mortality. And of course the meditator is right, as his talking (anyway, thinking) horses clownishly show with their overtones of children's stories and animated cartoons. On the other hand, the horses do out–sing him with their lyrical vision of trees in the wind. And talking horses are not always clownish. The horses most relevant in a classical context are the ones that speak to another Orphean hero, another man doomed by the strength of his response to loss. In the *Iliad*, Achilles's horses speak to him after "the light from [his] fair elaborate shield [shoots] into the high air."[10] What the horses say to Achilles acknowledges both the true nature of temporality and the limits that mortality puts on life and beauty; their poetry is elegiac, Orphean:

---

[10] This and the following quotation from the *Iliad* are somewhat modified from the Richmond Lattimore translation (Chicago: University of Chicago Press, 1951).

But for us, we two could run with the blast of the west wind
Which they say is the lightest of all things; but for you
There is destiny to be killed in force by a god and a mortal.
                    (xix, 415–17)

Ashbery's horses also say something worth hearing. They speak for the conciliatory power of elegy, and their image of the wind, like that of their Homeric doubles, suggests something that transcends the harshness of destiny "day after day"—a "music" that is either the breath of poetic inspiration or the simple freedom of air. The horses' Orpheism may be naïve, but that compromises them only so far; after all, they're only horses.

"Syringa," at any rate, is not the first poem to associate Orpheus with a horse, as the lyrical comedy of this episode may be meant to remind us:

But O to you, Lord, say what to consecrate to you
who taught all created beings their ear?
My memory of a spring day,
a spring evening, in Russia—, a horse . . .
                    (RILKE, *Sonnets to Orpheus*, I, 20)

Ashbery's polyvocality in "Syringa" seems to meet the demand of that other Orphean poet, Rilke, who called for the demigod himself to live in "the double realm" where being and not-being are conjoined and where "the voices grow / eternal and mild" (I, 9). Ashbery's richly detailed and heterogeneous text can be read as an attempt to fill in the gaps left behind by Rilke's extremely elliptical ones, so that the double realm can take on particularity— not in a referential concreteness, which is illusory anyway from the standpoint of a double existence, but in a concrete rhythm of consciousness and a language that can respond to it. Carter, in turn, tries in his "Syringa" to represent the movement of that rhythm, to tap the pre-conscious sources of that language.

VI

In both Carter's case and Ashbery's, the polyvocal style that articulates the double realm drastically alters the meaning of time, an effect that is by no means limited to either "Syringa." Earlier, I pointed out that Carter's polyvocality diverts emphasis from the linear progression of his music to its vertically generated duration. One way to develop this point is to say that in its dynamic layering, Carter's music resembles the prolongation and transformation of a single enormous chord—a chord of specifically modern cut. Twentieth-century music makes frequent use of "referential sonorities": chords that are not tonally functional, but that act "tonally" as recognizable textures of pitch, color, spacing, and rhythmic position. A mature piece by Carter essentially consists of a referential sonority that sustains itself continuously. In works like the Second and Third String Quartets and the Double Concerto (1961), this sonority—call it the gesture-chord—is not made up of pitches but of rhythmic and intervallic consistencies, of expressive repertoires. In the Piano Concerto (1965) and the Concerto for Orchestra, Carter began to "double" the gesture-chord in the pitch dimension by forming large background chords of twelve registrally fixed notes. Either way, the process of the music coincides with a kind of pulsation or turbulence within the primary multi-leveled sonority.[11] From a linear standpoint, the music is likely to seem static, because its multiple activities are always engaged in shaping and reshaping the vertical arrangement. But it is just the linear standpoint, which Carter derides as the one "in which first you do this for a while, then you do that" (*WEC* 270), that the music radically alters. By varying his tempos continuously, by sustaining a polyrhythmic texture for his layered voices, by filling each level in the gesture-chord with intense activity, Carter makes the linear movement of his music so fluid, so organic, that the listener cannot possibly measure it. Each moment, each texture of a composition merges seamlessly into the next (no matter how different) within a rhythmic whole that does not guide the ear but envelops it.

Not that Carter tries to negate the linear dimension, to fashion "crystalline" sound-structures like Varèse or to evoke the mantra-like stasis of minimalist composers like Steve Reich or Philip Glass. Carter *is* concerned with the projection of his music through time, and takes pains with it. He is especially prone to use the coalescence or dispersal of voices to pattern a work or to indicate closure. Thus the Double Concerto for Harpsichord and Piano with Two Chamber Orchestras begins by gradually differentiating its voices—one belonging to the instrumental group associated with the harpsichord, the other to the piano group—and closes as the voices gradually break down and merge together. And the climax of the *Symphony of Three Orchestras* is an apocalyptic series of tutti chords in which the three voices of the work implode into one. Carter's music is also powerfully, even aggressively, linear at the level of the individual voices. Nevertheless, the polyvocal whole composed of these voices absorbs their linear impetus into the resonance of a temporal order that persists instead of progressing. Ultimately, the role of linearity in Carter's work is supplementary, contextual. The listener does not so much hear the overarching shape of change as live through it:

[11] In a small way, the third of Carter's *Eight Etudes and a Fantasy* for woodwind quartet (1950) provides a simplified model for this effect. In this piece, Carter explains, "the three notes of a soft D-major chord are given different emphases by changes of tone-color and doublings" (*WEC* 347).

In a piece that deals primarily with the poetry of change, transformation, reorientation of feelings and thoughts, and gradual shifts of emphasis, as do most of my works . . . the matter of succession of material becomes very important, since how the ideas are formed and how they are related and connected gives expression to the poetry they evoke. Thus, the individual instant, the characterized sound or brief passage, like trees in a storm, gain an added meaning by their contexts.[12]

What Carter suggests by this passage is, among other things, the same doubleness of vision that Ashbery reflects in "Syringa." The flowing and fleeting of time is absolute, and the work of art is so formed that it submits to that flow without trying to wrench it into shape. Change, transformation, and reorientation are paramount. Yet the "poetry" lies in "the individual instant," the brief evocative passage that one is constantly tempted to treasure as it recedes.

Ashbery is perhaps less willing than Carter to preserve the linearity of his work. As Carter's polyvocal forms create a continuous gesture-chord, Ashbery's create a continuous moment of awareness for which there is no convenient name or image, but which might be called a texturing of consciousness. The texture arises from a continuous act of apprehension that is almost too full to be sustained. The eye "sharpens and sharpens" particulars until

no
Longer visible, they breathe in multicolored
Parentheses, the way love in short periods
Puts everything out of focus, coming and going.
("Fragment," DD 81)

Half vision, half blurred eyesight, this state of mind absorbs erotic, linguistic, and phantasmagorical elements without being typified by any of them. As the imagery of "short periods" and "multicolored parentheses" suggests, the traditional formula for transcendence is stood on its head in this poetry. Disincarnation, disembodiment prevail: it is the flesh that becomes the word—literally the sentence, the "short period"—with objects becoming a rhetoric for good measure. As a result, reality loses all its rigidity; it becomes whatever can be said of it in a free play of language that is only marginally (if at all) referential.

Since the stylistic turning-point marked by the 1966 volume *Rivers and Mountains*, this texturing of consciousness in Ashbery's work seems most often to be polyvocal, and its voices, like those in "Syringa," are at once disjunctive and continuous: each thrives on what the others leave out, each says what the others leave unspoken. In at least one poem, "Litany," this latent

---

[12] Elliott Carter, liner notes to the recording of his Concerto for Orchestra (Columbia M 30112).

structure takes the foreground as an explicit principle, as if to dispose of the envy that Ashbery once admitted to feeling for the polyphony and polytonality available to composers.[13] "Litany" is written as two independent columns of poetry that face each other across the page, and it has actually been performed in simultaneous readings with the poet's blessing.

A more subliminal design, but still one more formalized that that of "Syringa," appears in the "Fantasia on 'The Nut-Brown Maid.' " At first glance, this poem appears to be a dialogue between two persons, "He" and "She." Each stanza begins by qualifying, reproving, or going one better than something in the stanza preceding:

> [HE]
> For those who go
> Under the green helm know it lets itself
> Become known, at different moments, under different aspects.
>
> SHE
> Unless some movie did it first, or
> A stranger came to the door and then the change
> Was real until it went away.
> (*HD* 80)
>
> HE
> You are like someone whose face was photographed in a crowd
> scene once and then gradually retreated from people's memories,
> and from life as well.
>
> SHE
> But the real "world"
> Stretches its pretending into the side yard
> Where I was waiting, at peace with my feelings, though now,
> I see, resentful from the beginning . . . .
> (*HD* 84)

As the antiphonal rhythm establishes itself, however, the traditional pattern vaporizes before the reader's eyes. There is actually no way to distinguish between "He" and "She."[14] Both voices speak in the same style, or medley of styles, and both display the same vagaries of attitude. The one-upping "unless" and reproachful "but" of the quoted stanzas are empty, purely formal divisions—signs of a stanza-structure, not of a self; the two voices are really

[13] John Ashbery, quoted by David Lehman in "The Shield of a Greeting," in *Beyond Amazement: New Essays on John Ashbery*, edited by David Lehman (Ithaca: Cornell University Press, 1980), pp. 111–12.

[14] See also John Koethe, "The Metaphysical Subject of John Ashbery's Poetry," in *Beyond Amazement*, pp. 87–100.

one voice. "He" and "She" are, in fact, not antithetical to each other but conjointly antithetical to the implied persona of the author. "Fantasia" is not antiphonally divided between a male and a female voice, but polyvocally divided between an integrated authorial ego and a separation of that same ego into male and female principles. The presence of this intrapsychic division is confirmed toward the end of the poem when "He" and "She" are banished from the scene and the authorial voice takes over again with an extended passage of prose-poetry. But here again, the style and attitude of this new persona are indistinguishable from those of "He" and "She"; their voices still sound within his. The poem thus ends with an attempt at Romantic irony that is deliberately left to fizzle: the ego is still orchestrated into a polyphony of concentrated and dispersed identity.

Like their counterparts in Carter's music, Ashbery's layered voices fluctuate widely in the textures that they create, but their basic "chordal" relationship is constant. As a result, nothing can be said to "happen" in an Ashbery poem except a duration. The poetry simply writes itself out on

> the front page
> Of today, looming as white as
> The furthest mountains, and oh, all kinds of things
> Caught in that net and shaken.
> ("Fragment," *DD* 91)

This point comes across clearly in "Syringa," which ends only by reaching the point of origin that it has never left, the memory of what happened "in some small town, one indifferent summer." Nothing has changed but the clock; and the poem has been a kind of fable about itself, one of the "Fables time invents / To explain its passing" ("Years of Indiscretion," *DD* 46).

Ashbery's style rests on a transcription of those fables. As a rule, an Ashbery poem does not articulate a process, but simply lets a textured consciousness persist shimmeringly for a given duration, which is presented as something like an *objet trouvé*. Within that duration, the voices of the poem participate in the continuous flow of the present without imposing any shape on it or experiencing what Richard Howard calls "the invoked anxiety of closed form."[15] The nature of this flow is to be quirky, inconsistently coherent, and, contrary to conventional expectations, non-linear. Time flows, but not in a straight line; it flows every which way. Ashbery's poems, accordingly, though they have meditative voices to them, are not the meditations that they are often said to be. They are uncertain reflections in "a randomness, a darkness of one's own" ("The Ice-Cream Wars," *HD* 61), a darkness in which the mind "happens along" but does not change, though its objects

---

[15] Richard Howard, "Sortes Vergiliane: *The Double Dream of Spring* by John Ashbery," *Poetry* 117 (1970–71): 53.

do. In their form, these poems suggest a new way of defining subjective time in which the continuity of the ego dissolves experience instead of integrating it. The mind becomes the only constant presence, and it presides over a continuous recession of objects into absence, some of which it is reluctant to let go.

One consequence of this is that Ashbery's work marks a radical shift away from the style of subjectivity that has prevailed in most poetry since the nineteenth century. Ashbery, as a rule, likes to show how the mind goes rather than where it goes. For most poets after Wordsworth, the mind has "gone" in a pattern of conflict and resolution, or crisis and resolution, prompted by the inherent instability of subject-object relationships.[16] But Ashbery, by situating his poetry in the kind of temporality I have just described, makes conflict and crisis impossible. A horizon of calm frames the tumult of integrations that confronts the reader, even when the extremities of loss are figured in as they are in "Syringa." The ego need not be arrested by the "Gang-wars, ice cream, loss, palm terrain" ("Bird's-Eye View of the Tool and Dye Co." *HD* 27) that keep accosting it; there is always an alter ego. "Perennially, / We die and are taken up again" ("Two Deaths," *HD* 37). The poetry thereby transcends the pattern of self-aggrandizement, anxiety, and disappointment that leads

> To pain,
> And the triumph over pain, still hidden
> In those low-lying hills which rob us
> Of all privacy, as though one were always about to meet
> One's double
> ("Houseboat Days," *HD* 38)

and so, by the tradition of the *Doppelgänger*, to meet one's death. Such sublime doings may always take part in a poem, may stem from one of its voices, as from the Orphean voice in "Syringa"; but the poem is never determined by them. The cool mezzo always tempers the fiery bass who enriches the sound of her voice.

"What I am writing to say is, the timing, not / The contents, is what matters" ("Fantasia on 'The Nut-Brown Maid,' " *HD* 85). Both Ashbery's timing and Elliott Carter's are ways of ramifying the present which upset our unacknowledged illusion that time is simple. With Carter, this takes the form of continually superimposing different metrical structures, all of which are themselves in constant change. Given so many shapes, polyvocally fused together, time loses the quality by which we customarily identify and measure

---

[16] The classic discussion of this pattern remains M. H. Abrams, "Structure and Style in the Greater Romantic Lyric," in *From Sensibility to Romanticism: Essays Presented to Frederick A. Pottle*, edited by Frederick W. Hilles and Harold Bloom (New York: Oxford University Press, 1965), pp. 527–60.

it—its periodicity. What remains is a kind of eddy, full of complex swells and pulsations. With Ashbery, something quite similar happens. The fluctuation of superimposed voices, desires, or layers of awareness replaces chronology as the way to tell—define, depict—time and dissolves the illusion of narrativity by which experience is customarily forced to make sense. And this creates an eddy of its own, each surge of which

> unrolls
> Its question mark like a new wave on the shore.
> In coming to give, to give up what we had,
> We have, we understand, gained or been gained
> By what was passing through, bright with the sheen
> Of things recently forgotten and revived.
> ("Blue Sonata," *HD* 66–67)

In this rich collage of a present, coming is going, giving is giving up, having is having had, and vice versa—actions that do not cancel each other, but that coexist in one bright sheen. Even more importantly, perhaps, in the ramified present to understand is to question, or more accurately it is to think and feel within the curve of a question mark that cannot be followed by an answer, but only by another question mark. Understanding is thus not a matter of knowing, but of being, and in particular of being in, of consenting to, time: "it's time / That counts, and how deeply you have invested in it." ("Saying It to Keep It from Happening, *HD* 29). To understand is to participate.

Only the trouble is that to participate in these terms is not easy—not, at least, for an ego that relies on a sense of its boundaries to manage the world, the ego that most of us have for most of the time. In the Romantic tradition, the breaching of ego-boundaries is permitted and desired in isolated moments of epiphany, "spots of time," "times of inherent excellence." "Such moments worthy of all gratitude," as Wordsworth calls them, are discontinuous from the rest of experience, which is thereby protected from them. The styles of Ashbery and Carter advance, perhaps advance beyond, the visionary tradition of Romanticism by adumbrating a breaching of ego-boundaries that is continuous, by positing an ideal reader or listener who has an ego without walls. At least two hardships are incurred by this. One, inevitable once the epiphanic movement has been decentered, is the loss of a graduated, quasi-erotic movement to a peak of ecstasy or illumination. The other is the necessity to relax the defenses by which the ego conducts its thankless task of mediating between desire and circumstance. Both of these difficulties find compensation in the plenitude that follows from polyvocal form, the sheer density of esthetic particulars that ranges from mere multiplicity to a virtual all-inclusiveness. But to enjoy that plenitude requires a readiness to be immersed in a complexity that can never be mastered, to embrace an imaginative world which repeatedly affirms that

> no part
> Remains that is surely you. Those voices in the dusk
> Have told you all and still the tale goes on.
> ("Self Portrait in a Convex Mirror," *SP 71*)

Not everyone is willing, of course. That is why Carter is criticized for a cerebrality that is admired in Bach, why Ashbery is attacked for an obscurity that passes for routine in Mallarmé. But there is a good deal to be said, even therapeutically, for an art that requires its audience to take anxiety off at the door. Carter speaks of the sensuous pleasure of "filling musical time and space by a web of continually varying cross references" (*WEC* 269), Ashbery of "filling up the margins of the days / With pictures of fruit, light, colors, music, and vines" (Landscapepeople," *AWK*). But just for fun, let Beethoven have the last word: "I must accustom myself to think out at once the whole, as soon as it shows itself, with all the voices, in my head."[17]

---

[17] Ludwig van Beethoven, note in a sketchbook for 1810; quoted in *Beethoven: The Man and the Artist as Revealed in His Own Words*. Compiled and annotated by Friedrich Kerst; translated by Henry Edward Krehbiel (1905; repr. New York: Dover Books, 1964).

Conclusion:
On Time and Form

Composers! mighty maestros!
And you, sweet singers of old lands, soprani, tenori, bassi!
To you a new bard caroling in the West
Obeisant sends his love.

The bard in question is, of course, Walt Whitman, and his carol is an ambitious, uneven, underrated poem, "Proud Music of the Storm." Close to unique in its extravagance, the poem is an explicit attempt to dissolve the boundaries between poetry and music by linking the two arts to a psychological rhythm—in this case a cathectic rhythm in the original erotic sense of the term. The fascinating results include a strong intimation that the ego is essentially feminine, a definition of poetic inspiration as a visionary musicopoetics, and, most importantly for our purposes, a form that epitomizes the movement of gestural convergence.

"Proud Music" disguises itself with an old-fashioned, indeed outmoded, genre: it is a later version of the Augustan musical ode, a form that celebrates different aspects of musical expression on a scale of ascending power and one that developed, as John Hollander has shown, into a means of commenting on the poetic tradition.[1] What Whitman does is to superimpose a dynamic pattern based on the principle of maternity over the ceremonial pattern of the ode. This more primary rhythm envelops the processional movement of discrimination and praise with a turbulent liquidity. Impatient with boundaries in any form, it breaks unpredictably into brief, ecstatic fusions of subject and object:

> The *Creation* in billows of godhood laves me.
>
> Give me to hold all sounds, (I madly struggling cry),
> Fill me with all the voices of the universe,

[1] John Hollander, "Wordsworth and the Music of Sound," in *New Perspectives on Coleridge and Wordsworth*, edited by Geoffrey Hartman (New York: Columbia University Press, 1972), pp. 67–73.

> Endow me with their throbbings, Nature's also,
> The tempests, waters, winds, operas and chants . . . .
>   (138-41)

The basis of such fusions and defusions is the power of the poet's auditory imagination to transform any natural sound into music. There is no secret about the source of this power; it is the singing voice of the poet's mother, heard in infancy:

> Ah from a little child
> Thou knowest soul how to me all sounds became music,
> My mother's voice in lullaby or hymn
> (The voice, O tender voices, memory's loving voices,
> Last miracle of all, O dearest mother's, sister's voices).
>   (59–63)

The primary bond between mother and child, mediated through the mother's voice, becomes the principle of receptivity by which the poet unites with nature—"The rain, the growing corn, the breeze among the long-leaved corn." As a woman, the primal singer is the mother of the poet's body; as a voice, she is the mother of his ego, the "base" (basis/bass) of the "composition" that is his identity:

> The strong base stands, and its pulsations intermits not,
> Bathing, supporting, merging all the rest, maternity of the rest.
>   (38–39)

In response to this feminine presence with which it is always half-merged, the (masculine) self adopts the internalization of the maternal voice, the voice of primary creativity, as its central dynamic principle. Whitman recapitulates the birth of his ego from maternal song by becoming a maternal singer himself. He both gives birth to music from the sounds of nature—the "hidden orchestras" and "serenades of phantoms" tossed on the night air—and reintegrates the sound of actual music with a primary ecstasy and envelopment. Throughout the poem, he shuttles from a language of impregnation that defines his creativity as feminine—what he hears "fills" and "inflates" him; he feels it "bending me powerless, / Entering my lonesome slumber-chamber"—to a style of prophetic declamation that unifies "man and art with Nature" in a return to "the far-back days the poets tell, the Paradiso."

In the final strophe, Whitman's procreative faculty appears as the imaginative power to hear unwritten poetry as he once heard his mother's singing voice in "lullaby or hymn," and to bring forth what he hears in prophetic or bardic form. The recognition of this link between remembered music and emergent poetry—"the clew I sought so long"—seems to revive a poetic and personal vitality that has been flagging. An unprepared shift from the present tense to the past distances and shapes the music of the storm:

> Then I woke softly,
> And pausing, questioning awhile the music of my dream,
> And questioning all those reminiscences, the tempest in its fury,
> And all the songs of the sopranos and tenors . . .
> . . . .
> I said to my silent curious soul out of the bed of the slumber-chamber,
> Come, for I have found the clew I sought so long.
>
> (143–46, 149–50)

Within the hazy interval of his pause, Whitman recasts the perceptual and emotional volatility of the poem as a form of temporality, a "new rhythmus" that gestates

> Poems bridging the way from Life to Death, vaguely wafted
>   in the night air, uncaught, unwritten,
> Which let us go forth in the bold day and write.
>
> (163–64)

The "personified dim shapes" of music in the wind and trees are no longer brought into focus as the sounds of "sweet varied instruments"; instead they are recollected as an ecstatic indeterminacy, the duration in which the passage from life to death becomes a vision that inseminates the mind. So far, what we might call maternal time has directed the structural rhythm of the poem as a background movement of merging, blending, and "laving" that harmonizes "all the voices of the universe." Here, the background briefly becomes the foreground as the womblike slumber-chamber floats a "refresh'd" life-cycle in embryonic form: an aimless wafting in which limitless possibilities rest. The rhapsodic form of the whole poem is redefined as its shifting "chords left as by vast composers" appear retrospectively as the "rhythmus" that prepares the birth of new poetry and the new birth of the poet.

Whitman's maternal temporality is reminiscent of the generative intervals that we saw in connection with Wordsworth, Beethoven, and Ives. More generally, we can observe that most of the poems and compositions studied in the preceding chapters have included a similar interval in which time breaks into the foreground as a palpable force. In some cases—the *Andante con moto* of the "Appassionata," Panthea's vision of concentric spheres in *Prometheus Unbound*—the work during these intervals seems to be representing a pure movement of origination, the surprisingly turbulent exten-

sion of one moment into another. Rilke, in a poem from *The Book of Hours,*
identifies this phenomenon as the source of continuity within the self:

> I am the rest between two tones
> that sound together in discord only:
> for the tone of death wants to mount—
>
> But in that dark interval the tones,
> trembling, are reconciled.
> ("Mein Leben ist nicht diese steile stunde,")

Following this clue, we might speculate that Rilke's "dark interval" of temporal connection is thrust into the foreground in order to serve some ego-
need: for dialectical recognition, for a renewal of identity, for a sense of security or power in sheer being. Ordinarily, the movement of time is not
presented directly to consciousness; instead, it is displaced onto the action,
the poem, the composition that organizes it. With music and poetry, the texture of temporal displacement is especially dense, a plural, "polyphonic"
process. But at sensitive moments—beginnings, endings, junctures—a reversal is always possible: displacement can give way to a heightened representation of pulse, periodicity, or ec-stasis. In part, the "chronophany" that
results is incorporated into the work as a projected form of subjective time.
The discontinuity in the work testifies to the continuity within the (maker's, perceiver's) ego. And this allows the ego, whose dynamics provide the
model of completeness for the work, to appear as the source of closure,
whether closure is achieved or not. In most cases, the possibility of convergence turns on how this pattern is realized or negated.

Chronophanies represent an expressive limit. From the discursive point
of view, they do not make sense and resist being made sense of. In general,
they constitute the most dissociative breach that a cathectic rhythm can
make in a legible discursive surface. (Where the surface is problematical, as
in the work of Ashbery and Carter, the reversal of temporal displacement is
apparent almost continuously.) In "Proud Music," for example, the closing
identification of maternal time with poetic inspiration violates both the visionary fabric that has been built up and the framework of the musical ode.
As the poetic present breaks down, Whitman informs us for the first time
that he has been dreaming, and goes on to surmise that the music that has
laved him in "billows of godhood" was not really music at all. At the same
time he echoes rhetorically the very music that was *not*

> the sound of winds,
> Nor dream of raging storm, nor sea-hawk's flapping wing nor harsh scream,
> Nor vocalism of sun-bright Italy,
> Nor German organ majestic, nor vast concourse of voices, nor layers of harmonies
> (156—59)

and so on. The motive for the chronophany that follows is the need for sepa-rateness, individuation: if the poet is to "carol" like the singing mother, he must stop playing the infantile role in which he hears an Imaginary music "lapsing, bathing me in bliss."

One effect of chronophany is to make structural rhythms self-referential. Any poem or composition that exposes "the way time feels as it passes" nec-essarily incorporates a reflection on the course of its own unfolding. (It is important to add that this reflection does *not* necessarily take precedence over other kinds of significance.) Moreover, if a work with a strong cathectic rhythm does not yield a chronophany, the very absence of one may become a palpable quality and produce the effect of self-reference dialectically—say, if a work conspicuously tries to avoid an exposure of sheer time, to expunge it or to defend against it. One example is Chopin's Prelude in F♯ Minor, the only piece in Opus 28 with a conventional contrastive middle section, com-plete with a new theme, a new tempo, and a new key. In its dissociative sur-roundings, and heard against the dissociative effects of its own pedalling—which, as Thomas Higgins observes, causes "a considerable blurring of en-tire half-measures" at syntactic junctures[2]—the piece loses all formal inno-cence. Its symmetrical structure appears as a transient attempt to resist the free, truncated, unbalanced temporality that prevails throughout the set. Likewise, the absence of chronophany in "The Thorn"—emphasized by the tub-thumping rhythm of the poem—corresponds to the inability of the char-acters to break the concentric circles of their common obsession, together with the inability of the poet's voice to do it for them. In this case, the fore-grounding and concretizing of time must be produced by the reader, in a reflection on the act of reading. Where dialectical patterns like these are lacking, a self-referential temporality may still appear in diffuse form throughout a work, usually as the result of problematized boundaries. Whit-man's "Proud Music" uses the merging and "lapsing" of musical sounds to articulate its cathectic movement until the break at the final strophe. In works like his String Sextet in G major, Op. 36, and String Quartet in B♭ ma-jor, Op. 67, Brahms makes a diffuse self-reference primary by minimizing the tempo differences among his four movements, thus creating a single meta-tempo for the entire composition. Flexible within narrow limits, this "higher" tempo produces a substantial slowing of musical time, a kind of sonorous slow-motion. Taken together with a consistently thick and rhyth-mically complex texture, this gives the music the air of defensively warding off all non-musical perception, so that there is an edge of urgency even to the most relaxed moments.

Within the orbit of Romanticism, the intrusion of exposed time into a work is regularly associated with visionary intensity, with sublimity, with

[2] Thomas Higgins, in his edition of Frederic Chopin, *Preludes, Op. 28* (New York: Nor-ton, 1973), p. 65.

what Ives called the "showers of the absolute." A chronophany usually appears as a disorienting gap within the rhythm of perception; charged with ambivalence, impossible to rationalize fully, it both magnifies and erodes the consciousness that is occupied with it. Poetically, the reversal of temporal displacement is almost always sudden and vertiginous, and it is frequently accompanied with images of chasms, abysses, or gulfs. Instances range from the "fallings from us, vanishings" of Wordsworth's "Intimations" Ode to the tantalizing "Open" of Rilke's *Duino Elegies* in which "the flowers / endlessly open" ("die Blumen / unendlich aufgehn") to the "wished-for disappearances" of Stevens's "Auroras of Autumn," with their "form gulping after formlessness." Musically, the same mode of transcendence is linked to a weakening of boundaries, whether sectional, stylistic, or harmonic. Most chronophanies in music are introductory or transitional; the shocking silence of the piano during the recitative in "Erlkönig," after four minutes of continuous pulsation, stands as a rarer closural instance. Otherwise, chronophanies tend to occur in brief pieces or movements with an uncertain or transitive identity—Chopin's E♭ Minor Prelude, the *Andante con moto* of the "Appassionata." Most chronophanic episodes are conceived generatively; when they are not, they often embody drastic discontinuities from the main body of the work. In the grotesque operatic parody that mediates between the March and Finale of Beethoven's A-Minor String Quartet, Op. 132, the syncopated sliding of the first violin over a thick *tremolando* presents a degraded form of rhythmic plasticity that the concluding Rondo is asked to transfigure. In Bartók's Concerto for Orchestra, the static introduction to the first movement takes fifty measures of mysterious *pianissimo* to establish tonal centers on F♯ and E, the chromatic neighboring tones of the actual tonal center of the movement, F.

Chronophanies may sometimes appear in a poem or composition autonomously; the self-observing, self-consuming close of Yeats's "Byzantium" ("Those images that yet / Fresh images beget, / That dolphin-torn, that gong-tormented sea"), the fading "heartbeat" in the last of Berg's Three Pieces for Orchestra, and the ominous tick-tock in the Funeral March of Beethoven's "Eroica" Symphony are all instances. They are more interesting, though—at least to me—when they are not simply patches of vision, hushes, drones, or thrummings that just happen, but integral parts of a larger rhythm. As Eliot says in "Burnt Norton," "Words move, music moves / Only in time," but

> Only by the form, the pattern,
> Can words or music reach
> The stillness, as a Chinese jar still
> Moves perpetually in its stillness.

I am skeptical about the stillness, but the point about patterning is essential.

What a chronophany exposes is the *kind* of time in which a poem or composition moves, at the same time as it forces us to confront and interpret the presence of temporal movement. In making our response, we will inevitably have to deal with that movement in generic terms—a need that leads us back to the workings of paradigmatic structural rhythms.

II

We have been dealing with three primary large-scale rhythms, each of which assigns a distinctive structure and significance to temporality. Taken together and paired with their opposites, the three map out a fairly full set of relationships between gestural time and cathectically shaped form. Romantic repetition belongs to a polarity that posits time as blockage or liberation, compulsion or ec-stasis. Temporality here is primarily situated in consciousness, secondarily in objects, and the works that realize it tend to resist closure. The polarity that includes generative form posits time as the medium of connection or disjunction, integration or separation, maturation or decay. It situates temporality in an exchange between consciousness and objects, and produces works in which closure is strongly heightened. Recurrence—a deferred continuity found in the return of what has been lost or disavowed—is a frequent feature in generative rhythms. Sometimes called repetition by critics, recurrence lacks the compulsive, excessive quality of Romantic repetition, but does sometimes border on it. "Uncanny" episodes— Wordsworth's visitation by "gleams of half-extinguished thought" at Tintern Abbey, the reappearance of the opening measures of Beethoven's Piano Sonata in A Major, Op. 101, before the finale—mediate between the two forms of return.[3] Finally, transitivity belongs to a polarity that posits time as the vehicle of wholeness or fragmentation, identity or dissociation. The emphasis here is on how either subjects or objects take up a discrete time, just as bodies and things take up a discrete space. Temporality lodges in the consistency of self-unfolding that supports ontological identity; transits of identity work by shifting the basis of that consistency. Closure is readily available in transitive works, but it is often lacking in security. Sustained bursts of seemingly rootless intensity are common:

> whirroos
> And scintillant sizzlings such as children like,
> Vested in the serious folds of majesty,
> Moving around and behind, a following,
> A source of trumpeting seraphs in the eye,
> A source of pleasant outbursts on the ear.
> (STEVENS, "A Primitive Like an Orb")

---

[3] On repetition and the uncanny, see my " 'That Other Will': The Daemonic in Coleridge and Wordsworth," *Philological Quarterly* 85 (1979): 298–320.

These classifications might be summed up by saying that time-as-experience is structured by the pair Romantic repetition/linearity; time-as-becoming by generativity/dialecticity; and time-as-being by transitivity/immutability. Further constructions are possible, of course, but it should be obvious that the categories embraced here provide a powerful resource for interpretation. In particular, if certain structural rhythms do have a certain primacy, we would expect elements of them to appear in various combinations as the constituents of other rhythms. Their imprint could thus be taken as the starting point for gestural analysis, either of individual works or of works taken in tandem.

Some such overlapping of paradigms has already drawn our attention—in the abrupt, discontinuous closes of Chopin's Op. 28 Preludes, for instance, with their link to Romantic repetition, or in Ives's and Stevens's reworking of generativity into a scene of mutual origination. Still, passing observations like these can only hint at the richness of a possible "shaping power," which deserves a detailed illustration of its own. To provide one, I will offer a closing analysis of a pair of works in which all three primary paradigms are at work. The effect of this triple overlap (and of others like it) is a structural rhythm based on the phenomenon of liminality. Partially as a test of method, the works chosen will be linked for once without the potentially deceptive plausibility provided by contemporaneity and by similarity in feeling. Rilke's meditative lyric "Orpheus. Eurydice. Hermes." is the poem. The composition is Beethoven's Fifth Symphony.

III

Before turning to the works, a brief comment about liminality is necessary. Liminal experience, the sense of inhabiting or passing across a threshold, is regularly represented in the literature of all periods. Before the nineteenth century, the thresholds in question usually appear as a space where two orders of being, higher and lower, sacred and profane, are simultaneously present. Examples (given by Angus Fletcher) include Homer's Cave of the Nymphs, Vergil's twin gates of horn and ivory, and Dante's Limbo.[4] In Romantic literature, this pattern is internalized, so that liminal movement involves a passage from a lower to a higher order of vision, usually accompanied by a heightening of the ego of the visionary. Divine imagery, reinterpreted by reference to the self, often reappears in this connection.[5] Both of the climactic episodes of Wordsworth's *Prelude*, the descent through Gondo and the ascent of Snowdon, furnish seminal examples. As a rule, the

---

[4] Angus Fletcher, " 'Positive Negation': Threshold, Sequence, and Personification in Coleridge," in *New Perspectives on Coleridge and Wordsworth*, pp. 133–64.

[5] See my "The Return of the Gods: Keats to Rilke," *Studies in Romanticism* 17 (1979): 483–500.

threshold itself is a narrow strip of space, a defile, set in a mediating position between other significant spaces. In music, the effect of such a space (felt as an indeterminate moment) is created by the mystification of introductory or transitional passages, or by the reduction of a musical segment to a bare minimum of content or duration—as, for instance, in Bach's substitution of a single phrygian cadence for a slow movement in the Third "Brandenburg" Concerto. In most cases, too, the appearance of a liminal defile is chronophanic.

In "Orpheus. Eurydice. Hermes.," Rilke uses a liminal space, "a pale strip of path like bleaching linen," to articulate a dialectical antagonism between Orpheus and Eurydice during their failed ascent from Hades. Orpheus, "mute and impatient," carries out a refusal to complete the work of mourning, while Eurydice, "soft and without impatience," gradually completes it *for* him without his knowledge or consent. What resolves the unacknowledged tension between the two is a generative rhythm that leads to the crossing of the threshold. Like the Orpheus of "Syringa," the Orpheus of this poem is guilty of a mistake—in fact of the same mistake: an overinvestment of the self in what has been lost. But Rilke's poem is neither polyvocal nor significantly ambivalent, and while it recognizes the pathos of Orpheus's error, it judges his failure to be both just and desirable. Orpheus's effort of resurrection is a violation of the ontological integrity of death. His passionate devotion to Eurydice is not, as he thinks, a vindication of her life but a possessive degradation of the death that she has died.

Orpheus's misguided effort reveals and betrays itself as a form of Romantic repetition. Captivated by Eurydice—so much so that his ego cannot exist apart from his relationship with her—Orpheus cannot yield to the demands of mourning and surrender his attachment to her image. His descent to Hades is essentially a narcissistic attempt to reunite the image with the woman: to repeat Eurydice like a refrain. The dissociative result, the imprisonment of the self in the stalled moment, appears in projected form as a pair of landscapes. Orpheus's underworld takes the form of a fragmentary repetition of the upper world—one that, all too tellingly, disfigures and decreates the things that it repeats. The forests of Hades are reminiscent of the trees that once danced to Orpheus's songs, but they are nothing more than embodied absences; Rilke calls them "wesenlos" (unreal), with pointed emphasis on the literal meaning of the compound "being-less." Bridges are said to hang over nothingness, and a "blind pool" ("blinde Teich") hangs at a distance over its bottom like a rainy sky. In their insubstantiality, these repetitions externalize the "world of mourning" ("Welt aus Klagen") that arose in Orpheus's imagination after Eurydice's death.[6] By clinging to the images of the past and reproducing them in song, Orpheus could so repeat the actual

---

[6] Rilke's *Klagen* differs from Freud's *Trauer*; the distinction seems to be between a form of mourning that incorporates its own expression and one that does not.

world that "everything was once more there" ("alles noch einmal da war").
But the things that he repeats are "there" only in the "being-less" sense of
that-which-is-mourned. In the world of mourning, "everything" is disfigured by the lack of substance, set forth under "a mourning-heaven of mis-
featured stars" ("ein Klage-Himmel mit entstellten Sternen"; "entstellten":
disfigured, misrepresented). Strikingly, too, Rilke's list of "everything"—
wood and valley, path and village, field and stream and animal—conspicuously omits Eurydice, whose absence cannot be undone by the phantasmal
world that it inspires. This omission, which foreshadows the failure of Orpheus's quest, is the core of the poem.

For her part, Eurydice is immune to both the allure and the terror of Orpheus's Romantic repetitions. Made "new" with her "great death," she cannot be encompassed by Orpheus's visions, which is why he is not permitted
to see her except in departure. In contrast to the insubstantiality that haunts
the obsessed Orpheus, what surrounds Eurydice is absolute fullness. She is
said to be full the way a fruit is full with "sweetness and darkness," and
what "filled her like fullness" ("erfüllte sie wie Fülle") is the condition of
her being-dead ("Gestorbensein")—something that can neither be repeated
itself nor produce a repetition of anything else.

This division between the former lovers is acted out as a conflict in transitivity, or more exactly as the intimate detachment between one self in transit
and another. Both Orpheus and Eurydice are immersed in changes of identity, but their streams of metamorphoses move in opposite directions. Orpheus, in a foreshadowing of his eventual fate, is effectively dismembered by
Rilke's figurative language. Objectified and depersonalized, his hands hang
down from the blue mantle into which his ego metonymically dwindles; his
left hand is said to have grown into his lyre (the source of his mourning-
world):

> seine Hände hingen
> schwer und verschlossen aus dem Fall der Falten
> und wussten nicht mehr von der leichten Leier,
> die in die Linke eingewachsen war.
>   (18–21)

> his hands hung
> heavy and clenched from the fall of the folds,
> and knew no more of the light lyre
> that into the left had grown.

Also objectified, Orpheus's senses are sundered ("entzweit") both from each
other and from him, and their alienated forms misfeature him degradingly.
His sight runs in front of him "like a dog" ("der Blick ihm wie ein Hund
vorauslief"); his hearing, by a kind of perverse synesthesia, lags behind him
"like a smell" ("wie ein Geruch"). By the end of the poem, seen from Euryd-

ice's standpoint, Orpheus is reduced to a mere "someone or other" ("irgend jemand") with an unrecognizable face. Eurydice, in contrast, constantly metamorphoses into new forms of fecundity and potentiality: a "new virginity" that is also a pregnancy, a young flower, a fallen rain, a hundredfold harvest ("hundertfacher Vorrat").

Every such movement into fullness by Eurydice alienates her further from Orpheus; every addition to her intactness also adds to his fragmentation. The poem closes when this process reaches a natural end. Orpheus's failure becomes Eurydice's success: released at last from the possessiveness of life, Eurydice moves back across the threshold into the purely generous being of her death. Of course, that being does not seem generous to Orpheus, yet in a way he simply refuses its generosity as too impersonal. Eurydice's self-consummation is in no sense a willed rejection of Orpheus, even though Rilke's poem is; her affirmation of Orpheus's loss does not proceed from a dialectical negation of his effort at recovery but only from the intrinsic fecundity of her own effortless state of being. In order to reach this conclusion, Rilke must find a way to efface the dialectical thrust of the poem in favor of a generative interval. This he achieves by a simple but exquisitely graduated transition in point of view. For roughly its first half, the poem is narrated with Orpheus as its center of consciousness. The result is that the ascent through the underworld, Orpheus's literal-minded effort to draw life dialectically out of its opposite, is riddled with his anxious impulses to ward off resistance from "the pair of light ones" (Eurydice and Hermes) who always seem to lag reluctantly behind him. Orpheus's failure, however, is not shown from this agonic perspective; in fact, it is not shown at all. In the process of describing Orpheus's world of mourning, the poem distances his turbulent, impatient consciousness and grows sensitive to the presence of Eurydice. Her power as an object elides his as a subject and appears as the direct source of his song:

> . . . *sie.*
> Die So-geliebte, dass aus einer Leier
> mehr Klage kam als je aus Klagefrauen.
> (46–48)

> . . . she.
> The so-beloved, that from a single lyre
> More mourning flowed than from all mourning-women.

Before one is fully aware of the change, the poem has gone on to make Eurydice its new narrative center. And since her being-dead is essentially a dissolution of all relationships between self and other, Orpheus appears only as a dim, remote figure, "dark in the bright exit," as he loses her a second time. He is held in the poem at all, perhaps, only by the Rilkean narrator's will to repudiate him as an alter ego. Eurydice's release thus seems to emerge not from anything in Orpheus, but only from her experience of her new condition, the death "so new that she could fathom nothing" ("also neu . . . dass sie nichts begriff"). Orpheus has nothing to do with her; she does not even know she is being lost.

Turned inward as if near childbed, Eurydice finds that being-dead is a new way of inhabiting time, one that paradoxically both disperses and concentrates the self. Described by a series of past participles with prefixes that signify distance and dissemination—*aufgelöst, hingegeben, ausgeteilt*—she moves organically into a state of pure potentiality, the condition, in Wordsworth's phrase, of "something evermore about to be." This "giving out" of the self is consummated in the climactic line of the poem, where it merges into a new taking-on of self: "She was already root" ("Sie war schon Wurzel"). (As in the "Ode to the West Wind," the completion of a radical transit of identity appears in a metaphor that closes a long chain of similes—a passage from the latent sundering of likeness to the intactness of being.) Filled to overflowing with generative temporality, Eurydice is incapable of grasping contingency, accident, the indeterminacy of human events. Thus, when Hermes cries in anguish, "He has turned around," she can only answer: "Who?" Orpheus, meanwhile, has unwillingly broken off from Romantic repetition with a gesture so senseless, so arbitrary, that it seems self-destructive. Yet even his turning around has become subtly organic. Orpheus looks back for Eurydice *only because she is already gone*: "already root."

IV

Beethoven's Fifth Symphony takes a more humanized route into liminality than Rilke's anti-elegiac poem; its threshold leads to the light, not to the darkness. The work is perhaps the most rewarding example of overlapping paradigms in music, in part because by treating it as such we can clear off some of the cobwebs that surround it, the results of an excessive fame that subliminally obscures and even degrades the music. Beyond that, all of the most striking features of the Fifth can be connected to its paradigmatic play. In fact, the symphony accumulates the paradigms dramatically, one by one, and superimposes them "polyphonically" in sustained chronophanies as each new one emerges.

The first element to become prominent is the transit of identity, which operates over the form of the symphony as a whole. Like the "Eroica" and the Ninth, Beethoven's Fifth is a re-thinking, a detailed problematizing, of the formal impulses that support the Classical symphony. This process in each case is founded on features of the first movement, and in the Fifth the detonating force is the emotional weight that Beethoven gives to the elaboration of the famous initial motive. The motivic concentration of the opening *Allegro con brio* is often misconstrued as its most radical element, a notion that mainly suggests a failure to listen to Haydn. What is unprecedented about this music is its aggressiveness, the sheer vehemence with which it works and exhausts its motivic material, the intensity with which it turns the presence of a motive into an assault on the listener's nerves. This ruthless expressivity is aimed at producing a crisis toward the close of the movement. Within the Classical style, a first movement in a minor key allows the composer a choice in the working out of the sonata form: the "second group" material, which is presented in the relative major during the exposition, may be recapitulated either in the tonic major or the tonic minor. Beethoven's choice in the Fifth is the tonic major, but as every listener knows his recapitulation is followed by a ferocious C-minor coda of more than a hundred measures, measures that contain the most emotionally violent music in the movement. The startling vehemence of this gesture breaks up the equivalence of C major and C minor as possible home tonics and becomes a testimony to the failure of C major to resolve the tensions produced by the music's sonata form. More subversively still, the collapse of the tonic major, taken together with the relentless C-minor hammering at the main motive during the coda, suggests a failure of the sonata form itself to resolve or even to relieve the music's aggressiveness. The result is that a dialectical antagonism springs up between C major and C minor, a coiled tension that will have to be resolved through the totality of the work. The symphony as a whole thus acquires its widely recognized goal of C major—but not just any C major; rather, one that is free of its dialectical vulnerability to the minor, a C major that *cannot be followed.* This projection of the harmonic and gestural tension of the first movement onto the scale of the whole is what motivates—necessitates—the reappearance in each movement of the basic rhythmic cell that begins the work. The symphony—which is to say symphonic form—is being redefined: it is no longer a sequence of integral movements, a generic whole that consists of the sum of its parts, but a dynamic weaving-together of non-integral movements to form a whole that cannot be specified in advance. Procession gives way to process—which is also why the Fifth is the first symphony to violate the discreteness of its subdivisions, in the fusion of the third and fourth movements and the return of the third in the fourth.

Beethoven proposes to resolve his large-scale tension through a generative rhythm, but before he makes a move in that direction he establishes the need for it as concretely as possible, and at the same time specifically points to C major as its goal. These new orientations occur in one of the least understood features of the symphony, the second theme of the slow movement. This theme, blaring out raucously in trumpets, horns, oboes, and drums, has been described by countless program annotators (and by Tovey, who should have known better) as parading forth in a "triumphant" C major, but I would imagine that most listeners have always been shocked and disturbed, even frightened by it, even on repeated hearings. It is sudden, aggressive, and deliberately overemphatic as a gesture, and seemingly quite ir-

rational in what it emphasizes. Its C major is a mediant of the tonic A♭;
reached through a complex passing dissonance on which the whole orchestra
pounces *fortissimo* for a full measure, the key sounds both remote and arbitrary (Ex. 56). In addition, a simple reduction of the theme itself reveals it to

EXAMPLE 56. Beethoven, Fifth Symphony, second movement.

be little more than an assertion of the C major triad—in other words, an anticipation of the similar, this time naked assertion that constitutes the first
theme of the finale (Ex. 57). The modulation to the blaring *Andante* theme
is, in short, an advance parody of the critical move to C major on which the
fate of the whole work will depend, and its ferocity and tonal instability
clearly demonstrate the need for some generative means to produce the final
resolution.

   That means is found, of course, in the transitional passage that links the
second *Allegro* and the finale. Beethoven is, if not the inventor, then at least
so thorough and radical an explorer of this kind of passage that later com-

EXAMPLE 57. Beethoven, Fifth Symphony, themes of second movement and
finale.

posers have tended to shy away from it. His transitional spells have a different, though always a problematical, meaning each time that one appears in a
major work. In this case, the aim of the transition is to produce a chrono-

phany that is both liminal and generative. Liminal, because the passage is to lead, or so it appears, from the plane of harmonic contingency to the "absolute" C major that the symphony is seeking—in emotional terms, to lead from raw aggressiveness to its sublimation in ebullience. Generative, because the liminal movement is to dispel the dialectical tension between C major and C minor—a tension that has been pointedly reanimated by the contrasting sections of the second *Allegro*—and to evolve the one key from the other.

The major/minor dialectic melts away as the result of a mesmerizing harmonic ambiguity. The transitional passage begins with a pedal point on the third, A♭–C, as if to restore the A♭ major of the second movement. The music, however, does not sound like A♭ major because of the emphasis produced by its most famous feature, the timpani ostinato on C that pulses ceaselessly throughout the episode. Stripped of shape and direction, the music enters an inchoate phase; renouncing temporal displacement, it seems to surrender to the same germinal temporality that Rilke assigns to the dead. (The tone-color, with low strings enveloping the timpani, the cellos and violas closely spaced, suggests a sonorous image of a brimming, self-involved darkness.) This feeling of indeterminacy deepens when the first thematic fragment to emerge from the thrumming abyss launches itself in A♭ major only to end up in the nerveless grip of an exposed C-F♯ tritone (Ex. 58). Gradually, however, the generative impulse clarifies itself. Over the incessant pedal and ostinato, the music shifts little by little to C minor and C major. This harmonic movement proceeds without a trace of cadential feeling; there is no sense of arrival, only of a constant liminal brooding. The result is that the antithesis between C major and C minor is transformed imperceptibly into a continuity. The minor emerges seamlessly from the uncertain A♭ major that precedes it, and runs just as seamlessly into the C major that emerges from it. This music is, in fact, centered on a tone—even a tone and a timbre—rather than on a triad; its referential base is the timpani's throbbing, softly insistent C. The "dissolve" of the minor to the major sounds more like a change of intensity than a change of harmony: a strengthening of the primary tone by the gradual accumulation of bright, consonant intervals; an almost acoustic phenomenon in which the overtones of the timpani are reinforced by the first violins. (The increase in harmonic security is articulated by an increasing melodic smoothness and a rising registral contour.) It is on this basis that the finale, beginning on a tonic cadence, can offer what seems to be an inviolable C major, and that the first theme of the finale can be, even must be, spun out from a fanfare on the C-major triad.

None of this can stand, of course. Its collapse is precipitated when the development section of the finale erupts unexpectedly into a harsh return of the symphony's motto rhythm. The earlier reappearances of this figure have all seemed to be legitimate extensions of the motivic concentration of the first movement into the enlarged area of symphonic unity. This time, protracted and noisy, the return sounds like an ugly spell of Romantic repetition, dominated by the persistent tattoo of C's and G's in the horns, trumpets, and timpani against a harmonically mobile background. The impression is confirmed by the unmistakable instance of repetition that fol-

EXAMPLE 58.   Beethoven, Fifth Symphony, transition to finale.

lows shortly afterward with the same rhythm: the C-minor return of the second *Allegro* in its soft, ominous texture, telescoped with a version of the transitional passage that Beethoven makes uncanny by omitting the basses and timpani. This celebrated episode is a sublimely reckless gamble with the tensions of the symphony. The captivating C minor of the revived second *Allegro* undermines the C major that the finale had seemed to make secure; but at the same time the return of the music to its liminal defile allows the recapitulation to emerge as the exposition had, with a generative continuity that makes its tonality radiant. The trouble is that a generative movement cannot resolve the tensions introduced by Romantic repetition, so Beethoven is also committing himself here to an arbitrary closure. Like the "Appassionata" Sonata, the Fifth Symphony drives toward resolution by compounding its dilemma.

Unlike the exposition, the recapitulation of the finale must be genuinely invulnerable in its tonality. Beethoven responds to this need by emphasizing the dominant rather than the tonic in his spectral version of the transitional passage; for the last twenty-three of thirty-two measures, he reconciles the major/minor antithesis with an ostinato on the dominant triad, which is the same for both modes. The melodic line also adds support: most of it is confined to the tones of the dominant-seventh chord, with a telltale E or E♭ pointedly absent. The music is simply in C major/minor. At the same time, as if to defend doubly against any further dialectical violence, Beethoven draws on yet another liminal pattern, one that has been latent throughout the symphony and only now comes into its own. This is not a harmonic pattern but a timbral one.

Back in the first movement, just after the start of the recapitulation, an unaccompanied oboe solo appears out of nowhere and briefly dissolves the aggressiveness of the music. As with the famous C♯ dissonance in the finale of the Eighth Symphony, but on a vaster scale, nothing is made of this for a time. Then, in the liminal passage of the finale, the solo oboe recurs to echo its entry in the first movement. Moving through an equivalent melodic contour, a long-breathed descent from G to D, the oboe once again mediates between tension and release, once again marks off an inchoate duration that must be traversed before a recapitulation can establish itself. This time, though, the "liminalized" oboe can help to dissolve what it could only defer before—the violent C minor that haunts the symphony.

With so many continuities to envelop it, the C major cadence prepared by this episode is overpoweringly full—"heroic sound / Joyous and jubilant and sure," to borrow from Stevens again—and the outcome of a chronophany in which musical time appears as an impulse toward, a cathexis of, the tonic. But whatever the jubilance, nothing can be sure about this music until the ghost of Romantic repetition has been put to rest. Beethoven withholds the arbitrary gesture required for that until it is almost too late for one. Then, in the late measures of the coda, he unleashes a wildly extravagant curtailment. The episode resembles the maniacal note-pounding at the close of the "Appassionata" in being itself a kind of exorcistic parody-repetition: twelve measures of *fortissimo* tonic and dominant chords, followed by twenty-nine explosive measures of the tonic chord alone. The raucous dance of expulsion ends, as E. T. A. Hoffmann observed, with a series of tonic chords that follow what seems to be the end—chords that are precisely measured so that their outbursts are unpredictable to the ear:

> The closing chords . . . are strangely positioned. To be specific, the chord which the listener believes to be the last is followed [by an irregular series of rests and repetitions]. The perfect calmness which the heart feels as a result of the several closing figures that are linked together is destroyed by these single struck chords and pauses.[7]

The vehement exuberance of this close, however, is a fully sublimated form of the aggressiveness that boils over in the parallel measures of the first movement. What is more, the passage as a whole even veers toward a closure compatible with the organic thrust of the symphony by virtue of the continual climactic brightening of its sonority. Led by the piccolo, the high wood-

---

[7] E. T. A. Hoffmann, from the *Allgemeine Musikalische Zeitung,* July 4 and 11, 1810, translated by F. John Adams, Jr. Reprinted in *Ludwig van Beethoven, Symphony No. 5 in C Minor,* edited by Elliott Forbes (New York: Norton, 1971), pp. 150–63.

winds mount three times to sustained piercing cries, articulating the sense of a direction successfully pursued, while the static, overinsistent C-major harmony, secure on its side of the threshold, defies the faintest peep of a minor inflection to sound.

We might say, borrowing a phrase from D. H. Lawrence, that the symphony at this point reflects on the long course of its liminal movement to proclaim, "Look! We have come through!" Rilke's Eurydice, who also crosses a liminal bridge to confirm a transit of identity, who also moves through a generative pattern toward a release from Romantic repetition, bears much the same message. Though she follows a passive, regressive course where the symphony suggests a determined will to develop, the aims that Rilke gives her are much the same as the ones Beethoven gives his music: to depart from "impatience" by crossing a threshold; to stay on the other side.

V

It is conventional to call poetry "musical" when it is mellifluous, conventional to call music "poetic" when it seems especially expressive. The phenomenon of convergence shows, perhaps, both the emptiness and the inevitability of these conventions. The music of poetry and the poetry of music are one and the same thing: the shaped flow of time produced by the unfolding of a structural rhythm, especially where that rhythm has a cathectic basis. And this remains true of any poem or composition whether or not it is considered in convergent relationship to another work. The gestural "level" of a work is a thing of independent and, I think, of central importance. In it, two vital interests coincide, two basic dimensions of our temporal experience. One is the heightened realization of the radical connectedness that is the special domain of music and poetry, and that corresponds phenomenologically to our lived sense of being continuous selves in a continuous world. That sense may, it is true, be largely illusory, but it cannot be renounced without pain, nor can it be permanently banished from the ego, which stubbornly revives it after any number of disillusionments or deconstructions. The other dimension is that of cathexis, in the revisionary sense I have tried to give the term: the process by which we invest perception with feeling in a mobile, endlessly displaceable way, and by which we acknowledge that investment only indirectly even as we depend on it. Something essential to us seems to hinge on our ability to fuse these two activities—poetically, musically, perhaps erotically, too. Our impulse seems to be to flood the channels of passing time with a sense of the relationships that constitute us, so that they can there acquire a sense of tangible presence. The study of convergence, or of gestural rhythms wherever they may arise, takes place within that imperative, and derives what importance it has from our persistence in it.

Glossary

Appoggiatura. A dissonant sonority on an accented beat that resolves by step into the prevailing harmony.

Augmented-sixth chords. Chromatically altered chords treated by composers of the Classical period as belonging to the major and minor keys. The bass note of these chords normally occurs on the sixth degree of the minor scale or the lowered-sixth degree of the major scale; all the chords contain the characteristic interval of an augmented sixth between their bass and soprano notes. Augmented-sixth chords are found in three forms, traditionally called Italian, French, and German. The normal resolution of these chords is to the dominant. During the nineteenth century, augmented-sixth chords with the bass note a semitone above the tonic, resolving to the tonic, also came into common use.

Augmented triad. A major triad with its fifth raised by a semitone.

Circle of fifths. The twenty-four major and minor keys differ in the number of sharps or flats that they contain in their scales. If we start with C major (no sharps or flats) and change key by adding one sharp at a time, each key will occur on the fifth degree—the dominant—of its predecessor: C, G, D, A, etc. If the same procedure is followed with flats, each key will occur on the dominant of its successor: C, F, B♭, E♭, etc. The same patterns obtain for minor keys. In equal temperament, the procedure will eventually lead in a complete circle back to the original key. Modulation or harmonic progression along the circle of fifths is frequent in the Classical period.

Deceptive cadence (Interrupted cadence). A progression from the dominant to an unexpected chord, most commonly the submediant (V–vi), where a full cadence (V–I) is anticipated.

Deconstruction. Broadly speaking, an effort to find the crucial area in which a discourse questions or undermines what it affirms. Largely inspired by the work of the contemporary French philosopher Jacques Derrida, deconstruction has provoked controversy because of the claim that *all* discourse, including deconstructive discourse, is somewhere self-subverting. However, deconstruction should not be understood as a method of invalidating or deriding the texts that it considers; as Derrida has repeatedly emphasized, the deconstructionist is always dependent on the texts he deconstructs. A deconstruction is a supplement, not an attack.

Defamiliarization. The most common translation of the Russian term *ostranenie,* used by the formalist critic Viktor Shklovsky to designate a making-strange of familiar objects or phenomena. Shklovsky and his school, the Russian Formalists of the 1920s, regarded defamiliarization, the renewal of perception, as the primary purpose of art.

Différance ("with an a"). A term, coined by Jacques Derrida, intended to emphasize that the French verb "différer" means both "to differ" and "to defer." According to Derrida and others, language is based on a system of differences, or distinctive oppositions, rather than on the availability of determinate meanings that can be made present in and through an act of communication. Discourse, as a result, has only one power—to differ from other discourse. And since the process of differing is impossible to limit, the discourse that *differs* in order to mean must also *defer* a full or secure grasp of its meaning. *Différance* designates the activity of differing/deferring by which meaning is simultaneously constituted and withheld.

Diminished-seventh chord. A diminished triad (q.v.) with a minor third added above the fifth. This arrangement produces a chord that consists only of minor thirds, a property that may be used to render the chord tonally ambiguous or even to suspend the feeling of tonality altogether. In the Classical period, the diminished-seventh chord most often carries a dominant feeling; the chord has in fact been regarded as a dominant minor-ninth chord with the root omitted.

Diminished triad. A minor triad with the fifth lowered by a semitone.

Dominant-seventh chord. In root position, a dominant triad with a minor third added above the fifth (G–B–D–F in C major). There are three inversions, all of which are used. The dominant-seventh chord is a lynchpin of Classical tonality. Its resolution is always to the tonic triad, normally without any intervening harmonies; and it may substitute for the dominant in a full cadence (or a deceptive cadence). *See also* Inversion.

Eleventh chord. See *Higher dominants.*

Enharmonic equivalance. The identity, on the keyboard, of two notes that are written differently, for instance B♯ and C. Ideally, the difference in notation indicates a difference in melodic and harmonic function or meaning, so that enharmonic relationships in actual compositions indicate a reinterpretation of musical material.

Fourth-chord. A chord of three or more notes that may be spaced so that each tone forms a perfect or augmented fourth with the tone(s) adjacent to it. Fourth-chords are frequent in the music of Scriabin, Schoenberg, and other composers working in atonal idioms; the fourth-chord does not occur as such in tonal harmony, though ornamental dissonances sometimes produce the characteristic fourth-chord spacing.

Full cadence. A progression from the dominant or dominant-seventh to the tonic at the end of a musical phrase. The effect is often compared to that of a period in a sentence.

German sixth. See *Augmented-sixth chords.*

Half cadence. A progression from the tonic to the dominant at the end of a musical phrase; the effect is often compared to that of a semicolon in a sentence.

Higher dominants. In root position, chords formed by adding one, two, or three thirds above the seventh of a dominant-seventh chord. These higher dominants—ninth, eleventh, and thirteenth chords—are resolved in various ways, but in general their resolution proceeds to the tonic triad. The most important thing about these sonorities is the clear dominant character that organizes the dissonance of their upper tones.

Interrupted cadence. See *Deceptive cadence.*

Inversion. A chord is said to be inverted if its fundamental tone is not also its lowest tone. An inverted triad may either have its third in the bass (first inversion) or its fifth (second inversion).

Logocentrism. As defined by Derrida, the conviction that meaning in all of its forms is established and stabilized with reference to some form of presence (divinity, truth, nature, consciousness, etc.).

Melodic cadence. A concluding fragment of a melody that brings it to a point of rest or closure. Full melodic cadences usually end on the tonic note, most often approached by step. Half-cadences usually end on one of the notes of the dominant or subdominant triad.

Metonymy. A type of rhetorical figure in which one term signifies another by virtue of an association or contiguity between the two terms. Thus Byron writes,

> I stood in Venice on the Bridge of Sighs,
> A prison and a palace on each hand

to evoke oppression and power in the history of the Venetian empire. Metonymy is frequently regarded as an opposite of metaphor, which signifies by virtue of a resemblance between terms. Some literary theorists argue that all figurative language can be categorized as metaphoric or metonymic; others use a fourfold scheme, derived from Renaissance rhetoric, that supplements metaphor and metonymy with synecdoche and irony.

Neapolitan sonorities. Traditionally "pathetic" and subdominant in character, Neapolitan sonorities are those based on the flat supertonic—i.e., on the tone a semitone above the tonic. In the Classical period, the *Neapolitan sixth* is in frequent use. This is a flat-supertonic triad in first inversion (F–A♭–D♭ in the key of C; note that the A is also lowered in order to give a major triad). The normal progression of the chord is to the dominant. In the nineteenth century, composers began to use Neapolitan triads in root position.

Ninth chord. See *Higher dominants.*

Ostinato. A musical figure that is repeated continuously, most often in the bass.

Parataxis. In traditional rhetoric, the arrangement of clauses or phrases without connectives; more broadly, any non-connective juxtaposition of structural elements in a work of art.

Pedal, Pedal point. A single note or chord, most often in the bass, that is repeated or sustained continuously amid changing harmonies. The dissonances that normally result do not "count" in the harmony, which is defined (in the short term) without reference to the pedal.

Polyrhythm. The clearly articulated superimposition of two or more independent rhythmic patterns.

Pulse. The basic unit of musical time, regarded as a subjective, psychological phenomenon. Pulse is correlative to, but only sometimes identical with, *beat*, which is the basic unit of musical time regarded as a chronometric phenomenon.

Relative major, Relative minor. Major and minor keys are said to be *relative* to each other when they share the same key signature; for example, A major and F♯ minor are relative keys, each having three sharps. In the nineteenth century, relative keys were sometimes treated as equivalent.

Root position. A chord is said to be in *root position* if its fundamental tone (or *root*) is also its lowest tone. Root-position triads are normally necessary to establish a firm sense of key.

Six-four chord. A triad in second inversion, i.e., with its fifth in the bass; the bass note is always doubled in four-part harmony. Various types of six-four chords occur; the most important of them is the "cadential" six-four. This chord contains the tones of the tonic triad, but it is not stable; its function is dominant, and it must be resolved to the dominant.

Thirteenth chord. See *Higher dominants.*

Sequence. The repetition of a melodic pattern at different pitch levels.

Tonicization. The establishment of a non-tonic key as a temporary tonic, with its own dominant and the authority to organize fairly extended harmonic progressions with reference to itself.

Tritone. The interval of the augmented fourth, called "tritone" because it consists of three whole tones. In the Middle Ages, use of this interval was interdicted as "diabolus in musica," the devil in music. Tritones are unlike other intervals in that, if a tritone is sounded in isolation, the ear cannot tell which of its two tones is the fundamental (root). Tritones are therefore a frequent source of tonal ambiguity and instability.

Voice-leading. The technique of writing the different parts ("lines" or "voices") of a polyphonic composition so that each part independently forms a good (clear, consistent, expressive) melodic contour.

Index